Margaret Anglin,
A Stage Life

M.A. in 1912: "lambent red-gold hair," "limpid grey-green eyes," and "that lovely haunting voice."

Margaret Anglin, A Stage Life

by John LeVay

 Simon & Pierre

Toronto, Canada

We would like to express our gratitude to The Canada Council and the Ontario Arts Council for their support.

Marian M. Wilson, Publisher

Cover photo: M.A. as Rosalind, 1913.
Photo by Arnold Genthe.

Photos courtesy of Basile Anglin, pp. 30, 43, 96, 125, 230, 278, 286, 289, endpapers; by Schweig, 172.

Photo by Peyton, opposite title page; New York Public Library, 12, 53, 57, 103, 117, 182, 191, 293; by Blum, 17, 86; *Saturday Night*, 18; courtesy of Naomi Le Vay, 26, 36; *Theatre Magazine*, 68, 108, 140, 206, 218, 257, 267; by Otto Sarony, courtesy of Naomi Le Vay, 78; Metro Toronto Public Library, 150, 158; courtesy of Dr. Adrian Anglin, 241; *Globe and Mail*, courtesy of Herbert Whittaker, 304.

ISBN 0-88924-206-2

1 2 3 4 5 • 93 92 91 90 89

Canadian Cataloguing in Publication Data

Le Vay, John
    Margaret Anglin, a stage life

ISBN 0-88924-206-2

1. Anglin, Margaret, 1876-1958. 2. Actresses - Canada - Biography. I. Title.
PN2308.A64L44 1988 792'.0924 C88-094938-4

Design: Christopher W. Sears

Editors: Marian M. Wilson and Peter Goodchild

Printer: Hignell Printing Limited

Printed and Bound in Canada

Order from
Simon & Pierre Publishing Company Limited/
Les Éditions Simon & Pierre Ltée.
P.O. Box 280 Adelaide Street Postal Station
Toronto, Ontario, Canada M5C 2J4

ANTIGONE

To Margaret Anglin

Clear on the moonlit California air
    A voice from out the deathless ages breaks!
Brave with the courage of a god, and fair,
    Antigone the true, the tender, wakes!
O hero days renewed, that we behold
    One of the bright immortals live again,
Pouring her pure, high passion in the mold
    of classic art to melt the hearts of men!

Ah, mournful eyes! A silver voice that shakes
    The night with tragic sorrow, sing anew
The glorious womanhood thy soul partakes,
    The virgin love, the faith forever true!
Beauty and power are thine, and noble zeal,
    Lady of mighty dreams, to crown thy high ideal!

Charles Phillips

Berkeley: Hearst Greek Theatre, June 30, 1910

Acknowledgements

I should like to thank, first and foremost, my parents, Bertrand and Naomi (Anglin) Le Vay, who most congenially put me up and put up with me throughout the period of the writing of this book, and who suffered my Anglomanic folly almost gladly.

Miss Basile Anglin (M.A.'s unofficial secretary in 1927) was, perhaps, the most substantial contributor, in terms of memorabilia, and her multifaceted generosity will live in my memory. The veteran actor and director Jerome Collamore (M.A.'s stage manager and assistant director in the thirties) favored me with a cornucopia of anecdotal letters which combine, in Horatian mode, "instruction with delight." Emmy (Tietz) Wittich (M.A.'s personal maid and domestic factotum from 1930 to 1946) was also generous in epistolary reminiscence, and has also earned my gratitude; as has Dennis Mills who read this work in manuscript with a kindly critical eye.

Thanks are also due to the entire Anglin clan of the city of Toronto, with special reference to Madeleine Anglin Mackay, who was a prime instigator of the biographical project and a keeper of scrapbooks. Mr. Frank M. Anglin of Ottawa kindly provided me with copies of the Mackenzie King letters.

I am also indebted to the following companies for permission to quote from published works: the Temple University Press (*Actors and American Culture*); Macmillan and Co. (*Broadway* and *These Things are Mine*); the Southern Illinois University Press (*Estranging Dawn*); E.P. Dutton and Co. (*Backstage with Henry Miller* and *The Great White Way*); Harper and Row (*Inside Looking Out*); the University of Toronto Press (*Timothy Warren Anglin*); the Indiana University Press (*Too Late to Lament*); Crown Publishers (*Mrs. Fiske and the American Stage*); the University of Oklahoma Press (*Dear Josephine*); Houghton-Mifflin (*The Damrosch Dynasty*); the Dartnell Press (*Great Names*); McGraw-Hill (*Matinee Tomorrow*); and Harcourt-Brace (*Stagestruck*).

Acknowledgement is also due to the Butler Library of Columbia University for permission to quote from the Randolph Somerville Papers, to the New York Public Library to quote from the Paul Kester Papers, and to Miss Dorothy Swerdlove, Curator of the Billy Rose Theatre Collection at NYPL for her oft-invoked expert advice and assistance.

And, last but assuredly not least, thanks to Dr. G. Arnold Johnson, whose doctoral dissertation "The Greek Productions of Margaret Anglin" was an invaluable resource.

Contents

Illustrations

End papers: M.A. and the cast of *Lady Windermere's Fan* (1914): a long and fruitful connection with Wildean comedy, in which M.A. played roles from ingenue to dowager over her lifetime.

Abbreviations

AAC	Benjamin McArthur, *Actors and American Culture* (Philadelphia: Temple Univ. Press, 1984).
Amb	Margaret Anglin, "The Ambitions of an Actress," *New York American*, June 1915.
B	Brooks Atkinson, *Broadway* (New York: Macmillan, 1970).
BWHM	Frank Morse, *Backstage with Henry Miller* (New York: Dutton, 1938).
C	Jerome Collamore, Letters to John Le Vay (1985-86).
DD	George Martin, *The Damrosch Dynasty* (Boston: Houghton-Mifflin, 1983).
DJ	*Dear Josephine* (Norman: Univ. of Oklahoma Press, 1963).
ED	Maurice F. Brown, *Estranging Dawn* (Carbondale: Southern Illinois Univ. Press, 1972).
EWW	*Everywoman's World* 1) Margaret Anglin, "My Career" (December 1916); 2) Margaret Anglin, "My Career" (January 1917); 3) Margaret Anglin, "My Career" (February 1917); 4) Margaret Anglin, "My Career" (April 1917); 5) Richard M. Winans, "The Woman Part of Margaret Anglin" (May 1917).
FAD	Lewis C. Strang, *Famous Actresses of the Day in America* (Boston: L.C. Page, 1902).
GC	Paul Sheren, "Gordon Craig's only American Production," *The Princeton University Library Chronicle*, Spring 1968.
GN	Thoda Cocroft, *Great Names and How They are Made* (Chicago: Dartnell Press, 1941).
GSAS	Daniel Blum, *Great Stars of the American Stage, A Pictorial Record* (New York: Greenberg, 1952).
GWW	Allen Churchill, *The Great White Way* (New York: Dutton, 1962).
H	*Hearst's International Magazine* 1) Margaret Anglin, "Playing Greek Tragedy" (July 1915); 2) Margaret Anglin, "Some Experiences with Richard Mansfield" (October 1916); 3) Margaret Anglin, "With the Empire Theater Company" (November 1916); 4) Margaret Anglin, "With *Zira* and *The Great Divide*" (January 1917); 5) Margaret Anglin, "Greek Drama and Theatrical Management" (March 1917); 6) Margaret Anglin, "An Actress in the Making" (September 1919); 7) Margaret Anglin, "My Australian Tour" (February 1917). The original typescripts of these articles sometimes provide supplementary material, and I have included such material under the *Hearst's* rubric. The

originals in question are in the Montrose J. Moses Collection in the William Perkins Library of the University of North Carolina at Durham.

ILO   Harding Lemay, *Inside Looking Out* (New York: Harper and Row, 1971).

J   Gordon Arnold Johnson, "The Greek Productions of Margaret Anglin" (unpublished Ph.D. dissertation, Case Western Reserve University, Cleveland, 1971).

K   Paul Kester Papers (letters to and from Margaret Anglin, 1898-1933), New York Public Library Collection.

LDJ   Eugene O'Neill, *Long Day's Journey into Night* (New Haven: Yale Univ. Press, 1956).

MAP   Lena Ashwell, *Myself a Player* (London: Michael Joseph, 1936).

MFAT   Archie Binns and Olive Kooken, *Mrs. Fiske and the American Theatre* (New York: Crown, 1955).

MT   Ward Morehouse, *Matinee Tomorrow* (New York: McGraw-Hill, 1949).

MTL   S. Morgan-Powell, *Memories that Live* (Toronto, Macmillan, 1929).

NAT   Emily Kimbrough, *Now and Then* (New York: Harper and Row, 1972).

P   Otto Preminger, *Preminger: An Autobiography* (Garden City, N.Y.: Doubleday, 1977).

Plu   Margaret Anglin, "A Plunge into Theatrical Management": unpublished article (1916), intended for *Hearst's*. Montrose J. Moses Papers, loc. cit.

S   Randolph Somerville Papers: letters from Margaret Anglin to Randolph Somerville (1931-46). Butler Library, Columbia University, New York.

S   Maurice Zolotow, *Stagestuck* (New York: Harcourt Brace, 1965).

SOS   William Winter, *Shakespeare on the Stage* (New York: Moffat-Yard, 1915).

Str   Margaret Anglin, "The Stride of the Theatre": unpublished article 1916), intended for *Hearst's*. Montrose J. Moses papers, loc. cit.

TLTL   Maurice Browne, *Too Late to Lament* (Bloomington, Indiana Univ. Press, 1956).

TTAM   George Middleton, *These Things Are Mine* (New York, Macmillan, 1947).

TTCC   Doris Arthur Jones, *Taking the Curtain Call* (New York, Macmillan, 1930).

TWA   William M. Baker, *Timothy Warren Anglin* (Toronto: Univ. of Toronto Press, 1977).

W   Emmy (Tietz) Wittich, letters to John Le Vay (1985-86).

Wha   Margaret Anglin, "What Happened to *The Great Divide*"; unpublished article (1916), intended for *Hearst's*.   Montrose J. Moses Papers, loc. cit.

WVM   David D. Henry, *William Vaughn Moody* (Boston, Bruce Humphries, 1934).

An unknown when she opened in *Cyrano de Bergerac*, M.A.'s poetic and beautiful Roxane was hailed by the New York critics. (1899)

Introduction

No memory of having starred
Atones for later disregard
Or keeps the end from being hard.
(Robert Frost, "Provide, Provide")

Margaret Anglin, the "unchallenged first practitioner of anguish" of the American stage (*N.Y. Times*, 9.1.58)* or, to use the words of the *Time* (20.1.58) obituary, the "sad-eyed, junoesque tragedienne," was an essentially happy person: good company in her leisure time, "a formidable raconteur" (K, 4.5.14), possessed of a "delightful Irish wit" (GSAS, 21), and, above all, happy in her life's work—and she was, as we shall see, a prodigious worker. Though she made her name in tragedy and melodrama, she herself was heard to observe at mid-career: "Comedy is, in fact, closer to my own natural temperature of spirits" (*Green Book*, Aug. 1911). Therefore, despite our epigraph, this story is to be, as she surely would have had it, a happy story: our marking will be *allegro, ma non troppo.*

We shall not dwell on the melancholy years of decline and neglect, nor shall we depict the hurt, confused and perplexed face of the aging diva losing her grip. We shall certainly not wish to close with anything like Arnold Johnson's sombre valedictory:

> During the last year of her life, it was said that Miss Anglin
> refused to utter a single word. Miss Anglin had stilled her
> own voice—a voice which in the performance of Greek
> tragedy had awed so many people. (J, 281)

And therefore we acknowledge these things at the outset. We shall doubtless need to think about the seeming inevitability of the disregard and near oblivion which overtook one who was conceded to be "America's best emotional actress" (*Woman's Home Companion*, Apr. 1921) and even, at her apogee, "the greatest tragic actress of our time" (*N.Y. Evening World*, 21.2.18)—essentially the fall from public favor of "the grand manner" and "high-style"—but that, too, may be almost tacitly taken for granted.

What we must clearly, and happily, be most interested in are the years of power, prestige and brilliance—the three-decade period delimited by her "glowing" Roxane of 1898 and

---

*In newspaper and letter dating, the order is day, month, year.

her final "majestic" Electra of 1928. She had formidable rivals in her prime—Minnie Fiske, Julia Marlowe, Viola Allen, Maude Adams, Jane Cowl, Blanche Bates, Ethel Barrymore—but looking back over that thirty-year period in 1928, few would have denied her the pro tem queenship of the American theatrical castle. For Miss Anglin was not only an actress of power and imagination, she was the last of the great actor-producers of the American stage. "Unexcelled," "unrivalled," "peerless," are adjectives often elicited by Margaret Anglin in her prime, and in the spring of 1927 we find the distinguished New York Critic, Burns Mantle, putting this rhetorical question: "Who is the greatest American actress of Margaret Anglin's time, if it be not Margaret Anglin herself?" (*N.Y. Evening Mail*, 16.4.27).

As for Margaret Anglin's nationality: despite the fact that she was, in her day, the most famous member of a distinguished Canadian family, and daughter of the Speaker of the Canadian House of Commons, we shall routinely refer to her (as do most library catalogue cards) as an "American actress." She lived in the United States almost continuously from her eighteenth to her seventy-fourth year, became a U.S. citizen (by marriage) at thirty-five, and clearly came to think of herself as a (not unworthy) laborer in the vineyard of "American culture," and possibly as a prophet without honor in her own country. "But of course I'm still a Canadian," she told Rose MacDonald of the *Toronto Evening Telegram* on 17 February 1943, "but I like being an American, too. I think it is very nice to belong to both countries."

But S. Morgan-Powell, in his *Montreal Star* (9.1.58) obituary, remarks ruefully that "Canada has never in any way given any national recognition to Miss Anglin's great achievements [in the theatre]"—and yet, he boldly concludes,

> There is no Canadian woman in any field of art who has brought more credit to her native land by her achievements. Now she is beyond praise or blame, but not beyond remembrance.

The fact that "Canada's Forgotten Great Actress" had "come home" to die is fraught with an irony which was bitter to Powell, a bitterness which we may well leave virtually untasted in this exercise of happy memory.

One thing more should be said at the outset, and that is that I have shrunk from the modern practice of referring to famous women by surname alone. The actress Dorothy

In 1919 M.A spent the summer, as she did most years, at Cedarwold, her "picturesque hacienda" in the Catskills.

Stickney recalls that her husband, the actor-author-director, Howard Lindsay,

> could never bring himself to call her anything but *Miss Anglin*. I remember that many years after their association together she asked him to call her Margaret and he simply could not do it. His respect for her and his awe of her were too great. She never ceased to be a great lady. (J, 40)

The dashing Alfred Lunt avowedly felt the same way, and one would not wish to put oneself above Messrs. Lindsay and Lunt in such a matter.

The beginning of a letter (probably written in 1925) from another of Miss Anglin's colleagues to her husband suggests a way out of the difficulty of which I have been glad to avail myself. The actor Irving Pichel (later a director at Paramount) cautions Howard Hull:

> I hope M.A. is going to take things a bit easily. Her indomitable capacity for killing herself with frantic spurts of overwork really ought to be curbed. (J, 156)

And we find Howard himself, in a letter of somewhat later date, saying, "I am exultant because M.A. has thought well of me." The "M.A." designation seems to have been the normal way of referring to the great woman among her more senior colleagues, and it constitutes a useful and respectful short form with a respectable degree of precedence.

The kind of response that Margaret Anglin elicited at the top of her career is typified by the opening sentences of an article in the *Toronto World* of 20 December 1913:

> Queenly Margaret Anglin spent some hours in Toronto yesterday visiting her brother Arthur Anglin, 70 Grosvenor Street; Miss Anglin did not devote the whole of her visit to her family, however. She graciously reserved a few moments for the press. . . .

And forty years later, at the sad neglectful end, we find Miss Ethel, her devoted dressmaker of many, many years, addressing her, perhaps in a *lapsus calami*, as "dear Lady Anglin." This was, in Arnold Johnson's words, "a commanding and awesome personality" (J, 227), as well as a kindly and gracious one, and we shall, by and large, bear that in mind. And since the imperious is likely to get more play in this study than the affable, Thoda Cocroft (M.A.'s twenties press agent) should be allowed to plump for the latter quality at this point:

With her there was none of the remote sparkle of Mrs. Fiske, who was quick-flowing cool water. Miss Anglin was, by contrast, a warm, gushing torrent which poured itself directly into your heart. Never have I encountered anyone else in the theatre who established herself in a brief interview on such a warm, human plane and without even the suspicion of artifice. (*GN*, 57)

Finally, it should be noted that Margaret Anglin was a person of some literary skill, a talented composer of magazine articles, a lively and literate letterwriter, and a notorious reviser of scripts—but she held no brief for herself as a writer:

Had Miss Anglin never thought of writing her memoirs? [she was asked in her sixty-eighth year]. Well, she had been approached on the subject, but it was just one of those things she had never got around to, and furthermore she doesn't care for the idea of having someone else do the writing, adding, "though I myself have no literary bent." (*Toronto Evening Telegram*, 17.2.43)

She never did get around to her memoirs, and so, at last, someone else *is* doing the writing, in a spirit of which he fondly hopes M.A. would approve.

President Harrison attended the premiere of *Cyrano de Bergerac,* when M.A. "flashed upon the Broadway scene like a newly discovered gem." (1898)

Chapter I

Childhood, Adolescence and Theatrical Beginnings: 1876-1896

If there is nothing like the air one breathes first, why did I not grow up a lobbyist, or, more important still, an advocate of "woman's rights"? (M.A., *Bohemian*, Nov. 1906)

On 3 April 1876, Margaret Anglin commenced her striking and singular life with the striking and singular circumstance of being the only person ever to be born in the Canadian House of Commons. Her father, the Honorable Timothy Warren Anglin, P.C. (1822-96), was, at the time, Speaker of the House and had domicile apartments in the Parliament Buildings in Ottawa.

Timothy Warren Anglin was born 31 August 1822 in County Cork, Ireland, the son of Francis Anglin, a substantial landlord in the village of Clonakilty, and an officer in the civil service of the East India Company. His paternal grandfather, Jeremiah Anglin, a contractor, was the builder of a substantial part of that village and owner of a housing estate called "Myrtle Grove," which he bequeathed to his heirs. T.W.'s maternal grandfather was Timothy Warren, an estate agent from Fermoy, County Cork.

"T.W. was, apparently, preparing for a legal career when the Great Famine hit Ireland in 1845 and forced him to turn to schoolteaching in his home town" (*TWA*, 9). He was, by all accounts, even in his early twenties, a man of a conservative cast of mind, and one must regard with some scepticism the rather persistent allegations that he was at one time an active member of the revolutionary Young Ireland movement. His departure from Ireland would appear to have been prompted by economic rather than political pressures. By 1849 the famine of four years' continuance had rendered Ireland a virtual wasteland, and so, after granting freehold status to all of his tenants, on Easter Monday of that year Anglin embarked for Canada.

His quick establishment of himself as a solid citizen in the country of his adoption, in spite of the social handicaps of his race and religion, is a tribute to his strength of will and spirit. Three months after settling in Saint John, N.B. he became editor (and subsequently owner) of the newspaper the *Saint*

John Freeman. Twelve years after his arrival he was elected to the parliament of the crown colony of New Brunswick. He served in the government for five years, was elevated to ministerial rank, led the anti-Confederation faction, and was (in 1866) defeated on that issue. A year later, however, having accepted the fact of Confederation, he was elected to the federal parliament of Canada, in which he served for fifteen years (1867-82) and was for four years (1875-78) Speaker of the House. Upon the loss of his seat in parliament in July of 1882 he returned to the newspaper business in Toronto as editor of the *Tribune* and editorial writer for the *Globe*.

William Baker's political biography, *Timothy Warren Anglin: Irish Catholic Canadian*, gives an extended portrait of this careful, conscientious, conservative (Liberal) politician, and a briefer one of his second wife, Ellen McTavish Anglin (1843-1923), daughter of Alexander McTavish, a Scottish-Catholic Canadian, and a successful merchant of Saint John. From this source, as from others, we can gather that whereas T.W. was a notably straitlaced, earnest, no-nonsense, not-amused Victorian gent, Ellen was pretty, charming and sociable, and had minor but distinct musical and histrionic talents and a lively taste for theatricals of all polite varieties. Otherwise, Margaret's artistic leanings in general and theatrical leanings in particular would be hard to account for in terms of heredity: though it may be added that T.W. was recognized even by his opponents as "a fluent and forcible speaker" with "an amazing memory" (TWA, 8).

Mary Margaret was the seventh of Timothy and Ellen's ten children, and one may say a lucky seventh, though her name reprised the first names of her two earlier-born sisters who had died in infancy. Margaret, indeed, was to be blessed not only with prevailing good fortune but with extraordinary physical hardihood. She was always the liveliest of the Anglin children and seems to have been a born actor—a fact that she imagined was mystically perceived by Oscar Wilde. Wilde was a guest of her father's in Ottawa in May 1882 when Mary Margaret was just past her sixth birthday, and forty years later she could still remember "clearly" being "held playfully up in the air by Oscar Wilde at a garden party" and that Oscar "wore a happy smile and a brilliant sunflower in his buttonhole." She thought he had an obscure premonition "that the small bit of frilly pink and white creation he was so merrily tossing about in his gleeful mood would some day produce his plays" (EWWI).

A year earlier, when she was "scarcely five," M.A. had taken her first step towards becoming "what [she] was *born* to be." She produced, for a couple of sentimental elderly nuns, in the convent garden which adjoined the Anglin garden in Saint John, her very first "speaking piece." She spoke a poem called "Little Pearl Honey Dew." Perhaps she brought tears to those pious wistful eyes. In any case, she claimed that this "part" was "the only one" she had "never forgotten" (*Bohemian*, Nov. 1906).

Another memory of very early days was that of "a large, beautifully illustrated Shakespeare of my father's" in which she took a "wild delight." She was about four at the time,

> and the books were too heavy for me to lift, so they were put on a stool, or sometimes on the floor of the library, and I would coax for stories while I looked at the engravings. . . . All the stories resolved themselves into fairy stories, and here I gained my first acquaintance with Miranda and her father, with Puck and Titania. For me all fairies dwelt in Ireland and everything beautiful happened there. (Amb)

It is likely enough that T.W. obliged with some well-honed plot summaries. It is more than unlikely that he had anything to do with the emergence of Fairy Erin as an imaginative icon. It is in fact interesting to note at this point that, globetrotter as she became, M.A. never actually set foot on the "auld sod" of the land of her dreams.

Another of her dramatic performances that she could remember took place in Saint John when she was "not yet six" and had to do with a play of her own devising, based upon *Pinafore* (1878), and entitled *Dick Deadeye*, whom she took to be the real hero of the opera. "It was," she says, "a tremendous, soul-moving drama, of sighs and tears, love and hate, of romance and tragedy"—very much the type of thing that was to be the making of her as a professional actress. Her first audience was a slackjawed, "astounded and bewildered gardener," and her first critic the family dog, "Dalmatian Jack," who at the emotional climax of her performance inflicted a severe bite on her right leg. This critic was shot the next day—Miss Anglin's wishes with regard to abusive critics were not always so swiftly and signally honored (EWWI). This taste for domestic histrionics apparently died hard, for, during her Loretto years (*aet.* 7-12), "Margaret," according to Baker, "was frequently to be found out in the stable acting out plays for her schoolmates" (TWA, 5).

She appears indeed to have been undaunted by the rough reception of her first Saint John appearance, for she tells us (*Metropolitan Magazine*, 1.4.02) that when she was "six years old" she appeared in her convent-school's Christmas concert (solo) in the role of Santa Claus and gave a speech describing the wonders of the North Pole and the advantages of being good for goodness' sake. It was, she believes, delivered with *brio* (not, certainly, with *sang froid*), despite the fact that her "great bushy white beard" fell off half way through her harangue. "I finished my recitation to the last word," she recalls, "made my bow, and walked off the stage with unshaken dignity."

From the age of a few weeks till "the delectable age of seven" Mary Margaret lived, for the most part, with her mother, three brothers and one sister in Saint John, while father spent half the year in Ottawa and the other half in New Brunswick with his family. It does appear, however, that occasionally during those seven years M.A. (and presumably her siblings) again called the Speaker's apartments home. For when the Parliament Buildings were destroyed by fire in 1916, M.A. spoke of the destruction of "one of the finest examples of Gothic architecture on the continent" as a loss to "the world" and "a personal loss to me." "I do hope," she said, "that the structure will be rebuilt exactly as it was when I was a child and romped through the stately corridors and lofty chambers." She also recalled "an ancient librarian" reminding her (in 1914) that when she was four or five she rushed up and embraced the feet of "a very fine marble statue of Queen Victoria that stood in the great hallway, . . . and cried because [she] could not have a great big doll just like that." "The room in which Miss Anglin was born [the article concludes] is still intact, but the flames have effaced all semblance of a human abode" (*Pittsburgh Dispatch*, 9.2.16).

When, in the summer of '83, T.W. took over the editorship of the *Tribune*, the Anglins moved to Toronto. Their spacious brick house on University Avenue later became the Chinese Institute. Here, M.A. recalls, T.W. was often visited by the eminent British historian Goldwin Smith (1823-1910). Little Mary-Margaret was deeply impressed by that august personage, but she was, she allows, "too young to derive much profit from such knowledgeable associations" (*Toronto Telegram*, 17.2.43). While their new house was being completed, the Anglins lived at the Rossin House Hotel, which especially featured, in M.A.'s fond recollection, "ice cream three times a day" (*Bohemian*, Nov. 1906). All too soon, however, she was bundled off to day-school, where "lovely ice cream" was replaced by "ugly bread and cheese," and obsequious hotel attendants by the imperious nuns of the junior convent school of Loretto Abbey (Bond Street).

While her general academic accomplishment at the Abbey was unspectacular, her penchant for reading aloud expressively and charmingly was early recognized and abetted by the good ladies of Loretto. She recalls being invited at the age of nine to recite at the St. Patrick's Day concert a piece appropriate to "the Irish-Canadian spirit which reigned supreme at Loretto" (H6). She chose "The Exile of Erin" by the Scottish-Presbyterian poet Thomas Campbell. No doubt she put a little extra into the lines:

> Erin! an exile bequeaths thee his blessing!
> Land of my forefathers, *Erin go bragh!*

In any case, she was well received, and found herself in no way averse to the ovation.

"And so," she says (*Theatre*, Dec. 1905), "I fell into the habit of 'speaking pieces,' and the nuns encouraged me in it. Miss Jessie Alexander taught me elocution as they called it then." Miss Alexander soon became Mary Margaret's favorite teacher ("the dearest little woman imaginable"), and when to her potent influence was added that of "the beautiful Mrs. Scott Siddons," whose vibrant Shakespearean program M.A. heard one thrilling afternoon, the die was cast—she started learning "all of Juliet by heart": she was twelve years old. Her mother made her recite Shakespeare to the famous Belgian actress Madame Rhea. Madame Rhea smiled and sighed (Amb).

Jessie Alexander still remembered many years later (*Toronto Star*, 7.12.13) how, at one of her elocution lessons devoted to the proper speaking of the tumbling trochees of Longfellow's *Hiawatha*, young Mary Margaret adroitly changed seats so that she might be the one to perform the strong emotional passage leading up to the death of "the lovely Minnehaha." "O the long and dreary winter!/ O the cold and cruel winter!" chanted the sweet ten-year-old voice, and Miss Alexander was impressed. Nearly fifty years later (to a string-quartette background) Margaret Anglin read the proem to *Evangeline* to a glittering gathering at the Pleiades Club in Toronto, and was moved to tears when Jessie Alexander appeared to present her with a huge bouquet of roses (*Mail and Empire*, 13.4.34).

Though extempore playlets in the stable were looked upon by T.W. with amused indulgence, and recitations at school concerts with guarded approbation, play-going fell unquestionably into the category of *les jeux défendus*, so that M.A.'s childhood experience of the professional theatre was virtually non-existent.   It happened, however, that a schoolmate's father was manager of the Grand Opera House, and with that friend, from the manager's box (which was so situated as to give glimpses of backstage business) she dimly recalls having seen matinee performances of *Pepita*, *Humpty Dumpty*, and *Fantasma*.   The plays were soon forgotten; the theatrical atmosphere was not (*Bohemian*, Nov. 1906).

Prior to the Opera House matinees, her only experience of the theatre had been "a children's performance of *Pinafore* in a skating rink," and a matinee *Mikado* with mother, brother Wanny and sister Eileen.   "And that," she says (*Bohemian*, Nov. 1906), "was the extent of my youthful theatre-going—with one dramatic exception"—one episode of reckless daring.   One gloomy Saturday afternoon, when she was ten, she secretly borrowed her father's never-used "complimentary season ticket to a new theatre."   Then, with seven-year-old Eileen in tow, she crashed the gates of the New Theatre. Despite trepidation at entrance and wicket, all went well till the curtain rose. Then, as guilty creatures sitting at a play, they were to sup full with "horrors," and to feel the sting of "retributive justice":

> The play was one of Western life: *The Danites* [Joaquin Miller's thriller about a murderous band of Mormon vigilantes].   Pistols and knives seemed to pervade each and every act.   We had been seated in the first row, and there, with lowered heads, terrified and holding hands, decided we would never, never commit such an awful deed again.

Given the egregious prominence of *Mrs. Dane* and the hit Western, *The Great Divide*, in M.A.'s career, the deep impressiveness of *The Danites* might be fancied to be forebodingly significant.

Finally, at twelve-and-a-half, Mary Margaret, after much ardent pleading, was allowed to go (with Mother) to the Opera House to see *L'École du Sacré Coeur*, *Sault au Récollet* ("the Sault"), some five miles north of the city.   This was a tough but "good" Catholic school in which one might well be expected to acquire moral fibre, genteel deportment, and serviceable French, in that order.   Its "stern, if kind, *régime*" (H6) included a 5:45 A.M. to 8 P.M. day, scratchy black uniforms, "skimming the ice off the wash-basin," bathing in one's shift, and no Christmas vacation. Still, it had produced the great opera and oratorio diva Madame Albani, and it did offer to M.A. as schoolmates, if not classmates, (Marie) Louise Edvina (1880-1948), herself a famous Marguerite (and Tosca) and "the first London Louise," and Aloysia Thompson, daughter of Sir John Sparrow Thompson (1844-94) who was to become the fifth prime minister of Canada (EWWI).

At the Sault, as at Loretto, Margaret's brightness ran less to studiousness than to sociability. She was a brisk, outgoing girl who was much more adept at "skating and tobogganing" (EWWI) than at devotions and *devoirs*. Margaret was somewhat noticed at the Sault for voice and "presence," but not at all for academic excellence, as the almost invariable grudging notations of "*assez bien*" (H6) on her report cards witness.

The Sault confronted the extroverted natural-born Speaker with a markedly uncongenial environment:—in that no-nonsense institute, says M.A. "the French nuns would have none of elocution" (Theatre, Dec. 1905). But, surprisingly enough, however little Mesdames du Sacré Coeur may have thought of elocution as a school subject, they did allow that the producing, "pour les soirées concertantes," of "des petites pièces de théâtre" served to develop the memory, poise, and pronunciation of their pupils, and Marie Marguerite was a headliner in several of these playlets. In particular she remembered her first big part, that of the Vulture in a playlet entitled *La colombe et le vautour*—she was mightily pleased with her flamboyant rendition of the Vulture,

> until my high spirits were rudely subdued by the criticism of the Mother Superior, a distinguished Belgian lady of noble birth, who, with a regretful note of regard, yet in no unkindly tone, said to me, "Ma fille, tu es trop théâtral." There is in my mind no reason to believe that I did not profit by her candid and helpful remark. (EWWI)

One may fairly safely assume that she continued (unofficially) to regale her colleagues with "speaking pieces," and her abilities in this kind must have been recognized, however grudgingly, by her teachers, for, as one of her classmates recalled, "She was the girl who was chosen to read the address at the annual distribution of prizes. Ahead of all the graduates, too, mind!" (Maclean's, April 1914). Another classmate remembered that when Mr. and Mrs. Anglin attended the annual School Concert Night in June of 1891, Mary Margaret,

Photos courtesy of Naomi Le Vay

Timothy Anglin (1822-1896) served for fifteen years in the federal parliament of Canada, four as Speaker of the House; M.A.'s mother, his second wife Ellen (1843-1923), loved theatricals of all types.

who had declined to appear in the play in deference to her father's disapproval of theatricals, quite stole the show with an eleventh-hour unscheduled recitation of "a scene from Shakespeare," which T.W. was apparently liberal enough to applaud (*Theatre*, August 1913).

Indeed, one of the oddest things about Margaret Anglin's career is that the illustrious T.W. never saw his illustrious daughter perform; but perhaps we should allow Miss Anglin to tell us about that in her own way:

> Certainly [she avows] I inherited neither taste nor talent for the stage from my father, for when he and my mother came to Buffalo to see me my first year on the stage, he went to the theatre but he did not see me play, for he kept his eyes rigidly closed. Thus, since he never came to another performance of mine, my father never saw me on the stage.
>
> But my mother, while a domestic woman, had a taste for amateur theatricals. She was a warm friend of Lord and Lady Dufferin. Lord Dufferin was a relative of Sheridan's and he and his wife liked the things of the playhouse and frequently gave amateur theatricals at Rideau Hall, the home of the Governor General, just out of Ottawa. My mother appeared in several of the little home-staged plays, and enjoyed her performances, and liked the atmosphere of the stage. If, therefore, I inherited my bent for the stage it was undoubtedly from my mother. (*Theatre*, Dec. 1905)

We can, in fact, derive a little pleasant puffing for Ellen McTavish Anglin as an amateur diva of poise and presence from Lady Dufferin's Journal:

> I was able to be present at *Le Maire de St. Brieux*. The music is very pretty and the whole play excellent. It is very interesting to bring out a new thing on one's own stage, and even the author and composer must have been satisfied with the actors and singers who played in it, . . . The prima donna, Mrs. Anglin, both sang and looked charmingly. (*EWWI*)

T.W., however, was not to be numbered among Ellen's fans, and the stringency of his anti-stage bias (at least where his womenfolk were concerned) may be illustrated by the *Sweethearts* anecdote. Lady Dufferin had chosen to produce W.S. Gilbert's musical comedy of that name with Ellen Anglin as lead singer, and Lord Dufferin had adjourned the House so that Mr. Speaker could have no excuse for not attending. But astoundingly, dramatically, "my father deliberately absented himself from the performance"—the front and centre seat of honor remained reproachfully empty. (*EWWI*)

Margaret's three-years-younger sister, Eileen Warren, was moved to follow in her elder sister's footsteps. She was for some time a regular with the Lancers company and had a fairly steady run of small parts. Indeed, she lived with Margaret in New York, more or less under her patronage, on and off from 1898 until her marriage in 1910 to Capt. C.T. Hutchins, U.S. Navy attaché-elect to Peking, and her removal to that city. M.A.'s six-years-older brother, Arthur, was, apparently, a stellar performer in collegiate plays (in French) at Collège Ste-Marie in Montreal. Arthur was to go on to become one of the premier corporation lawyers in Canada while Margaret was bearing away the bell on the American stage. The first-born of the family, the Right Honorable Francis Alexander Anglin, K.C., P.C., LL.D., Chief Justice of Canada (1924-33), as Supreme Court judge, Grand Cross Papal Knight, Imperial Privy Councillor, and surrogate head of the Government of Canada, would appear to have had precious little time for things theatrical. He was, however, in his younger days, chief tenor soloist of the St. Michael's Cathedral choir, and the composer of original scores for the motets "Ave Verum" and "Salve Regina" (*Toronto Star*, 6.3.33). A third elder brother (by three years) Timothy Warren, Jr. (Wanny), also followed Margaret to New York where he pursued a shady business career and was an occasional worry (and charge) to the actress. Her five-years-younger brother, Basil, who became a petroleum industry executive, also ended up in New York, and proved to be the main prop of Margaret's declining years. The last of T.W.'s ten children, and the seventh to survive infancy, was Alexander Edward (1883-99), a bright, winning lad, who died of consumption three days after his sixteenth birthday. His funeral was paid for by the ever-generous Margaret (K, 6.6.99).

Sometime during the summer of 1893, Mary Margaret, just turned seventeen, a year away from graduation, enlisted her mother's sympathy in her yen to slough off the dreariments of convent school for the adventure of acting school. T.W., needless to say, was not supportive of the project, even though the course at the Empire Dramatic School was described to him as "a course in dramatic reading," conducive to a drawing room and collegiate career as a professional elocutionist. However, when Ellen assured T.W., "If she will, she *will*," and proceeded to produce the tuition fee out of her own purse—she had "secretly sold some prize lace flounces" (*TWA*, 255)—T.W. reluctantly agreed. But, as M.A. puts it, "My father remained a bulwark of disapproval." Though he never begrudged her a generous allowance, he never alluded to his daughter's chosen profession, and "never allowed the subject to be mentioned in his presence" (Amb).

According to M.A., it came to her, "as though an oracle had spoken," in Chicago, in the midst of the heady divertissements of the Columbian Exposition, that she was "destined to be a dramatic reader" (EWW1). The "friends of the family" who had taken her to Vanity Fair helped her to go directly to New York where, by way of "a letter from Mr. Shepard, manager of the theatre [sic] in Toronto, to Mr. Augustus Pitou, one of the foremost managers in New York," she found herself ushered into the courtly, ironic presence of the veteran English actor-teacher Nelson Wheatcroft, the principal of the Empire School (Amb).

At the school she had "a hall bedroom—plenty of heat in the summer, a deal of cold in winter, a cracked pitcher, and a springless bed" (*Maclean's*, Apr. 1914). But everything seemed like luxury after the self-obliterating austerities of Sacré Coeur. She later boarded out with another girl student and began her long career of monetary mismanagement by treating her friend to such theatrical delights as Fanny Davenport's Cleopatra, Julia Marlowe's Juliet, and Ellen Terry's "ardent" Portia and "glittering" Beatrice—"O there be players that I have seen play—"and failing to find money for car-fares and lunches, leading to unscheduled crash diets and forced marches (Amb).

While ostensibly studying to be a "public reader" under the able tutelage of Mr. Wheatcroft and his wife, the American actress Adeline Stanhope, Margaret took part in several quite well-attended school plays. She also managed to persuade Miss Stanhope to teach her the part of Rosalind (Amb). As her first public *platform* appearance was as Santa Claus, it seems fitting enough that her first public *stage* appearance should be "in a little one-act play by Martha Morton, entitled *Christmas*, which was produced at one of Mr. Wheatcroft's matinees at the Empire Theatre" (*Every Month*, Dec. 1898). She also recalls a school matinee appearance as Little Em'ly in *David Copperfield*, of which production she remembers only the line addressed to her by one of the Dickensian heavies: "There are doorways and dustheaps for such as you." "It seems prophetic," she says (H6), "in view of all the sinners and outcasts my managers have since forced me to play."

What she refers to as "My First Professional Appearance" (EWW1) was as an extra in Belasco's *The Girl I Left Behind Me* (a

With her mother's support and father's disapproval, M.A. studied as a "public reader" in Montreal, taking part in several school plays; here aged 14, Sacré Coeur. (1890)

melodrama in which she was subsequently to play the lead). She and her boarding-house friend faithfully and punctually appeared for six evenings and two matinees during the week's run, went broke on car-fares and new hats (specially purchased for their big parts), and for the last two days were reduced to walking the two miles from the school to the theatre. At the end of that epoch-making week, she recalls, "we were handed the munificent sum of $5 each for the entire week's work, and in addition we were told that we were no longer required" (H6).

Just after this episode, she found herself at cross purposes with a play called *Cross Keys*. As a student addition to a professional cast, she made her first appearance fiercely straitlaced into a too small gown, so that she presented an apoplectic visage to an apprehensive audience, and prompted one of the backstage regulars to call out "Number eighteen!"—stage lingo for rouge. In her second appearance, as the result of a late call, she astonished another audience by entering through the lake (EWW1).

Her big break came in August of 1894, just three months past her eighteenth birthday (and less than a year after her arrival in New York), when, by her own account, she somewhat fortuitously landed a part in a play being produced at the New York Academy of Music:

> My first engagement [M.A. recalls] was with *Shenandoah* [a Civil War "romance"]. Mr. Charles Frohman, when he engaged me, didn't remember that he had seen me in any of the school plays, so that I could not flatter myself that any merit of mine appealed to him. It was rather sheer good fortune, for in the distribution of half a dozen students from the school among the season's plays I happened to fall to the cast of *Shenandoah*. I played a small part called Madeline West. . . . Then one night Margaret Robinson, who played the part of Mrs. Everill, fainted, and I was thrust into her part, playing that of Madeline West also. While doing my best for Mrs. Everill, under the circumstances, I was not reassured by hearing the voice of [producer] Alf Hayman in the corridor saying, "Take that girl off!" (*Theatre*, Dec. 1905)

She was, however, warmly reassured by the affectionate regard she elicited from the author, "the lovable Bronson Howard." Howard, by then the author of a dozen successful plays, was all of fifty-two years old in 1894, but to the trepidant rookie actress he seemed a rock of ages,

> a venerable old gentleman—one I held in awe but loved because he was so kind and generous to me. "We will hear from you some day, my dear," he said to me, and for that instant I could scarcely speak, so boundless was my gratitude. But my

exultation was short-lived, for along came a lady attached to the company with the comfortable rejoinder: "Oh, yes, she'll be heard, for she outroars the cannon!" (H6)

Just before she was admitted to the Empire company, Nelson Wheatcroft had decided that "Anglin was an impossible name," and Mary was no good either, and so henceforth his young and highly recommended graduate would be called Margaret Moore (after the author of *Irish Melodies*), and that, indeed, is how M.A. appears on the '94 *Shenandoah* program (Bohemian, Nov. 1906).

She remained with *Shenandoah* until the spring of '95, and in the course of that nine months "played every female part in it." Having served the company so faithfully and adaptably, she naturally expected Mr. Frohman to present her not only with an accolade but with a substantial contract, but the impresario appeared to have quite forgotten the existence of the "painfully thin," sad-eyed teenager who had unaccountably caught his fancy nine months earlier. So she "accepted a position in Buffalo stock" and while with that company she played (among others) "the girl in [Richard Mansfield's version of] *Dr. Jekyll and Mr. Hyde* and the more subtle Mrs. Linden in *A Doll's House*" (H6). She apparently learned the part of Agnes Jekyll without rehearsing with the company, for she told the *St. John Progress* (31.7.97), perhaps disingenuously, that

> She had never seen the play done before the night of the performance, and on that evening when she saw the gentleman who played the title role as Mr. Hyde, he was so entirely horrible that she actually shrieked with fright; there was no acting about it, and, later, when he is supposed to take her by the throat, she was simply paralyzed with fear.

On another occasion she was "dismissed for 'incompetence'" in the midst of one mid-day rehearsal, only to be "re- engaged two hours later, in time for the evening show" (EWW 1).

Otherwise those ten or twelve weeks in Buffalo stock exist in her recollections simply as a distinctly unthrilling "maze of hard work." "The munificent salary was fifteen dollars a week," but then one was gaining valuable, if hard-earned experience; one was becoming a trusty trouper and a good companion; and ultimately one attracted the attention of the stylish, if somewhat unstable, actor-manager Charles Rohlfs and his consort, the novelist Anna Katherine Green, for both of whom she conceived, in spite of all, she says, "an almost affectionate regard" (H6).

M.A.'s Shakespearean appetite was modestly indulged in Rohlfs's production of *The Merchant of Venice*, in which she played Nerissa and understudied Portia. Unfortunately, that show ran only a fortnight and Portia never fell to her lot. "Mr. Rolfe [sic] was also playing Molière [unspecified] and *The Leavenworth Case"* (H6). This last was Anna Green's own dramatization (1891) of her popular novel (1885) of the same title. M.A. played a harrowed but spunky Eleanor Leavenworth, while the suitably manic-depressive Rohlfs took the part of the hopelessly impassioned secretary, James Harwell, who kills Eleanor's husband and then kills again to cover his tracks. After twelve weeks Rohlfs abandoned his rather ragtag tour and drew back, for the nonce, *pour mieux sauter,* and Margaret Moore was again an actress in search of a character.

During her *Cyrano* success in '98 she gave (in an unguarded moment) this description of the Rohlfs tour to an importunate interviewer:

> We were barnstormers; nothing more nor less, and when we entered a town we felt like burglars. If you had seen the plays we gave and the properties and scenery (announced on the billboard as "Same cast and production as seen for 150 nights in New York") you would know why we felt guilty. Our manager didn't feel guilty. He said he felt abused. He had a grudge against the local public because they wouldn't rush up to him with their hard-earned money. And he had no kind feelings for us either, though we were working entirely without pay. No one was able to draw a cent of salary during the entire twelve weeks we were together. All we got was food and lodging, and how the manager hated us because we had to eat. (Rpt., *Cleveland Plain Dealer,* 3.12.11)

Hard times in the country, to be sure: and when Margaret received a hundred dollars in a letter from home, the harddone-by manager (presumably Rohlfs himself) "borrowed" it from her and never paid it back. Needless to say, after reading this piece the "far-famed" Anna Green Rohlfs wrote to Miss Anglin "assuring me in no uncertain terms of the depth of my ingratitude," but without offering to repay the hundred dollars.

Shortly after the demise of the Rohlfs company, M.A. (still as Margaret Moore) was able to catch on with the William Morris company and travel with them into Michigan and the mid-west. In one of her roles the nineteen-year-old M.A. was called upon to play the mother of the forty-year-old Morris. She remembers Morris handing her one of his own grey wigs while "he himself put on my make-up of dark smudges and heavy lines to portray the hollow cheeks and crow's feet of a face of old age" (*EWWI*).   Her Birthday Book contains this cryptic entry for 3 April 1896:

> This is all very well—being an actress—but playing Nadia in *Michael Strogoff*, with William Morris, at the National Theatre, Philadelphia, isn't all it might be.   And one wonders whether the ghost will make its appearance this week.

It was with Morris, too, that M.A. played the lead in David Belasco's suspense melodrama, *The Girl I Left Behind Me*, the play in which she had made her first "pro" appearance, as a super.   Morris, a good-looking and effective actor of the flamboyant school was, years later, for M.A.'s benefit, rather unfairly dismissed by Howard Hull in two words: "O trumpery! O Morris!"

Exactly one month after that twentieth birthday entry, T.W. Anglin died of a stroke in Toronto, and Margaret, on being called home, terminated her coolly amicable connection with "the brisk and businesslike Mr. Morris" (*H6*).

The passing of T.W. represented a kind of grievous emancipation to his daughter.   Her tears at his graveside welled up from deep-seated conflicting feelings of regret and release.   The high-principled, puritanical, Victorian gentleman had been a figure both forbidding and admirable to the somewhat wilful and whimsical young Mary Margaret, and his death, in considerably reduced circumstances, represented both a heartfelt loss of a steadfast authority figure and a welcome liberation from a source of inhibition and reproach.

Margaret's sense of family dignity, and noblesse oblige, held somewhat in abeyance by the steady decline in her father's fortunes since the mid-eighties, was given a boost by the presence among the official mourners of such politico-legal luminaries as Sir Oliver Mowat, Sir Frank Smith, Sir Glenholme Falconbridge and Sir Charles Moss (as the latter two were soon to become).   The *St. John Globe* (4.5.96) closed its obituary with a simple and telling tribute to this all too Job-like "perfect and upright man":

> He was as widely esteemed for his blameless private life as for his conscientious public-spiritedness. . . . Possessed of a great memory, a great capacity for work, a facile pen, Mr. Anglin shone as a writer, and as a speaker there were few men who were superior to him.

She might have felt a challenge to excellence in those words too.

In any case, after recovering her equilibrium after the shock of her father's death, and recovering it again after a fall from a horse, she obtained an audition with "America's premier romantic actor," James O'Neill—and her rise to stardom may well be considered to have begun with that fortunate interview.

With O'Neill's Empire Company, M.A. played the female lead in five plays in twelve months, including Virginia in *Virginius*. (1896)

Chapter II

The Road to Stardom—O'Neill, Mansfield, Sothern: 1896-1900

> I remember the almost too secure feeling of the Empire
> Company. I also remember the non-stop Charles Frohman
> eating his ever-present, never-lit cigar at rehearsals.
> Somebody had to be nervous. (M.A., *H3*)

The Kilkenny-born James O'Neill at forty-seven was a
handsome, "romantic-looking," square-built man, hale-fellow-
well-met—a man of indomitable feckless cheerfulness,
variegated with "streaks of sentimental melancholy and rare
flashes of intuitive sensibility" (*LDJ*, 14). His intuition did not
fail him in the case of Margaret Anglin. He was himself
possessed of a fine, flexible voice, excellent stage presence, and
a gift for poetical delivery, and he immediately recognized all
of these qualities in the twenty-year-old hopeful before him,
and so he engaged the rather flimsy looking 110-pound girl
without hesitation, although she recalls that

> I was first given only the ingenue roles. But not long after I
> came into the company I changed places with the leading
> woman, and strange to say we remained friends throughout
> that year's engagement. (*H6*)

An early and notable instance, this, of the Anglin charm
sweetening a potentially bitter relationship. In the case of
Hamlet, she tells us, "I began as the Player Queen, but after
the first week I was promoted to Ophelia, and played it for
that entire year" (*Amb*).

In the just under twelve months that she stayed with
O'Neill, M.A. took the female lead in five plays which O'Neill
was then playing on tour, more or less in rotation:—these
were *Hamlet*, *Virginius* (Knowles), *The Lyons Mail* (Reade),
Richelieu (Lytton), and *Monte Cristo* (Dumas-Fechter), in which
M.A. played Mercedes, while O'Neill "lived" the dual roles of
Dantès and the Count. O'Neill's experience with *Monte Cristo*
(which M.A. shared for ten months) constitutes what Benjamin
McArthur (*ACC*, 45) calls "the most famous example of character
entrapment" in the annals of the American stage. O'Neill
played *Monte Cristo* more or less continuously for seventeen
years (1883-1900) during which time he played the dual role
more than five thousand times. Needless to say he became

almost totally identified with the Count in the popular theatre-going mind, and he came to feel this identification as a histrionic straitjacket.   Doubtless O'Neill told his young colleague to avoid at all costs the character-entrapment morass, and, on the whole, she was conspicuously successful in doing so.

The Birthday Book entry for 3 April 1897 reads as follows:

> One's third birthday as a professional, and things might be worse—even though one has to play two performances this day: Mercedes in *Monte Cristo* at the matinee, and Virginia in *Virginius* at night—and all this with James O'Neill, at the Metropolitan Opera House, St. Paul.

This busy time she describes (*Theatre*, Dec. 1905) as "a comfortable year"—the comfort, perhaps, deriving from her willingness to let herself be carried along by the current of O'Neill's egotistic optimism.   Though O'Neill's normal manner was bluff, breezy and off-hand, he reserved a kindly and avuncular attitude for his bright young protégée and co-star, and they got on famously together. And if Margaret was pleasantly patronized by James O'Neill, she was able to return the compliment to the eight-year-old Eugene O'Neill, an ubiquitous backstage pixie, whose indulgent and complaisant idol she readily became.

When the O'Neill tour came to Toronto in November of 1896, Miss Anglin was, not unnaturally, the centre of attention.   The *Globe* drama critic who covered the performance of Sheridan Knowles's (1820) Roman-Christian melodrama *Virginius* at the Grand Opera House, after a brief perfunctory tribute to Mr. O'Neill's "impressive, picturesque and powerful" Virginius, goes on to say:

> The occasion had a special local interest in the debut of Miss Margaret Anglin, of Toronto, who essayed with unquestioned success, the role of the heroine, Virginia. Miss Anglin more than justified the praise of her friends by her charming presentation of the role.   An attractive and winning personality, a well modulated, musical voice, and artistic appreciation and intelligence, enable her to give a singularly grateful exposition of the character.   Virginia's artlessness, her modest love and filial tenderness, were portrayed with an unaffected charm that proved quite convincing.   Miss Anglin made a

conquest of her audience with her first scene, and was subsequently recalled and presented with several handsome bouquets. (*Globe*, 3.11.96)

When the same production appeared in Ottawa on 11 November, it received this notice:

The most noteworthy event of the season occurred here this evening, the occasion of Mr. James O'Neill's appearance at the Opera House. More than usual interest was attached to his programme through his leading woman, Miss Margaret Anglin, a native of this city, daughter of the late Hon. Timothy Anglin. Miss Anglin's efforts were appreciated with much applause by a large and representative audience, which included several members of the Cabinet, Secretary of State R.W. Scott and Premier Laurier. The Premier took occasion to compliment Miss Anglin on her work, and as an admirer and staunch friend of her father felt proud of her success. (*Journal*, 12.11.96)

The *Globe*'s response (4.11.96) to her Ophelia is a trifle more guarded:

Miss Margaret Anglin made a very pleasing Ophelia, full of maidenly modesty, shrinking like a sensitive plant from the painful situations in which she became involved, and into which she was forced by her father to play so prominent a part. She looked charming in the character, and when greater experience enables her to overcome the difficulties of the mad scene, her Ophelia must hold a high place in the repertoire of the young actress.

Whether she was significantly stronger in the mad scene when she played it three years later in San Francisco (in Henry Miller's production) is a moot point. Her own adjective for her Ophelia is "misty" (*N.Y. Times*, 5.3.16), which quality might well tell against a strong mad scene. In any case, Alan Dale, several years later, harked back to M.A.'s "wonderfully sweet and fresh" Ophelia as the only memorable thing in O'Neill's rather "fusty musty" *Hamlet* (*N.Y. American*, 4.3.12).

Many years later the eminent Canadian critic, Hector Charlesworth, was to recall that

She was an exquisite Mercedes in *Monte Cristo*, but had a much better opportunity as the persecuted Virginia in Sheridan Knowles' Roman tragedy, *Virginius*, once a favourite with the public. She made a wonderful picture in classic robes. It was a foretaste of later triumphs in the Greek drama. (*Globe and Mail*, 13.2.43)

She wore a white chiton and a white rose as Virginia. "Do you remember," said O'Neill a dozen years later on a backstage visit, "the night I forbade you to wear a red rose in your hair when you were ready to go on as Virginia?" "Imagine," says the emblem-conscious M.A., "wearing a red rose as Virginia!" (H3)

During her stay in Toronto in November 1896 the twenty-year-old Margaret Anglin was interviewed for the *Globe* (7.11.96) by an excessively refined young lady called Miss S.P. (Donna) O'Grady, who seems to have known the actress as a schoolgirl:

While awaiting her coming I speculated freely upon the change in one's appearance a few years make. Yet here the alteration was not great; a graceful young creature with a clever, delicate face and eyes sweetly expressive; a woman fully grown. I noted, too, the long slender hand and tapering fingers, the artistic hand. Miss Anglin's chief charm is her voice, so full of musical cadences that it is a pleasure to hear her speak. However, she is loath to speak about herself, deeming it egotistical; but all questions are answered with a gentle, well-bred courtesy. . . .

She admitted she had no fad, "unless a love of horses and horseback riding could be considered one. . . . No, I do not ride a wheel. I am afraid you will find me very commonplace."

Beauty, brains and ability combined with youth and a charming personality. Commonplace, indeed!

Miss Anglin is a cultured gentlewoman, and besides possessing dramatic talent of an unusually high order she is a brilliant musician, speaks French fluently, and wields a facile pen.

In the course of the dressing-room interview, M.A. transformed herself for the part of Jeanette Lesurques in Charles Reade's (1854) romantic comedy *The Lyons Mail*, and Miss O'Grady was able to improve the shining moment with a burst of fine writing:

Presently before me stands the quaintest figure imaginable. With auburn curls tossing over neck and shoulders, a great bunch of deep crimson roses is fastened among the tresses, the piquant, smiling face aglow with colour, the gaily striped skirt and coquettish bolero, a peasant maid with twinkling feet in absurd little slippers. Dear heart! what a contrast to the poetic Virginia and the frail, gentle Ophelia. A pretty, pretty picture. Involuntarily I sigh: such a glancing image of fleeting sweetness.

We are also indebted to Miss O'Grady for the incidental intelligence that Miss Anglin, at this early stage of her career, was generally "accompanied on her travels" by her still slightly stage-struck mother, who was thus able to act as both fan and duenna.

M.A. never ceased to think with affection and gratitude of James O'Neill ("that sterling actor" [Bohemian, Nov. 1906]) as the person most instrumental in getting her started on the road to theatrical stardom. Twenty years after their stage association she remembers him as "the delightful and lovable James O'Neill," and recalls that "from the first of our acquaintance Mr. O'Neill was considerate and gentle." In the heady times of her first big parts he was her friend, philosopher, and guide. "His many kindnesses," she declares, "will be treasured always as a golden heritage of my life upon the stage" (EWW1).

It was O'Neill who persuaded her to keep her own name (barring the Mary) rather than adopt the more euphonious Margaret Moore as her stage name. "Moore," he assured her, "is a very run-of-the-mill name, and could lend no distinction, whereas Anglin is singular and arresting." "And it was he," she generously concedes, "who first taught me to read Shakespeare" (H6). In his onward and upward exhortation to Margaret at their professional parting of the ways, O'Neill, the phrasemaker, was heard to say, "And, Mary, you must do Shakespeare, you have the Irish Sea in your voice" (Amb). "Oh, ay," said Miss Anglin, "like the howling of Irish wolves against the moon." But she never forgot those fancifully challenging words.

It was, in fact, in response to an offer from the Canadian-born play promoter and producer William F. Connor to sponsor her in a Maritime tour of *As You Like It* (featuring herself as star and director) that M.A. parted from O'Neill in the summer of '97. It was a very green (mostly Canadian collegiate) outfit that the twenty-one-year-old directrix had in tow, and "so ill-prepared were the actors" for the opening night at the Yarmouth Opera House that they had taken the desperate remedy of "pinning their lines to the boughs of the trees in the Forest of Arden" (H6). This expedient led to a somewhat puzzling performance, so that the next day's *Yarmouth Sentinel* (24.7.97) reported that "Miss Anglin's company played *As You Like It* as they liked it."

Whether or not they liked her *As You Like It*, Maritime theatre-goers certainly liked M.A., if one can judge from the description proffered by the *St. John Progress* (31.7.77):

> She is charming in manner and attractive in person, with a dainty, svelte figure, a riante sparkling face, and brilliant conversational powers; in fact, a more thoroughly bewitching and interesting young lady it would be hard to imagine.

The *Progress* also notes that the precocious directrix (who normally does not give interviews) has already mastered "twenty-eight different parts," and that "she is accompanied by her sister Eileen [presumably a member of the troupe] and by her mother, who may well be proud of her gifted daughter."

While *As You Like It* was the feature of the hurly-burly Maritime summer of '97, M.A. & Co. also played (catch-as-catch-can) a comedy double-bill consisting of *The Mysterious Mr. Bugle* and W.S. Gilbert's *Comedy and Tragedy*, J.B. Buckstone's *A Rough Diamond*, Madeleine Ryley's *Christopher Jr.*, and W.S. Gilbert's *Pygmalion and Galatea*. It was while playing a vivacious Galatea to an inert Pygmalion that M.A. was approached by the New York impresario Daniel Frohman with the offer of a significant part in E.H. Sothern's production of *The City of Pleasure*, or, failing that, the role of Flavia in *The Prisoner of Zenda*, or, failing that, something nice in *Change Alley*. So she left her babes in the woods to face the remaining three backwater engagements without her, and "took the very next train back to New York" (H6).

As it happened, *none* of these plum parts fell into the eager hands of our heroine, and this fiasco may well have been the result of "a notice which appeared in the papers to the effect that I had proclaimed myself Mr. Sothern's new leading woman" (H6)—a totally false notice, well calculated to put everybody's back up and nose out of joint. In any case, Margaret Anglin, the Canadian headliner, was all at once reduced to dancing silent attendance upon the magisterial whim of the English-gentlemanly E.H. Sothern. Finally, she accepted, with winning modesty, the soubrette ("slavey") part of Meg, "the angel of the attic," in Belasco's domestic drama *Lord Chumley* ("I who had wanted to be a great Juliet!" [H6]). But when Sothern's beautiful and accomplished leading

Richard Mansfield played Cyrano to M.A.'s Roxane: they were "an oddly matched pair," though the play was a tremendous success. (1898)

woman, Virgina Harned, was taken ill, M.A., who had secretly understudied her, once again leapt from obscurity to stardom, this time in the title role of Anthony Hope's romantic comedy, *The Adventure of Lady Ursula*. And, all at once, from being an uncommunicative cloud-dweller, Sothern became "an angel of goodness to me," an "unselfish" colleague of great "warmth and solicitousness" (H6).

Her position of eminence in the Sothern company, however, was inevitably a temporary one. Sothern considered her too young for most leading-woman parts, and, in any case, he was still in possession of his permanent leading woman (and wife), Virginia Harned—though he was soon to swap her, in both capacities, for the equally delectable Julia Marlowe. And so, at the end of the *Lady Ursula* run, M.A. parted with Sothern (and Virginia) on friendly terms, in order to accept an offer from the other great star of the day, Richard Mansfield.

Her first meeting (in Washington) with the dashing Mansfield was characteristically disconcerting:

> The company was in the midst of rehearsals of *The First Violin*. The play was actually under way, and the actors were being worked and overworked relentlessly. I entered the auditorium of the theater and remained in the dark back of the last row. Everything about me was inky black. Suddenly up the aisle came the figure of Mr. Mansfield, and putting his arm about me he exclaimed: "Well, darling do you think that was good?" I am sure my embarrassment and amazement were no greater than his when he discovered I was a total stranger instead of his wife [Beatrice Cameron] whom he had left standing there a few moments before. (H2)

Mansfield was unwilling to encounter her again that day, and the flustered Margaret was fain to accept the distinctly niggardly stipend of "sixty dollars a week" proffered to her (apologetically) by Mansfield's business manager, the benevolent A.M. Palmer.

Word was already out that Mansfield was about to give Rostand's *Cyrano de Bergerac* its American premiere, and M.A. was hoping against hope that she would be offered the part of Roxane—"a most delicious *précieuse*, combining all the florid romance I had been accustomed to, and all the manner I most desired to try to put into it." Mansfield, however, gave her no encouragement in her hopes, and indeed let it be understood that he was "on the lookout for a blonde Roxane,"

and was "courting Ida Conquest" (*H2*). He kept M.A. cooling
her heels during the first week of rehearsals, not even
deigning to look in her direction; and it was not until she had
handed Palmer her resignation and accepted a part with a
rival company in a play called *That Man* that Mansfield called
her back and gave her the part that he probably always
intended for her, in view of her "aptitude for poetic
utterance." What he actually said to Palmer was, "Where is
that rather ugly little girl that always used to sit there—now
that I want her" (*H2*).

Rehearsals with the great man were no bed of roses. In
their very first run-through, Mansfield stopped her in mid-
sentence with the astonishing comment: "My child, your voice
is like a fog-horn. Pray, try to modulate it." And "at the end
of virtually every line he pulled [her] up with a sharp critical
halt." After that first humiliating day she confronted him
stonily at the stage-door: "Mr. Mansfield," she announced in
ringing tones, "you must be very careful what you say to me
hereafter." Mr. Mansfield "laughed consumedly," and
thereafter treated her much better (*H2*).

Nevertheless, the next day when M.A. unwittingly
upstaged him, Mansfield could not resist turning to A.M.
Palmer and saying very plonkingly:

> Mr. Palmer, I must say your young friend looks like being a
> star. . . . I think she should be featured in this play. . . . But
> I do not think, just yet, I can afford to *support* her. (*H2*)

Herbert Whittaker tells us of how the rather vainglorious
and overbearing Mansfield gained new respect for his pro tem
leading woman "after she had caught him making belittling
remarks about her in French. Miss Anglin, whose French was
impeccable, was not only able to correct Mansfield's grammar,
but to add some sharp Irish comments about his manners"
(*Globe Magazine*, 7.9.57). An even more widely circulated story tells
of how M.A. first gained a place in Mansfield's esteem by
way of a wittily turned compliment. The exchange went
something like this:

> **Mansfield:** Do you think, Miss uh, you can make yourself
> up pretty enough for Roxane?
>
> **M.A.:** I don't see why not, sir, if you can make yourself up
> ugly enough for Cyrano. (*H2*)

As Cyrano and Roxane they were (perhaps appropriately) an
oddly matched pair. He was forty-four, short, stocky and

choleric. She was twenty-two, tall, slender, and (seemingly) phlegmatic. And though they never did warm to each other, they played well to each other, and the play was an outstanding success.

This starring role in the first American production of an important Continental play was clearly M.A.'s most noteworthy and prestigious part yet, and by all accounts she brought it off with great charm and piquancy. The *N.Y. Tribune* (15.10.98) reviewer goes a little further than that:

> So exquisite [he rhapsodizes], so poetic and so beautiful was Miss Anglin's Roxane that it shone resplendent in a production altogether superb. Miss Anglin flashed upon [the Broadway scene] like a newly discovered gem.

The morning after the opening of *Cyrano* was to M.A. as the morning after the publication of *Childe Harold* was to Byron. "She awoke to find herself famous," as sister Eileen, who brought her the morning papers, was the first of many to say.

Few Broadway debuts can have been more striking, for many a critic over the years kept harking back to it, as did he of the *Cincinnati Commercial* (25.1.10), in the context of M.A.'s vivid portrayal of Helena Richie:

> It is now fully ten years since she thrilled us with her Roxane in the late Richard Mansfield's lavish and flamboyant production of *Cyrano*. . . . But who does not remember her charm and fascination in that marvellous and poetic creation? Who does not more distinctly remember its effect upon himself? For it was a work of tremendous instinctive talent if not absolute genius; it was one of those things that spoke direct to the individual; that penetrated all swaddlings of circumstance and education; that uttered a universal voice; that affected the innermost feelings.

More than half a lifetime later we hear the venerable Hector Charlesworth observing (*Globe and Mail*, 17.3.43): "Great as was Mansfield's triumph as Cyrano, it was also a triumph for the young unknown who played the dream-like lady of his adoration—since that night, Oct. 3 1898, the name of Margaret Anglin has been famous on Broadway." Speaking of the memorability of M.A.'s "flower-like" Roxane, Herbert Whittaker cites a first lady's fond recollection:

> President Harrison attended the premiere, and his wife remembered it, years after, as one of the greatest evenings she had ever spent in the theatre, dwelling particularly on the beauty of the new leading lady's performance. (*Globe Magazine*, 7.9.57)

Mansfield's growing respect for M.A. as a supporting actress and a contending intelligence did not, unfortunately, add any warmth to their obviously rather tetchy relationship. He clearly thought she was impossibly thin-skinned, always imagining slights—not to say saturated with *amour-propre*. Her words for him are "overbearing," "high-handed," "domineering," "egocentric," "irascible"—yet withal he had his moments of extravagant generosity and cordial geniality. "He was a great artist, a great manager," she concedes, "but all temperament" (*H2*). As a star in her own right, she did not have much time for temperament in others. One may imagine that they parted with a big sigh of mutual relief at the end of the *Cyrano* run, when, in terms of the new contract, Mansfield proposed to buy cheap and Anglin to sell dear. Nonetheless, in a pompous moment of weakness, which he almost lived to regret, Mansfield had told her, "If you remain with me you will have the same position as Miss Terry has with Mr. Irving" (*Amb*).

Two years later, when they were both playing in Boston, Mansfield invited M.A. "several times to his supper parties," and there she came to appreciate for the first time the wonderfully witty and multitalented man he was—his musical and literary skill, his story-telling genius ("in many tongues"). Still, she could see that, had she stayed with him, she would always have stood in his shadow (*H2*).

After leaving Mansfield, M.A. signed on with the Liebler Company to play Constance in Sydney Grundy's version of *The Three Musketeers*, with James O'Neill as d'Artagan and Blanche Bates as Milady. (The amiable Blanche insisted that Margaret should share with her the star's dressing room.) She endured a successful run of several weeks with a "nothing" part in this poor play, and then experienced the frustration of losing a good part in a good play as the piece died after three weeks of sparse houses. This play was Charles Coghlan's *Citizen Pierre*, in which the author took the title role while M.A. played the heroine, Héloïse Tison. On the one hand, she was sorry to see the play go under because she had discovered in Mr. Coghlan a model of "courtesy, kindliness, . . . superb diction and finished style." On the other hand, she was somewhat relieved by its early demise, since she found that "a play in which the guillotine and all the horrors of the sans-culottes figured prominently" had an unnerving way of delivering her into the clutches of the blue devils (*H3*).

It was while she was doing the *Musketeers* "nonsense" that she was scouted by Henry Miller, a rising "young" (forty) actor-producer, and when *Citizen Pierre* fell through she joined the

Henry Miller Stock Company for their 1899 tour. She was engaged "at fifty dollars a week less" than she was getting on the *Musketeers* tour, because, as she says, "Mr. Miller did not regard me at all in the light of a valuable acquisition to his company" (*Theatre*, Dec. 1905). That left her with $150 a week with which to maintain her "large apartment on 98th Street," in which on 1 February 1900 a *N.Y. Telegraph* reporter found the urbane Miss Anglin herself in a "trailing gown of mauve taffeta with yoke and half sleeves of black lace," her "poised" mother, "pert" sister [Eileen], "lounging" brother [Wanny], "trig" maid [Minny], and scads of books, photos and Turkish rugs. She was, by her own account, "sailing very near the wind" financially, but she had from the start subscribed to the idea that all her wealth ought to be devoted to establishing a life-style which might do honor to her chosen profession.

Ironically, given her grande-dame style and distaste for guillotines, the first New York performance M.A. gave for Miller was of the lowly Mimi in *The Only Way*, Freeman Wills's adaptation of *A Tale of Two Cities*. M.A. concedes that the play was a success, but "for eight weeks I shuddered beneath the shadow of the guillotine, and I hated it" (*H3*). It is a measure of her dedication to her art that nothing of her distaste for the play was evident in her acting—indeed, the *Criterion* (23.9.99) reviewer observes that

> Mimi appears as a protegée of Carton's, mutely, passionately in love with him. Miss Margaret Anglin makes Mimi second only in importance to [Miller's] Carton. Tender and subdued, she is never for a moment outside the character, always investing it with pathetic charm and intensity of devotion.

And many years later Hector Charlesworth was to recall that

> One of Margaret Anglin's most touching performances was that of the little seamstress, Mimi, in the original New York production of *The Only Way*. Those who in after years saw Lady Harvey travesty the role [could] have no idea how lovely it was when played by Miss Anglin. (*Toronto Star*, 18.2.43)

During the very busy summer of '98 Miller had used Margaret almost exclusively in English socialite parts, for which he decided she had a natural aptitude. (She was, as it were, to the manner born, and she managed the accent with ease.) Thus she played (usually opposite him) the Hon. Miss Neville in Charles Klein's *Heartsease*, Lady Jessica Nepean in

H.A. Jones's *The Liars*, the title role in *Lady Ursula*, and Lady Chetland in R.C. Carton's *Lord and Lady Algy*, apropos of which the *S.F. Chronicle* (1.7.13) critic remembers:

> Margaret Anglin was the first lady I had ever seen smoke a cigarette. She did it in *Lord and Lady Algy*. And how wicked and ravishing it was. No wonder I squandered my 35¢ weekly to see the performance repeated. Not that it ever was. At least I don't recall that the other plays called for just that brand of abandon.

The fact is, M.A. never did become a smoker and always more or less faked the performance on stage. This, notwithstanding the big ad she did for Lucky Strike in May of 1927—thus carefully worded:

> Certainly women of the theatre must be careful of their voices. The one cigarette, I have observed, which seems to protect the throat and give the greatest enjoyment is Lucky Strike.

Also, that summer, she played the part of Baroness Roydon in Leo Trevor's military melodrama of manners, *Brother Officers*. It was this highly congenial role, first essayed in San Francisco, that eventually got M.A. out from under the shadow of the guillotine and likewise out from under the shadow of Jessie Millward, the Empire Company's (imported from London) leading woman. After asking to be relieved of the role of Mimi, M.A. cooled her heels for a fusty fortnight as Miss Millward's understudy in *My Lady's Lord*. But when the Empire decided to feature *Brother Officers* in the new year (1900), Miss Millward generously, if a little rashly, told Charles Frohman to give the lead to Miss Anglin. So, once again M.A. was a leading woman, and again she made the best of the opportunity—this time to such effect that Miss Millward henceforth lived in the shadow of Miss Anglin.

The brother officers of the title are Lieutenant Lancelot Pleydell (Guy Standing), well-born, elegant and irresponsible, given to heavy gambling, loose living and piling up big debts, and Lieutenant John Hinds, V.C. (William Faversham), base-born and gauche, but brave, generous and true-hearted—the saver, first of Pleydell's life and then of his reputation. Of course both fall in love with M.A., "the very jewel of a girl" (*N.Y. Telegraph*, 17.1.00) as the early-widowed Baroness Roydon; but she chooses the wastrel aristocrat (while shedding a tear for the honest yeoman), so that she can reform him.   Of her rendition of the delicious young widow, the eminent English critic Clement Scott (then on a visit to America), wrote in January 1900:

> Before last night I had never heard the name of Margaret Anglin; it had not travelled to England. But what grace she has, what a sweet pathetic voice, what ease of movement, what absence of affectation, what genuine feeling, what moments of inspiration. Why, I could write a column about that love scene in the last act, womanly, tender, and touching to the core. (Rpt., *Munsey's Magazine*, Apr. 1906)

Until the third act, says Lewis Strang:

> Miss Anglin had been more passive than active. All the more surprising, therefore, was her plunge into tear-compelling emotion. With perfect sincerity and absolute fidelity to truth, she portrayed the heartbroken woman, not for one supreme moment—that would have been comparatively easy—but through a long sustained period of suppression and intensity. It was an unusually impressive instance of sustained power. (*FAD*, 298)

In the course of the west-coast portion of the Miller tour of 1900 the critic of the *S.F. Wave* (7.8.00) gave himself credit for discovering a superstar in the making in the person of the twenty-three-year-old Margaret Anglin. How is it, he asks, that the New York critics have not recognized the "superb quality" of this young actress?—

> Perhaps she has appealed to San Francisco audiences in a greater variety of roles and we have had better opportunities to form conclusions. She is really one of the foremost actresses on the stage today. Voice, temperament, intelligence, vivacity, facility, all are hers. Whoever would deny her genius should see the performance of *A Marriage of Convenience* at the Columbia Theatre in which Miss Anglin as the Countess de Candale had an opportunity to display her talent. It is an exquisite performance she gives, full of delicacy and charm and finesse—indeed as graceful a piece of high comedy work as we have ever had. In a few years this actress will have as great a reputation as Ada Rehan, and will surely rise higher than Maude Adams, Viola Allen, or Mary Mannering, who are now starring in the East.

A noteworthy part of the "great variety" of Miss Anglin's repertoire, which the *Wave* critic so rightly emphasizes, was provided in the summer of 1900 by Miller's new productions of J.K. Jerome's *Miss Hobbs* and R.C. Carton's *The Tree of*

Knowledge, in which M.A. had a comedy and a melodrama lead.   She also encored *Brother Officers* for her San Francisco fans, but not her other military play, *The Bugle Call,* a one-act English melodrama by Louis Parker "with a pile of unpronounceable names" (*N.Y. Sun,* 3.4.00), in which M.A. starred as the love-lorn Millicent Denbigh.   Apropos of this piece, M.A. recalls a performance in which Rose Eytinge was the one with the panache and M.A. was the one left holding the bag. At a critical juncture in the exposition of the plot, "Miss Eytinge, an actress of the 'old school,'" appeared to go blank on a speech and simply swept majestically off the stage, leaving M.A. and Mrs. Thomas Whiffen "high and dry as to what to do or say next":

> I have to smile [M.A. concludes] over the fact that in the papers next morning the critics were so enthusiastic about this exit of Miss Eytinge's that they berated us soundly, advising us to take a lesson from her, not realizing at what an expense [to us] Miss Eytinge had won their favors. (*H3*)

At the same time as she was in the process of replacing Jessie Millward as the leading woman of the Empire Company, M.A. was entering into negotiations with the novelist and playwright Paul Kester (1870-1933) for the American rights to his new play, *Sweet Nell of Old Drury,* which had already been produced in London.   Kester apparently quite agreeably, but not quite legally, ceded her the rights.   But Charles Frohman reneged on his promise to produce it for her:

> I did not know [says M.A.], when Mr. Frohman discarded *Sweet Nell,* that it was coveted by Miss Ada Rehan, whose managers took steps to secure it—what steps those were it is idle to go into now, but they remain vividly and bitterly in my mind. (*H3*)

The bitterness she felt was not against her distinguished colleague Ada Rehan (whose celebrated Shrew was to be a model for her own) but rather against the Syndicate (otherwise known as Klaw and Erlanger) which was out to establish a stranglehold on play production and promotion in the United States.   The Syndicate in effect forced Paul Kester to regain the rights to *Sweet Nell* from M.A. and to sign them over to Ada Rehan (as their client).

All this was not accomplished without some high astounding terms being directed against the Syndicate by an indignant Miss Anglin—terms which the Syndicate was not quick to forget. "Very well, then," said M.A., "if you will not let me give the play to the producer of my choice, I shall produce it myself." "If you do," shouted the voice of the Syndicate, "we will choke it out of every town you try to go to" (H3). And so, to the tune of those one-syllable words, the rights were returned to a cowed and sheepish Paul Kester.

In the event (poetic justice), *Sweet Nell* was not a success, and the play M.A. accepted as a *pis aller* was a big winner for her both money-wise and career-wise. Also the *Sweet Nell* affair (in which Kester's good faith was never doubted) marked the beginning of a long and warm friendship between the actress and the writer.

In the midst of her *Sweet Nell* woes, David Belasco offered her the lead in his production of his own Civil War melodrama *The Heart of Maryland*, but Charles Frohman, who had been doing a lot of tongue-clucking throughout the *Sweet Nell* episode, advised M.A. not to accept the part because it was tainted with the suggestion of premarital sex, and then proceeded to cajole her into playing the adulterous Felicia Dane in H.A. Jones's *Mrs. Dane's Defense.*

Perhaps Belasco would have been turned down anyway, because, according to Jerome Collamore, M.A.'s stage-manager of later years:

> Belasco, who was a notably erratic fellow, once put a heavy amorous rush on Mary, and she was, ever after that, leery of working with him. He came backstage one night, after a performance of *Brother Officers*, I think. Suddenly, in the midst of paying her a compliment, he grabbed her and kissed her passionately. When she pushed him away, he blushed and stammered like a schoolboy—though he was fat and forty and she a slip of a girl. "Well, really Mr. Belasco," she said, "I don't think this is the kind of relationship we want to establish." (C, 28.10.86)

And so the cool (and not entirely uncalculating) Mary-Margaret took the risk of playing the smouldering Mrs. Dane, and her acceptance of that challenge was indeed momentous, for her Felicia Dane was to establish her as a ship of the line on the theatrical high seas, or, as she puts it, more modestly:

> with the part of Mrs. Dane my beginnings must have ended—although an actress has her beginnings all through her professional life. (*Theatre*, Dec. 1905)

Chapter III

Mrs. Dane, Camille, Zira: 1901-1905

An actress that can express and rarefy large and deep emotions. (*Toronto Globe*, 22.9.05)

The commencement of the twentieth century proper provides a very convenient watershed mark in the career of Margaret Anglin, for it was in the final December of the old century that her first great indisputable star vehicle was launched, and indeed the premiere of *Mrs. Dane's Defence* was given on the last day of the nineteenth century (i.e. 31 December 1900).

Henry Arthur Jones is reported to have expressed a desire to have M.A. play Mrs. Dane, and he may have lived to regret that choice, for, according to Lewis Strang, she contrived, by means of her "peculiar quality of emotional and sympathetic appeal," to knock Mr. Jones's four-square morality play quite out of kilter. Not only was her acting "unquestionably the leading feature of the Empire Theatre performances," but in her rendition the villainess of the piece, an unscrupulous confidence-woman with an adulterously guilty past, was made to seem unconscionably attractive:

> So completely did Miss Anglin sway the sensibilities and conquer instinctive prejudices that the spectator was incensed when he saw Lionel Carteret, who loved Mrs. Dane, and who was disposed to marry her, past and all, return to his colourless girl love, while the woman who had erred, departed, crushed and hopeless. . . .
>
> Miss Anglin made one feel that Mrs. Dane had been made the victim of narrowness and of social bigotry, and consequently one could not help a moment of positive joy when he saw this creature of moods, rather than of sound judgement, walking away with the main interest, and leaving Mr. Jones's commendable morality shivering in its bare bones. It was the perverse triumph of the Sinner. (*FAD*, 300-304)

After viewing the premiere performance, the *N.Y. Times* (2.1.01) critic was convinced that M.A. was on her way to superstardom, and that "*Mrs. Dane's Defence* is likely to be remembered for the making of Miss Anglin." And Arnold Johnson remarks that "after this big success in an emotional role [*Mrs. Dane* had a run of 107 performances at the Empire],

M.A. with Henry Miller in *Camille* (1903): "There has been no Camille in the last fifty years who could touch her in the role" (Toronto's *Mail and Empire*); the New York critics were less kind.

the name of Margaret Anglin became indissolubly associated with 'emotional acting,'"—so that "by 1909 when she appeared in *The Awakening of Helena Richie*, she was generally conceded to be 'America's Best Emotional Actress'" (J, 45).

In her early prime Margaret Anglin was, to quote (once again) the *N.Y. Times* obituary, "the unchallenged first practitioner of anguish" of the American stage.   And Allen Churchill assures us, in *The Great White Way*, that she was "so effective as a tear-jerker" that members of her audiences "could be recognized by their red-rimmed eyes" (*GWW*, 143).

> Miss Anglin, however [adds Arnold Johnson], did not exhibit the excesses of the [emotional] style. According to Towse, her acting was realistic, a close imitation of nature and its depths of passionate and tremulous emotion. She could provide, however, the quivering cadences and bursts of frenzy, and she could cry, according to Dale, "several pints of tears." (J, 47)

And so the emotional triumph of *Mrs. Dane* was followed hard upon by an emotionally triumphant Dora in Victorien Sardou's "well-made" spy-melodrama, *Diplomacy*. Lewis Strang was again *almost* carried away:

> Miss Anglin could wring emotion from a keg of nails, if it were part of the play to do so, and therefore one had to wink considerably to dodge the moisture engendered by her Dora. Miss Anglin, too, has a voice that throbs and sobs, and at the sound of it a man must weep. With the aid of these natural gifts, therefore, she succeeded in presenting Sardou's formal pathos with a sympathetic appeal that was undeniably strong. (*FAD*, 310)

But if Miss Anglin's audiences were wet, Miss Anglin herself was in control, and Strang particularly commends the superb dramatic tact and "histrionic instinct" which enabled her to avoid the pitfalls of "bathos, morbidity, and hysteria" in a part which, as written, seems one of "pure sentimentality."   He praises her for distilling from a potentially mawkish part the true "pathos" of womanly high instinct and noble resolve in the face of the adversity of fate and the perversity of men.

The gracious elder actress, Rose Coglan, concluded her review of *Diplomacy* in the New York *Evening World* (16.3.01) with the generous words:

> Last, and not least, is Miss Margaret Anglin. I always said so! I recognized her wonderful ability when I first saw her in my brother's play of *Citizen Pierre*. She was dainty, womanly, and above all, natural.

> In the crucial scene of the third act with Julian she rose
> to magnificent heights, and won easily the recalls and
> applause given her by the enthusiastic audience. She has a
> great future.

Sometime in the spring of 1901, around her twenty-fifth
birthday, and in the midst of her great emotional successes
with Dora and Mrs. Dane, a golden gate of opportunity
appeared in M.A.'s primrose path, but her nerve failed her
and she sidled shyly past:

> When a message came to me [she recalls in *H6*] through a
> friend of Sir Henry Irving, asking if I would like to play
> Marguerite in his revival of *Faust*, my courage oozed. It was
> not the enactment of the gentle and sympathetic Marguerite
> that awed me, but the attempt to offer to the English public
> any successor to the unforgettable Ellen Terry.

In the spring of 1902 M.A. escaped the tyranny of tears for
the nonce with a refreshing plunge into the bubbly fount of
The Importance of Being Earnest which had a run of forty-nine
performances at the Empire beginning on 14 April 1902. In
this production she played a "delectably whimsical" Gwendolyn Fairfax opposite Charles Richman's "mercurial" Jack
Worthing. This was the beginning of a fruitful connection
with Wildean comedy. In her middle years the more
"mature" melodramatic roles of Mrs. Erlynne and Mrs.
Arbuthnot were to become Anglin mainstays in her own
productions of *Lady Windermere's Fan* and *A Woman of No
Importance*. As Donald Jones observes (a little inaccurately),
M.A. came by "her predilection for Wilde" naturally, "for
Oscar Wilde had once bounced her on his knee in her father's
home" (*Toronto Star*, 17.4.67).

Prominent among the other pieces in which she played the
lead for Charles Frohman in 1901-03 were *The Wilderness* (H.V.
Esmond), *The Twin Sister* (Ludwig Fulda) and *The Unforeseen*
(W.R. Marshall).

As Mabel Vaughan in *The Wilderness* she played the part of
a gold-digging vixen who comes to love and honor the
worthy middle-aged baronet (richly portrayed by Charles
Richman) whom she has, as she at first supposes, outwitted.
"This performance," says the *N.Y. Times* (15.10.01) critic, "is her
best yet":

> More than once she astonished her auditors by intellectual
> force, and at one point (the denunciation of her
> pusillanimous, harebrained, unscrupulous Lothario on his
> return to her after the marriage) held the situation in

complete control by her truth of feeling and her incisive precision alike of touch and speech. The scene is remarkable, too, for its cold, clear, absolutely ruinous rebuke of the vicious sentimentalism that so often passes for love, whether in plays or in actual life.

In *The Twin Sister* she played both Giuditta della Torre, the rather saccharine Countess of Albertone, and her own twin sister, the spicy Renata. As Giuditta she has become a little too much the devoted chatelaine and doting mother, and the Count, a handsome dog with a roving eye, is bored and begins to show a philandering streak. So Giuditta goes on a visit to mother and dispatches the dashing Renata to counter the Count's amorous proclivities. Charles Richman is, of course, instantly infatuated with the newcomer—Giuditta transformed by means of "a sprinkling of Titian powder on her hair" and "a wicked gleam in her eye." The Count is thus caught red-handed, and Giuditta discovers a new and useful side to her nature. It was all pretty flimsy stuff, but the critics were in general agreement that the Anglin-Richman combo wrapped it up with plenty of panache—Miss Anglin, in particular, giving an impressive display of "histrionic range."

The Unforeseen, "Captain Marshall's suspenseful melodrama," was precisely Margaret Anglin's cup of tea. In it she played Margaret Fielding, a high-souled, high-spirited heroine who escapes the clutches of a confidence-man to find (after many a snare and pitfall) heart's ease as the wife of a blind clergyman, whose sight is miraculously restored by her love. The part allowed her to pass from "sparkling banter" to "soul-stirring emotion," which was exactly the gamut her devotees expected her to run. "Miss Anglin," says the *Theatre* (Jan. 1903) critic, "never created a more charming impression than as Margaret Fielding."

Two items of more than passing interest in the 1902 summer stint in the west were two plays by Sir Arthur Wing Pinero. The first of these was *Trelawney of the Wells*, which gave a very real (controlled) emotional actress the opportunity to play a fictional (wayward) emotional actress, which she did reasonably convincingly. The second was *The Gay Lord Quex*, which challenged the reserved practitioner of cut-glass English with the character of the ebullient cockney social-climber, Sophy Fullgarney. "The part is a little foreign to you," ventured the *S.F. Chronicle* (12.7.02) interviewer:

Not more foreign than interesting [replied Miss Anglin]. . . . I think of her as a creature of impulse—emotion without logic, but

M.A. was "a delectably whimsical Gwendolyn Fairfax" in Oscar Wilde's comedy *The Importance of Being Earnest.* (1902)

with a large, foolish heart. The difficulty is to get her just vulgar enough, "innocently vulgar," as Pinero puts it. She has been a nursemaid with the usual twang of the trade, but she has also been associated superficially—with a backstairs view—with people of good society. She has a superimposed refinement that comes off when she is excited, and a Cockney accent that escapes under similar circumstances —I hope you won't think I forget it because I use it only occasionally.

In the following summer she had a brief run in *The Second Mrs. Tanqueray* in the role of the self-immolating Paula, which may or may not be thought of as a forerunner of her two big Phaedras, in 1911 and 1923. Incidentally, at this time (and perhaps always) she ranked Pinero far above Ibsen or Shaw—"Ibsen, oh, dreadful! . . . Pinero, oh, splendid!" (*Theatre*, March 1902).

"No," she said in the same interview, "I have not set out to be another Bernhardt; I simply want to do *some*thing that will allow me to be my own woman, and that is why I have vowed to essay acting to the top of my bent." And it was, of course, precisely this irreducible element of self-will, of self-seeking which was to constitute both her greatest strength and her greatest weakness both as a performer and as a person.

In a somewhat more cryptic vein she was to tell Robert Hunter of the *Brooklyn Eagle* (9.1.05) three years later:

> I sometimes think I do not belong in this life at all, but I am driven by some invisible dominating force not wholly understandable to find expression for my deepest feelings in acting.

One senses a nice ambiguity in the phrase "this life" as uttered by the sometimes "mystical" Miss Anglin.

Towards the end of May 1903 M.A. and the Empire Company closed the Boston Museum Theatre ("It having been decided to tear down that old historic playhouse" [H3]) with a one-week run of *The Unforeseen*. On the last night (1 June) M.A. declaimed ("with fine feeling") a nostalgic poem by William Seymour replete with the names of all the fine actors who had graced the Museum's boards throughout the nineteenth century ("names of the grand old actors that meant nothing to me" [H3]). There was an emotional tremor in her voice when she ended the tribute to the old theatre where oft the drama had set forth shapely legends of man's psychic life,

> And so refresh'd his soul, beneath the guise
> Of mimic worlds, as with Apollo's lute.

and when she predicted that the BM would surely arise phoenix-like from its ashes:

> Prophetic gleam of brilliancy to come
> Where Thespis finds a new congenial home;
> Thalia her disciples shall unite;
> Melpomene and Momus lend their light.

It is mute evidence of the high esteem in which the Anglin elocutionary prowess was held that this twenty-seven-year-old Canadian was elected to speak this pompous tribute to the American stage of yesteryear.

> No sooner was the curtain rung down on the Boston Museum [she tells us in *H*3] than I hastened—not back to my hotel—but to the steamer which was sailing for London the next day. I was at last to have one of my dreams gratified. I was to take my first trip to Europe. There had been a considerable amount of talk, while I was at the Empire, of Mr. Frohman's taking me to London for a season, and I was now on my way to have a conference with him.

"Upon her arrival in London," says the *N.Y. Telegraph* (24.7.03), "she was informed that her manager intended to make her leading woman of the Duke of York's Theatre for next season, and perhaps longer." He had in mind for her the title role in *The Sorceress*, Sardou's latest and "greatest" play (*H3*). Doubtless she accepted with delighted alacrity. While in London she spent a memorable afternoon in the elegant St. John's Wood home of that eminent critic and "most genial of men," Mr. Clement Scott (of *Poppyland* fame), whose treasure trove of theatrical memorabilia was made up mostly of "gifts in grateful recognition of his tribute from his many eminent actor friends" (*H3*). The sixty-two-year-old Scott, who had lauded M.A. in *Brother Officers* and who had provided the "impossible" translation of *Diplomacy* for the Empire production, was gallantry itself to the *spirituelle* twenty-seven-year-old prima donna.

At this time, too, she was wooed theatrically by both George Alexander and Beerbohm Tree, but she alienated the affections of these two very British (and slightly anti-semitic) actor-managers by solemnly declaring that she was still Frohman's girl and would make no move without his consent.

The *Telegraph* (24.7.03) goes on to say that after a diverting seven weeks in and around London, under the aegis of Mr. Charles Frohman:

Miss Anglin is now on her way to New York, and due to reach this port some time tomorrow. On Thursday morning [27 July] she will begin rehearsals with Henry Miller at the Criterion Theatre preparatory to assisting that player during his five weeks' Summer season in San Francisco. . . . Under this plan Miss Anglin's temporary farewell to America will be made a long distance from Broadway.

"In the California summer season of 1903," says M.A. (H4), "Mr. Dillingham and Mr. Miller made of me a 'star'—the first time I was ever so 'featured'—and gave me what then seemed [and *was*] a very large salary—seven hundred and fifty dollars a week." As a full-fledged star she was clearly expected to shine incessantly, for the 1903 summer tour included *Camille* (Dumas *fils*), *The Ironmaster* (Georges Ohnet), *The Lady of Lyons* (Edward Bulwer's romantic comedy of 1838), *The Taming of Helen* (Richard Harding Davis's romantic comedy of 1902), and Shaw's *The Devil's Disciple*, in which she played a nobly naive Judith Anderson to Henry Miller's crusty trusty Dick Dudgeon. Actually, M.A. had surprisingly little commerce with Shaw, the dominant playwright of her time—her only other Shavian excursion being into the title role of *Candida* some twenty-three years later, at the age of fifty. In 1903 she couldn't see that Shaw was any better than Jones or Pinero, and "couldn't imagine" what all the fuss was about (H4).

At the end of the 1903 summer tour, which went from San Francisco to the northwestern states, M.A. was told by Frohman, who was in a state of shattered nerves because of the disastrous fire at his Chicago theatre (the Iroquois), that he had abandoned his plan to star her in *The Sorceress* in London (he had, in fact, already sold the rights to Mrs. Patrick Campbell), but that she might as well go to London ("Micawber-like") and "wait till something else turns up there" (H4). M.A. emphatically excused herself from compliance with this maudlin piece of advice and from Mr. Frohman's sponsorship. A fortnight later she accepted the offer of Frank L. Perley to become her "presenting manager" (H4), and under his aegis had a success that winter with *Cynthia* and a failure that spring with *Camille*.

Unquestionably the outstanding Anglin-Miller collaboration in the 1902-03 tours was Miller's production of Dumas fils's *La*

Dame aux camélias (1849). It was received in the west with seemingly extravagant acclaim, and indeed such was M.A.'s personal triumph that on one occasion Messrs. Miller and Marx (the theatre manager) presented her "with the entire receipts of the performance, something over two thousand dollars, if I remember right" (H4). A note in *Theatre Magazine* of April 1903 observes that "Miss Anglin essayed the part of the Lady with the Camellias in San Francisco last summer and received no fewer than 18 curtain calls." The *S.F. Chronicle* (7.8.03) praised the Anglin Camille for its "subtlety, intelligence, and refinement of manner," while Louis Nethersole (who had just joined the Anglin-Miller team as business manager), the brother of Olga Nethersole, herself a highly acclaimed Camille, said that M.A.'s wonderfully sensitive rendition of soulful hedonism was one of "great and impressive originality—a veritable revelation to me" (Chicago Tribune, 15.9.03). There was (to comb the Chicago papers of November 1903) the lissome girlish form, "looking not a day over eighteen," the wavering wayward voice, "finely and expressively shaded," the "psychic" tinge, the "sweet pathos" —"Her Camille," says the *Record-Herald* of 10 November, "has Chicago by the throat."

Less subtle and refined than Miss Anglin's performance was that of Mr. William Courtleigh in the role of the Count de Varville whose token glove buffet one night broke Henry Miller's nose—which incident many years later evoked a retrospective headline in the *Chicago Herald Examiner* (11.1.20): "Count Broke Miller's Nose for Love of Anglin." And Miss Anglin herself recalls (H4):

> As I lay there on the bed in the last agonies of Marguerite's death scene—and taking as long a time about it as I possibly could—different characters, as they came on the scene, gave me whispered and varying bulletins, and my mind worked in all directions trying to improvise a loverless ending. Just when I was about to die a lonely and disappointed death, Armand appeared in the doorway, I gave a cry of joy, and the curtain was hastily rung down.

Frank Perley (referring to the summer 1903 production) told the Toronto *Mail and Empire* of 23 January 1904:

> Miss Anglin is a great favourite in the West. She played Camille out there last summer, and knowing critics who saw it say that there has been no Camille in the last fifty years who could touch her in the role.

They didn't quite say that in print, but the understandably partial Perley was reading between the lines.

Unhappily, by the time Mr. Perley had a piece of the action, the life and verve and spirit seemed unaccountably to have gone out of it. The New York production was a flat failure and received a particularly flatulent response from the critic of the prestigious *Theatre Magazine* (5.04) who opens his atrabilious review with these hard lines:

> The performance of *Camille* by Henry Miller and Margaret Anglin was a double disappointment. Western critics had praised both the former's Armand Duval and Miss Anglin's Marguerite Gauthier, but it must be frankly said that both these players, each of whom has gained distinction in less important roles, were lamentably and hopelessly at sea.

Miss Anglin, in particular, is excoriated for a performance that, besides being spiritless and unimaginative, was largely inaudible, and, as if that wasn't enough, there was the wig:

> Normally an attractive woman on the stage, Miss Anglin made herself look hideous by wearing a jet black wig, this probably being an attempt to fit Dumas' physical description of his heroine. There were, however, so many other points in which the actress did not fit the description that it was hardly worth bothering about the hair.

One shrinks from quoting more from this spate of *lèse majesté* (which continues, "Mr. Miller's Armand was on the same dead level of mediocrity"), but this deploring of the black wig and the "dull monotone" which marred M.A.'s Camille for this critic does serve to remind us of her two most "normally attractive" features—her "lambent red-gold hair" (complemented by "limpid grey-green eyes") and her "beautifully modulated musical voice."

In the midst of her ups and downs over three seasons with the tearful *Camille*, M.A. was having an altogether upbeat time with the effervescent *Cynthia*. In the title role of this rather flimsy romantic comedy (by H.H. Davies) she played a silly little butterfly wife, while Henry Miller played her adoring but exasperated husband. When *Cynthia* appeared in Toronto at the Princess in December of 1903, the *Saturday Night* (Dec. 1903) reviewer summed up the impressions of M.A.'s portrayal of a featherbrained darling who flirts with disaster and wins happiness-ever-after in these well-chosen words:

> To act the part of so foolish yet so lovable a woman requires art as light and as delicate as thistledown. But our Canadian Margaret possesses such a gift, and never came down the snowflakes on Canadian hills more softly and

daintily than fell the bits of brilliant folly from the lips of
Cynthia as Miss Anglin spoke the part. . . . The great charm
of Miss Anglin's art is its naturalness.   The tricks of the
second-rate actress, the trills and thrills of the lady who does
meller-drama were entirely lacking, and the audience found
itself quite at home with Cynthia, whether she reclined
bewitchingly in her pink dressing-room, or ate butterless
toast in dreary Lambeth lodgings. . . .

The audience fully appreciated Miss Anglin's art and the
charming personality behind it, and applauded her until she
appeared for the fifth time, bowing and kissing her
acknowledgements . . .

Another columnist for the same magazine gives, as a
human interest story, an account of the performance of "the
lovable and admired young actress" as "fairy godmother" to a
hundred enchanted children at a Christmas party at
McConkey's restaurant in Toronto.   She delineates the scene
thus prettily:

Pretty little mothers and wise nurses and a few
grandmothers flitted about watching that no shy or nervous
child was overlooked, and the fairy godmother herself,
looking a picture in a soft gauzy nut brown frock and brown
hat softly draped in white lace, whispered in many a little
ear sweet cheer and pet names and was followed by many a
fond gaze from her small guests. . . . After the feast there
was a Christmas tree round which the children sat in a huge
circle on the soft carpets of the Nile and Rose rooms, and
after the tree there was a hail of cheers for the hostess ("Ho!
for the Princess!") and a more remote augustness ("the
King!"). . . .
No one who saw Cynthia that evening could have
imagined that she had lifted a finger for anyone during the
day, much less have carried through that most exhausting
and exacting function, a huge children's party.

It is what Hardy might well have labelled a Satire of
Circumstance that this warmhearted woman who always had
a rare way with and feeling for children should have
remained childless.

After the aforementioned perplexing and depressing failure
of *Camille* in New York (Had the company just gone stale?)
and a truncated run of just sixteen performances, M.A.
whisked herself off to England to recover her spirits:

I took a little flying trip abroad this season [she told the
N.Y. Telegraph (11.9.04) in September] and bought a little

manor—a perfect dear of a place—in Surrey. It was one of those happy thoughts, don't you know? I happened to have the price in my purse, and I said "Deah fellah, wrap up that house for me, will you?" and he did and I have roughed it among the villagers for two months.

Incidentally, she met Charles Frohman in London in June. He was lunching at the Savoy with James M. Barrie when Margaret happened along one afternoon, but the shy "young" (44) Scot could not be prevailed upon to join the impresario and his bright young star the next day—Frohman having assured him that she had a pretty, teasing wit. "And so I was left wondering whether I should ever properly meet Peter Pan" (H7). And apparently she never did, but she and Frohman buried all remaining hatchets and remained fast friends until he went to a watery grave eleven years later (7.5.15) with the torpedoed *Lusitania*.

M.A. marked her return from the small-potato indolence of Surrey to the big-apple bustle of Manhattan by taking the bold step of presenting herself to the theatrical world (under Perley's management) as an actor-producer. She was twenty-eight years old. The play which was to initiate this new phase of her career was *The Eternal Feminine* (originally *Das Ewig Weibliche*) by Robert Misch (trans. Austin Page).

"The story," she says (H4), "is somewhat based on the *Lysistrata* of Aristophanes." The "somewhat" has reference to the fact that both plays feature militant women with Greek names—but whereas the tone of *Lysistrata* is satirical and scurrilous, that of *The Eternal Feminine* is romantic and sentimental. Nevertheless, *The Eternal Feminine* does represent the first glimmer of the Greek light of M.A.'s theatrical life. She tells us that she thought in 1904 that there was "no more amusing comedy than the *Lysistrata* in the whole long history of drama"; and it is interesting to note that twenty-two years later she told Irving Pichell that she loved the "broad fun" of *Lysistrata*, and would like to stage it at Berkeley, with herself, of course, in the title role (J, 267)—presumably in a bowdlerized version.

The Eternal Feminine was scheduled to open (appropriately enough, at the Hyperion) in New Haven on Saturday, 5 November 1904, but the exhausted M.A. collapsed on the morning of that day and the opening had to be postponed till Monday, 7 November, at which time,

despite a number of technical hitches, the big production was
declared a big success:

> and [says the *New Haven Evening Register*, 8.11.04] the
> postponement of the first night from Saturday in no way
> dampened the enthusiasm of the large audience.   Her
> reception was all that could be desired by her most ardent
> admirers. . . . [And it was fully deserved], for her
> interpretation first of the spirited queen and later of the
> queenly spirit in love were charming indeed.

The Eternal Feminine begins with the shipwreck of a
contingent of Greek soldiers under the command of Captain
Lysander (the darkly handsome Robert Drouet) on the idyllic
island of Halcyonae, which is under the autocratic rule of the
Amazonian queen, Antiope (the imperious Margaret Anglin).
The Greeks are impounded by the Amazons and allotted as
husbands to Antiope's lieutenants. They are allowed to escape
but promptly, in return, allow themselves to be recaptured, at
which time they capture their captors in amorous embraces,
and there is a happy confusion of mine and thine in the
halcyon isle of love.

> Comedy and satire though this play is [observes the
> *Washington Times*, 22.11.04], this wooing, all topsy-turvy,
> gives it its charm.   It discloses in Miss Anglin a gentle
> sweetness, a poetry of voice and motion, a grace of speech
> and ringing note of deep feeling which would adorn many a
> more noteworthy character than this Amazon queen. . . . The
> Lysander is Robert Drouet—a true patrician and a Greek in
> bearing.   But the quality that distinguishes Miss Anglin's
> impersonation most—the air of that early day—is never
> manifest in Mr. Drouet's acting.

A plug there for the superior imaginative quality of M.A.'s
work—her* ability to get inside characters, situations and
ambiences. "If this witty and refined piece of Grecian fantasy
. . . has more than fair acceptance in the United States [says
the *Milwaukee Free Press* (9.12.04) reviewer] it will be through the
fine effort of Miss Anglin and her support to bring out its
subtlest meanings."

In some of the earlier, more boisterous scenes the
Milwaukee News (9.12.04) critic discerns "a seeming taint of
superficiality" in M.A., a touch of "self-consciousness," such as
had in the past, occasionally, "impaired other of her
creations."   But in the climactic scene of Lysander's
succumbing to her wooing "she wins a true glory"; or as
Rodney Lee of the *Toledo Blade* (2.1.05) puts it:

When came the time of surrender, when "all/ Her falser self slipt from her like a robe,/ And left her woman," the beautiful Margaret Anglin radiant in the glory of her youthful enthusiasm, giving herself up wholly and unreservedly to the influence of the poet's spell, revealed hitherto unguessed power in the expression of the tender emotions of the heart. The beauty of that wondrous third act will be a haunting memory of greatest delight. Miss Anglin read the exquisite lines, unexcelled for purity of thought, loftiness of idea and elegance of diction by any of the modern writers, with full appreciation of their utmost significance, made their delightful rhythm more musical by the perfect modulation of her richly sympathetic voice, and by look and gesture imparted to them an indescribably affecting charm.

One could hardly guess from this rhapsody that the play was styled "a comedy satire," and perhaps, had it been truer to that label, we might not have read in the next column of the same paper:

Tonight, at the Columbus, *The Eternal Feminine* will have its final performance, as the tour has not been a financial success. Manager Frank L. Perley has faith in the beautiful play, but will shelve it for the time being, and substitute a new drama [*A Wife's Strategy*] by George Middleton, said to be an unusually strong piece of work

The production of *The Eternal Feminine* was, as the *Washington Post* (27.11.04) observes, "indeed lavish": with "highly effective" incidental music, composed and (sometimes) conducted by Professor Horatio W. Parker of Yale, elaborate sylvan and architectural scenery by Joseph Physioc, "gorgeous" costumes by Sir Percy Anderson of London, two dozen "name" actors, "a score of beautiful maidens, and a *corps de ballet*." It is not surprising that this play, with all that gorgeousness, especially all those delectable "spear-bearing, beplumed and sandalled Valkyries," pleased the gentlemen of the press. It is also not surprising that it ultimately sank in a sea of red ink—since it was, besides, "too poetical" and "caviare to the general."

The Eternal Feminine ran for 47 performances to fairly good houses and generally good report, but such was the extravagance of the production that it sustained a loss of some $16,000 (a loss borne in the main by Frank Perley who seems to have had a knack of backing losers). Miss Anglin's debut as a producer, if artistically auspicious, was financially calamitous, and henceforth backers tended to be a bit shy of

M.A.'s debut as a producer was financially calamitous; here M.A. is costumed for her role as Antiope in *The Eternal Feminine.* (1904)

her because of her free-spending ways. She was, however, personally comfortably off at this time, and nicely ensconced, as the *N.Y. Telegraph* (6.1.05) tells us, in "a charming house on West End Avenue," two blocks from Central Park, in which her most prized possessions were a Steinway grand piano and a beautifully housed 2,500-book library. She had as near neighbours her friendly theatrical rivals Henrietta Crosman and Maxine Elliott (Mrs. Nat Goodwin). She was also in possession of "a beautiful colonial country home, . . . at White Plains, N.Y., . . . where she lives almost entirely outdoors, mostly on horseback."

One of the odder spin-offs from *The Eternal Feminine* was the beginning of a peculiarly inappropriate association of the name Margaret Anglin with feminism. One critic of the play says quite simply that

> Lampito, counsellor to the Amazon queen, and Thyrissa, her confidante, are nothing other than Susan B. Anthony and Dr. Mary Walker in Grecian dress. (*Milwaukee Free Press*, 9.12.04)

One naturally assumed that their counsel was acceptable to M.A. as well as to Antiope and so one was not surprised to find Robert Hunter of the *Brooklyn Eagle* (9.1.05) asking her (as the star of a feminist play) to comment on militant feminism 1904-style. Her reply, ostensibly taken down verbatim, is quite astonishing in style, if not in content:

> I certainly believe in equality for women—the equality that a wife and mother already richly enjoys—but not in any assumption or usurpation of masculine characteristics or prerogatives. I am afraid I am a conventional woman, for I believe in nothing more strongly than that those conventions born of long social experience are not only tolerable but eminently wise and beautiful. There can be no question but that marriage is woman's happiest estate, and an unwonted independence on this subject must be due in the case of every natural woman to some unfortunate or embittering experience.

That kind of conversational style might be construed as either the cause or the effect of the circumstance that at this stage of her career she was "a very private person."

The aforementioned *A Wife's Strategy* was not, as it happened, nearly as "strong" a piece as the not very perspicacious Perley supposed, and it also turned out to be a box-office clinker, and closed after three weeks in Albany, Syracuse and Rochester.

Strategy tells the story of how Congressman Richard Allen (John Kellerd), a career-obsessed politician becomes involved in a blatant piece of influence-peddling in his campaign for re-election, and of how his faithful but exasperated wife, Mary (M.A.), gets an old-flame newspaper editor to publish the story and ruin Allen politically. In a somewhat scamped final scene the Allens are reconciled and vow to live virtuously, and apolitically, ever after.

Despite the *amor vincit omnia* ending, the winning of the audience's sympathy for the high-handed wife is a tall order, and only the conscientiously "sympathy-repelling" performance of John Kellerd and the "ardency and urgency" of M.A.'s portrayal of a woman in quest of affection and trust and honor in the marriage state brought the rather ill-made play anywhere close to its goal. Still *A Wife's Strategy* did M.A. no personal disservice in the eyes of the critics:

> By her acting of last night [says the *Syracuse Herald*, 19.1.05] Miss Anglin amply proved her right to be called one of the leading emotional actresses on the American stage. Her art has broadened even since the season so short a while ago that she won laurels in *Mrs. Dane's Defence*, and since she made the ideal Roxane to Mansfield's Cyrano. She has a charming stage presence and a graceful carriage that is a delight to the eyes of the beholders. To some of the older playgoers in last night's audience she vividly recalled Mary Anderson, both in her acting and in her personality. She made her audience forget the preposterousness of a wife's not only bringing about the defeat of her husband's dearest ambition, but of her own act laying him under the lasting stigma of having been defeated for office on account of his dishonorable practices.

The *Rochester Democrat* (21.1.05) also speaks of the extreme shakiness of the basic emotional prop of the piece and of the "awkwardnesses of technic in the first two acts [which] react unfavorably on the [stronger] third act."

> Whatever other question there may be about the play [*The Democrat* continues], there is no doubt that in *A Wife's Strategy* Margaret Anglin fully proved her right to stellar honors. Measured by the best modern standards of histrionism she played Mary Allen magnificently.

One can sympathize with the *amour-propre* of the twenty-five-year-old "rising" dramatist, George Middleton, smarting under such an outrageous hail of critical slings and arrows, and when one discovers that the actual staged version of the play was largely of Miss Anglin's devisal one can perhaps sympathize the more. "I knew the play was weak in many areas," concedes Middleton, "but the changes Margaret Anglin wanted so violated whatever integrity the idea had that I simply couldn't agree. So she put down the script, and I put down my foot. She put on her Persian lamb and walked out; I put on mine (Dad's) and boiled." That looked like a stopper; but soon Middleton was assured that the play would go on as scheduled. He eventually discovered that M.A., with "an acquiescent rewrite woman" in tow, had drastically revised the last two acts of Middleton's four-acter: "I learned," says Middleton, "that Acts III and IV were to be telescoped with a big scene to climax in a blaze of Anglinonics."

Because Middleton was stubbornly opposed to the rewrite, the principals in this piece of author-scuppering made themselves scarce:

> We were to open in Albany [Middleton recalls]. But my star wasn't on the company train. Neither were the two leading men; in fact I found, to avoid me, they, plus the lady playwright, had tiptoed up the day before and put in the "new ending" I had not even seen at the dress rehearsal. In fact, I seem to recall a headache came on that afternoon in New York just as she had reached it because she "hadn't felt equal to doing it." (*TTAM*, 70)

Not surprising, since the fretfully anticipatory Middleton was pacing the aisles like a caged lion during the rehearsal. Nor was the reduction to three acts acknowledged in the program: before the curtain in Albany the stage manager, Louis Nethersole, blandly told the audience, "We hope you will enjoy the play in three acts as much as you would have in four."

"The next day," says Middleton, "the press wires said, 'the author desperately tried to save his play by hastily condensing it from four acts to three.'"

> I sat [he ruefully remembers] with the astonished manager [Frank Perley]. When the new "big scene" came I said: "From now on I know nothing." In my version it was the husband who asked the wife's forgiveness. But not in Margaret's version. She went into the finest ground-groveling, please-forgive-me scene I ever saw. Amid strange, disjointed words, she sobbed and sobbed, and, behind her handkerchief, prompted the poor bewildered actor in his responses. Like Coquelin, Margaret never felt anything she

acted; she had perfect control over every nuance of
expression. She begged Hubby's forgiveness so well that I
almost forgave her myself. It was acting; but it wasn't my
play. (*TTAM*, 71)

When *A Wife's Strategy* failed after an ineffectual three-week
struggle for life, Middleton, a good-tempered young fellow,
asked M.A. for a signed photograph of herself in the role of
Mary Allen. When the photograph arrived it bore this
inscription: "To Mr. Middleton/ with kindest remembrances of
'A Wife's *Tragedy*'/ Margaret Anglin." "Her italics," says Mr.
Middleton,"—a characteristic piece of wit" (*TTAM*, 66).

Middleton, who had a fair amount of correspondence with
M.A. over the years (and "dined with her in Hollywood in
1928"), had mixed feelings about the great woman, containing
equal parts of admiration and antipathy:

While she lacked that ultimate lure of a warm, entrancing
personality [which was Julia Marlowe's], her training from
young womanhood, touring the provinces in Canada, had
made her a fluent mistress of stage mechanics. "You go
where you want; I'll find you," I heard her once tell an
actor. Her memory, like Huey Long's was photographic.
She could read a page and know it. An extremely cultivated
woman, with social background and personal charm, she
knew how to "protect" herself, and even held her own with
Richard Mansfield. Her wit matched his . . .

She was equally at ease in high comedy and agitated
emotion; but [David] Belasco thought her greatest asset was
a "vocal quiver" which brought your tears. Its effect was
automatic; no one could sob as she, nor better portray a
scene, as in *Mrs. Dane's Defence*, where, cornered, she would
try to lie her way out. Her capacity to project inner states
had inspired me with the hope that the sort of plays I
wished to write might lead to a permanent collaboration.
But she always had to have her own way, and that included
scripts. . . . (*TTAM*, 67-68)

—as we have seen.

That summer (1905), under the management of the good-
hearted but perhaps incompetent Frank Perley, M.A. went
again to San Francisco by way of Buffalo, where she tried out,
not very successfully, a new play called *Zira* (rhymes with
Myra) which was ultimately to become a hit:

That season in San Francisco was, I think, the happiest
experience of its kind I ever had. The work was very
taxing—frequently a new play every week, and extra
matinees of standard plays besides. But the most complete

harmony existed among the players, and with such a feeling everything in the theatre is possible. (H4)

The actors of that "excellent company" whom M.A. particularly remembered were Frank Worthing, George Titheradge, Edward Emery, Hall McAllister and Mrs. Thomas Whiffen. The plays the company did were *The Lady Paramount* (Henry Harland), *Frou-Frou* (Halévy and Meilhac), *The Crossways* (Hartley Manners), *Miss Mariana* (José Echegaray), *The Second Mrs. Tanqueray* (A.W. Pinero), *The Eternal Feminine*, the still evolving and experimental *Zira* (Miller and Manners), and *The Marriage of Kitty* by Cosmo Gordon Lennox, in which Frank Worthing was a "wonderfully hateable caddish hero" while Margaret Anglin was "an adorable pretty Kitty. . . . Adjectives fail to describe her grace, her voice, her ingenuousness" (*S.F. Chronicle*, 8.4.05).

In the midst of the tour ("one fine June morning in Denver") Frank Perley received a peremptory letter from "the then omnipotent theatrical firm of Klaw and Erlanger" adjuring him to dump that presumptuous upstart, Margaret Anglin, and assuring him that she was, as a business associate, both untrustworthy and insubordinate, as an actress simply "no good," and altogether in theatrical terms "a worthless proposition" (H4). The financially shaky (though "kind and loyal") Perley was eventually brought reluctantly to heel, but M.A. took *Zira* to New York where the cautious David Belasco promised to sponsor her in the spring, while the impetuous (though impecunious) Henry Miller offered to take a chance on her right away and to take out an immediate lease on the rather dingy little Princess Theatre—as co-author of the play, Miller was not, of course, acting entirely altruistically.

Zira opened on 21 September 1905 to a house so subdued and quiet "that we thought we had a failure on our hands," but at the final curtain the audience to a man and woman rose and cheered and set up a great "waving of [presumably wet] handkerchiefs," and thus "we realized the *Zira* had won its way." *Zira* was to have a mostly sold-out run of 128 performances in New York and to encounter an even more enthusiastic reception in Chicago. One can imagine Messrs. Klaw and Erlanger gnashing their teeth—and claws.

After the financial bath precipitated by her production of *The Eternal Feminine*, the financial sunburst of *Zira* was welcome indeed to one who was becoming fully accustomed to the affluent life-style, and the gratifying box-office success of this emotional melodrama may well have persuaded her, for the nonce, that she was still essentially an "emotional actress"—one that could make even a creaky emotional vehicle "go." In any case she had the distinct pleasure (and co-author Henry Miller the distinct displeasure) of reading in *Theatre Magazine* (Nov. 1905):

> The play is on no better a footing than *The New Magdalen* [the first play-version of Wilkie Collins' novel of that name]. The happenings are so improbable, so impossible, that only the acting of Margaret Anglin makes the play worth while. . . . Perhaps she lacks simplicity in her methods, but she is worth seeing for her effectiveness and virtuosity. She uses the old symbols, but they carry.

In short, declares this critic, she makes us "believe in and care about" an illicitly aspiring and daring young woman, despite her entourage of banality and absurdity.

Zira is the story of Hester Trent, a pretty, witty young woman who is the victim not only of a drunken spendthrift father, but of a profligate officer who faked a marriage in order to filch her maidenhead. While serving as a nurse in the Boer War, she witnesses the death of Ruth Wilding, a girl of good family who knows her guilty secret. Hester seizes the opportunity of swapping clothes and I.D. with the "dead" Ruth, and whisks herself off to London and the posh household of her new "aunt," Lady Constance Clavering. There she nobly joins forces with her "cousin," Rev. Gordon Clavering, a slum-ministering socialist clergyman. Not liking to use Ruth's name, she calls herself Zira (after Turner's caged tigress). But just as she is winning all hearts, the real Ruth Wilding (who had only been in coma) arrives, and they have a tremendous confrontation scene, in which Zira routs Ruth—and then confesses all. But, after all, Gordon stands by the unmasked Zira, and they pledge themselves forever to each other and to Fabian socialism.

The reaction of the *Evening Post* (22.9.05) critic is that of the *Theatre* critic writ large:

> The play itself, is weak alike in construction and characterization, mawkish and insincere in sentiment, flabby, lachrymose and specious in its morality, and generally inconsiderable from any literary or artistic point of view. But for the ordinary theatre-goer it has many alluring baits. It is full of sensation and distressful emotion; it is well larded with popular platitudes; it has an evangelical curate of the most latitudinarian and socialistic principles, and a

comic bishop for his tyrant; a drunken wastrel bubbling over with noble aspirations, and a heroine, who, barring the fact that she is a conscienceless impostor, is an ideal embodiment of all the Christian virtues. Thus does the modern stage hold the mirror up to nature.

He goes on to say that, while the first dramatization of *The New Magdalen* was a contrived and creaky affair, "this same fabric now, when laden with the weight of some additional absurdities imagined by Messrs. Miller and Manners, is absolutely crazy." It may be as well to confess at this point that while the play was still in rough draft (before the Buffalo opening), M.A., "with the help of Miss Charlotte Thompson, set to work and rewrote [her] own part practically from beginning to end." She also tells us that ("with the aid of a few notes pinned to my dressing-room mirror") she alone fabricated the big confession speech on opening night in Buffalo—and with such success that "that extemporized speech was incorporated in the play and spoken ever afterward, just as I 'made it up' that night in Buffalo. Later on, the first act of the play was rewritten to accord with it." (H4)

After his hard words for the play, the *Post* critic has some glowing ones for M.A. With special reference to the big confrontation scene he avers:

> No finer or truer emotional acting, of the melodramatic order, than that exhibited in her frenzied pleadings for some show of mercy, has been witnessed in this city since the best days of Clara Morris, and the final burst of hard and reckless passion, in which she defied her persecutor and fate was as inspriting as a trumpet call. Bernhardt herself could scarcely have done it better. It almost took the audience out of their seats, and the roar of applause that followed it, temporarily putting an end to the performance, was something that has not been heard in any theatre in this region for years. The scene was utter claptrap, but it was transfigured by the passionate and eloquent sincerity of the actress into the semblance of something great and noble. Miss Anglin has never done anything like it before, and the achievement puts her at once into the front rank of stars.

The *Boston Globe* (22.9.05) critic is even more outspoken in his praise of M.A.'s "supremely moving" performance of Zira. "In our generation," he declares, "only Bernhardt has matched it." And indeed the final seal of approval was placed upon M.A.'s *Zira* by the Divine Sarah when she announced that she would be willing to pay a hundred dollars to see a performance of "the big act." In a letter to the organizer of the "Russian Jews Benefit Night" to be staged at the Casino Theatre in New York on 21 December 1905 her manager issued this statement:

> Mme. Bernhardt says she is grateful to you for the opportunity of giving a special performance for the benefit of the Jewish sufferers in Russia. She will appear any time or anywhere you wish playing her new one-act piece, *L'Escarpolette*. She asks you to arrange for Miss Anglin's appearance on the bill in the big act of *Zira*. In this event Mme. Bernhardt will pay $100 for a box. (*N.Y. Telegraph*, 18.12.05)

Four years later Mme. Bernhardt told the *N.Y. Sun* (9.9.09) that "Margaret Anglin is one of the few dramatic geniuses of the day."

Still, in spite of all this enthusiastic acclaim, a *N.Y. Tribune* (22.10.05) interviewer was willing to goad her with the remark that, in the contemporary theatre, "emotional actresses are out." But she was ready with her reply:

> We are all emotional actresses that are any good. For a play that's any good must appeal to the emotions. It's only a difference in style, after all. Styles change. Hearts don't.

"Loyalty to heart" (Plu) was her histrionic watchword, and she strove to maintain this kind of truth as well in throwaway plays as in Greek tragedies. To give the audience "a sharp taste of how it *feels* to be this kind of character"—that was the end which all one's "technic" subserved.

Early in the continuously triumphant run of *Zira*, M.A. was visited at her hotel suite in Buffalo's Iroquois Hotel by her elder brother, Mr. Justice Francis Alexander Anglin, K.C. When no-nonsense Frank emerged he was put through this catechism by a bright young reporter:

> **Reporter:** So you are here in Buffalo as the guest of Miss Anglin?
> **Frank Anglin:** I am here, but I am not here as the guest of Miss Anglin.
> **R:** What relationship do you bear to Miss Anglin?
> **F.A.:** Her brother.
> **R:** Have you seen her in *Zira*?
> **F.A.:** No.
> **R:** Will you see the play before returning to Toronto?
> **F.A.:** No.
> **R:** Have you ever seen your sister act?
> **F.A.:** Now look here, what interest is that to the public? I have nothing to say as to my reasons for not going to see her play. (*N.Y. Telegraph*, 22.2.06)

Another footnote to the *Zira* success might be accorded to the spate of letters to the star from self-styled undiscovered emotional actresses, a few of which were produced for the delectation of the readers of the *N.Y. Mail* (10.10.05). One of the budding Bernhardts speaks of one of her pathetic recitations which prompted her teacher to compare her with "Mrs. [Patrick] Campbell, whoever she is"; and she suggests most forcibly that Miss Anglin should "send the money right away" for her passage to New York, so that she might live with and understudy the great woman. Another appeals to Zira in this way:

> Dear Miss Anglin—I've always been a great admirer of yours, especially in *East Lynne*. I seen you do it three times last year, and I thought you was grand. You made me cry awful. So please, dear Miss Anglin, won't you help me to go on the stage? I'm young (nineteen), beautiful (blonde), with golden tresses and blue eyes, and a good figure (so they tell me!), and I just know I could act. I'm waiting on table in a hotel just now, but that's just for "passy le temps," as the French say, for I'm an artiste at heart.

If the role of Hester Trent in *Zira* was "a winner" for Miss Anglin, the role of Ruth Jordan in *The Great Divide* was a triumph. And if the beginning of the new century with *Mrs. Dane's Defence* represents an early high water mark and turning point in her career, *The Great Divide* represents a second and perhaps even more striking new beginning, plateau, watershed mark, or what you will. And the fact that both the title of the play and the name of its heroine are of M.A.'s devisal indicates her awareness of the Jordan-crossing potential of the work which the playwright William Vaughn Moody had called *A Sabine Woman*. But *The Great Divide* clearly deserves a chapter to itself.

Photo by Otto Sarony, courtesy of Naomi Le Vay

The Washington papers gave *The Great Divide* mixed reviews, from "positive triumph" to "miserable play"; M.A. played Ruth Jordan. (1906)

Chapter IV

The Great Divide: 1906-1908

Some say the lark makes sweet division;
This doth not so, for she divideth us.
(Shakespeare, *Romeo and Juliet*, 3.5.29)

While M.A. was playing *Zira* in Chicago, Donald Robertson, an actor-manager of that city, sent her a manuscript of William Vaughn Moody's *A Sabine Woman* (Moody favored the indefinite article) and, as Ward Morehouse remarked: "It was Moody's good luck—and hers—for the script to be on the top of the pile beside her bed at her hotel—as she propped herself against the pillows for some midnight supper following an evening's *Zira* performance":

> "I just took the first script off the pile," Miss Anglin recalls, "and began reading. I got fascinated and couldn't put the damn thing down. My eggs got cold; the fuzz went off my Guinness' Stout. I read and read until I was through and I knew something had happened to me. I was crazy about the play." (*MT, 67*)

M.A. became a woman obsessed and a dynamo of activity. Within a week she had got hold of Moody (who was all but embarked for Spain) and arranged for a six-week option on the play, contacted her producer (Henry Miller) in New York and her manager (Lee Shubert) in California to clear a Chicago tryout, and made all the theatre arrangements at the Garrick. *A Sabine Woman* was put into rehearsal (using the "mostly English!" cast of *Zira*) on Sunday 8 April 1906, and opened four days later. "Her industry and enthusiasm [recalls Moody] were extraordinary. She told me that during that week she stuck pins in herself to keep awake" (*WVM, 171*).

When she asked Miller for his permission to produce, he said: "I think you're quite mad; but if you *can* do it, do it by all means" (*H4*). And Frank Morse records this exchange:

> "What did you tell her?" inquired Lee Shubert. "I told her to go ahead," was Miller's philosophic reply. "I knew she would, no matter what I said. (*BWHM, 20*)

When Moody arrived, "bronze-bearded and Western in his get-up of big hat and dressing bag" (*H4*), he was exceedingly agreeable. To the six weeks exclusive performing rights in the U.S., M.A. asked:

> "Would you mind including England and Australia?" "Madam," he replied, "you may have the rights to it in heaven. (H4)

Moody was, of course, present for the opening (as were his literary friends Edgar Lee Masters, Percy MacKaye, Hamlin Garland and Harriet Monroe), and just before the curtain rose, M.A. again asked Moody for his promised letter of option and urged him to produce it then and there with an eyebrow pencil and a piece of wrapping-paper; but Moody waffled and said "Let me think about it out front." The second act was such a huge success that Moody was literally compelled to take a curtain-call with his star to whom he presented "poems and flowers" (H4) but still no letter. "Apparently, being a novice in the theatre," conjectures Miss Anglin, "he was acting on bad advice" (H4)—the advice to put nothing in writing. And so he returned to his seat leaving M.A. empty-handed. And so she issued her famous ultimatum—"No letter, no third act." And this is how she described the show-down to Ward Morehouse:

> Mr. Moody came rushing backstage the color of an oyster. They all went searching for a lawyer, and who do you suppose they found? A Shubert lawyer! They went into a huddle below stage. We were all waiting on stage. I was called down to see the agreement and there it was (giving me a lot more than I had asked for), with Moody's signature. I got the thing pushed down into my dress and it came popping up in the third act which we began playing after a delay of an hour and ten minutes. Mr. Moody came back after the play and said he was terribly sorry for what had happened. There was no applause at the end of the play. The audience just sat there, impressed and kind of stunned. (MT, 68)

—or perhaps numbed.

But if M.A. remembers the lack of applause at the end, her stage director, Bertram Harrison, vividly recalls "fifteen almost volcanic curtain-calls [after the second act] for author and players" (BWHM, 22). Harrison, by the way, claims that it was he who first recognized the marvellous potential of the Moody script and lit a fire under the dubious M.A. He recalls a delay of "45 minutes" while the lawyer drew up a formidable document, followed by a rather *distrait* performance of Act 3—so that the lack of applause at the end might have indicated bafflement rather than dazzlement on the part of the audience. Maurice Brown, indeed, tells us that after a hiatus of "almost an hour" the third act was, not very surprisingly, "a disaster":

> Both the audience and the company had cooled. The male lead [the Englishman Charles Dalton] garbled his lines, omitting a portion of the act. Other players forgot their lines. The action was clogged. The curtain dropped well after midnight to perfunctory applause. Percy MacKaye later called the evening "hallucinatic," and Moody was to declare that he got ten years of experience in three days. (*ED*, 203)

Brown also informs us that the press got out the story that the dispute was over the split in royalties between author and producer and that Moody took it upon himself to publish a letter "defending Miss Anglin's dedication to her art against the imputation of commercialism" (*ED*, 204). He wished to make it perfectly clear that the document required was a simple cession of performing rights and had nothing to do with money. "Moreover," he added at the end, "I deeply regret that Miss Anglin, whose whole-hearted zeal for the artistic aspects of her calling is indisputable, should have been subjected to the annoyance of public misinterpretation of the incident." What he in fact signed, however, says Brown, "was a full contract of a dozen articles," devised by Shubert and Miller, "but apparently Miss Anglin did not know this" (*ED*, 117).

Moody clearly liked Margaret Anglin personally, but he had his doubts about her as an artist—she was all too well "trained in the overstated conventions of the American theatre." He was "not pleased with the constant pitch of intensity she brought to her roles," with her "cynosure stage presence," with her "applause-lust." "Applause," he observed sadly, after one of his post-performance suppers with her, "is the actor's currency and abacus by which all is reckoned" (*ED*, 205).

A Sabine Woman, given three more performances "before audiences of moderate size" (*ED*, 205), was allowed to bring down the curtain on M.A.'s Chicago engagement. Then it was off to New York for a series of conferences with Henry Miller and Lee Shubert in which it was agreed that Moody would revise the play over the summer and Miller would produce it in the fall. Moody readily acknowledged the influence exerted by Margaret Anglin upon his revision, and the tradition which ascribes to her the new title for the play and the new name for the heroine (Ruth Jordan instead of Zona Murchee) has a fair degree of credibility.

M.A. tells us that after the third or fourth performance she heard a couple on the street "confusing *The Sabine Woman* with a travesty called *The Sambo Girl* being given at another [Chicago] theatre at the same time" (*H4*). That was probably enough to convince her that "Sabine" ("suggesting a classicism which was wrong") would have to go. "Many," she said, "will not know what *The Sabine Woman* means, and those who do will not like it" (*N.Y. Mirror*, 20.10.06).

The Great (or Continental) Divide, with which in its southwestern manifestation Moody was on fairly intimate terms, is the eastward line of the Rockies, which, for our purposes roughly bisects New Mexico, and which divides, continentally, the eastward and westward river courses. In terms of the moral allegory of the play, it is the divide between Eastern "Puritan" conservatism and Western "free-thinking" liberalism.

The story-line of the revised play, though a trifle involuted, is easy enough to précis. Ruth Jordan, a high-toned New England girl, is (by a pointedly ironic concourse of circumstances, involving her fiancé) left alone in a cabin in the out-back of southwestern Arizona. She is made prisoner by three rambling drunken prospectors and offers herself to the tallest and least repulsive of them (Steve Ghent), if he will save her from the other two. So he buys off the Mexican "greaser" with a chain of gold nuggets and kills the other American in a "square" shoot-out, and rides off into the sunset with his Sabine Woman. In Act 2 Ghent strikes it rich and becomes a mine-owner; but Ruth finds the Mexican, buys back the gold chain with her own money, returns it to Ghent, and deserts him. In Act 3 a despondent Ruth is back home in Massachusetts with her family and son. One day Ghent, who has surreptitiously saved the Jordan family from bankruptcy, shows up, and asks to be forgiven for his rough ways. He reaffirms his love for Ruth and his zest for life, and tells her he accounts her eternally free. "I wish you'd come with me," he says, "but you belong here in your fine drawing-room with your Puritan ancestors, and I belong out yonder—beyond the Rockies, beyond the Great Divide." That is all Ruth needs to hear, and she says, "Tell me that you know that if I could have followed you freely I would have done it." And so he does that, and they ride off once again (this time in sweet accord, and baby makes three) into their brave new home in the west.

It was not until September of 1906 that Henry Miller could be persuaded to undertake the production of *The Great Divide* and the part of the male lead, the name of which he had changed, for no very clear reason, from Frank Stephens to Stephen Ghent. But once he accepted the challenge he went to it with a will and bulldozed all and sundry, including the bewildered Moody, into his manic *modus operandi*:

> Finally [says Frank Morse], on Sunday night, September 10, 1906, the cast and production arrived in Albany. It was here that William Vaughn Moody got his first genuine dose of the truly strenuous life. A dress rehearsal was begun at seven o'clock in the evening and ran until five the next morning. When daylight broke up the session, the unhappy author considered the scenery a joke, the company hopelessly incompetent and Miller himself utterly unable to play the part of Ghent. (*BWHM*, 26)

"The stage," said Moody, "resembled a stock exchange [or] a skating rink. . . . The company itself looked indescribably bad, the vulgarizing process sickeningly complete."

"But," as Maurice Brown attests, "the Monday night opening amazed him"; the performance was taut and spirited:

> The company pulled itself together in a way that astonished him, and the house was large and enthusiastic. The nightmare of dress rehearsal was forgotten and Moody began to warm to the idea of the strolling player's existence. The company set out for a week of one-night stands which took them to Amsterdam, New York, across New England to New Haven, and then to Atlantic City. In Washington the play settled down for a week's run in the Belasco Theatre. Moody was lightheaded from the tension of performances and rehearsals, rushing to and from hotels and trains, bickering over details of the text and interpretations of audience reactions, and drinking at the impromptu champagne suppers Miss Anglin liked after the performance. (*ED*, 208)

The stage seemed to be set for a big Washington success, "for the company had been playing to large and responsive audiences" (*ED*, 210). And indeed the *Washington*

Post, which was to be the main precipitator of the Washington fiasco, printed this glowing account of the Albany opening to herald the Washington run:

> Albany, N.Y., Sept. 10.—Miss Margaret Anglin and Henry Miller won positive triumphs tonight before a large and fashionable audience in Harmanus Bleeker Hall in the first performance of William Vaughn Moody's *The Great Divide*.
>
> This play is that with which they open the Princess Theatre, in New York, on October 1. It is one of the most intensely dramatic seen here in years. . . . The struggle between love and the forces of tradition gives Miss Anglin a splendid opportunity, of which she took full measure tonight. Mr. Miller made an equally strong impression as the dominant westerner. They were called before the curtain time and again after the remarkably strong first act.

When the young Frank Morse, then a cub reporter for the *Washington Times*, returned from the Belasco opening (Monday, 17 Sept.), he wrote "an afternoon follow-up of the laudatory review [he] expected to read the next morning, and went to bed wondering how and where Miller had found so fine a play." When he took in "the vicious denunciation of the drama and the cast" printed in the following morning's *Washington Post*, he "saw red," and so, apparently, did Miller, who that very morning "projected himself into the editorial offices of the *Post* to thrash the writer" (BWHM, 27).

This (mercifully brief) review, written by a reporter who was apparently "drunk when he saw the play" (BWHM, 29) and atrabilious when he described it, is, by reason of its disproportionate effect, worth quoting in full:

BELASCO'S OPENS BADLY

Henry Miller and Margaret Anglin
Struggle with a Miserable Play

> A melodrama, *The Great Divide*, by William V. Moody, opened at the Belasco most unsuitably last night. Henry Miller did the best he could to modify its crudities, but the task was too great for any actor. Margaret Anglin, who played opposite Mr. Miller, permitted herself to be so carried away by the play as to give some very fine impersonations of Charlotte Cushman as Lady Macbeth, but at other parts of the drama she restrained herself to a more moderate level and made the ghastliness of the whole proceeding a little less glaring.

The plot concerns a violent and wicked, wicked man, who invades the ranch house of a total stranger in the middle of the night and makes violent love to a middle-aged woman in a dressing jacket. He bargains for her with a Mexican for a necklace of nuggets, and shoots a miner.

Thus, having promised the woman protection and having received her promise to marry him, he goes forth with her into the dark, dark night. In the next act the woman is carried away from the husband, Henry Miller, and he, instead of being relieved and thankful, makes himself rich, finds his wife in New England, and after another violent scene she reveals her love for him in time for the curtain to go down and let the audience escape.

Mr. Moody, the author, is connected with the English department of the University of Chicago. Evidently he has read *The Virginian* and *To Have and to Hold*, and has had no mercy on them.   Mr. Miller made a speech after the second act, and thanked the audience for its forbearance.

Either Miss Anglin's stage directions in the first act were most extraordinary or she interpreted her part in a wonderful manner, for she juggled a bunch of flowers so wildly that the audience was alarmed, and then seized her bosom as though her heart were breaking, all for no apparent reason; but nothing came of it. The audience tittered. As a dramatic curiosity *The Great Divide* is worth seeing, but as a play it has no excuse for existence. The sympathy of the audience last night was with the actors. Laura Hope Crews and Charles Gotthold did very well and had parts that were humanly possible.

Frank Morse tells us that after he had redressed the balance by publishing a full-page laudation of the production in the *Times*, culminating with "the conviction that Henry Miller had come dangerously close to producing the long-awaited 'Great American Play,'" Miller "staged a second expedition to newspaper row for the purpose of demolishing the *Post* critic" (BWHM, 28).

The fuming Miller, with figurative horsewhip in hand, never did catch up with the forever-anonymous *Post* critic, who had in fact penned his last line for that prestigious paper—he was fired before the week was out. But the damage was done, for other papers tended to follow the *Post* line, and bad reviews continued to plague the play. The *Washington Star*, for instance, opined later in the week that Professor Moody and Mr. Miller had produced "a grossly immoral play."   Ward Morehouse remarks that "Margaret Anglin was disturbed, of course, by the Washington and Pittsburgh notices, but they did not upset her as much as did the apparent unconcern of playwright Moody, who would sit

Henry Miller in *The Great Divide*, which opened the Princess Theatre to wall-to-wall rave New York reviews. (1906)

for hours upon the porch of Pittsburgh's Schenley Park Hotel, smoking his pipe, meditating, and stroking his auburn beard" (*MT*, 68-69).

The chilly inhospitality of Washington and Pittsburgh hardly augured well for the New York opening, and when the dress rehearsal at the Princess went up in wrathful smoke, things looked black indeed. The rehearsal fiasco occurred when M.A.'s carelessly flung basket of flowers tripped up H.M. in one of his dramatic entrances. His satirical rebuke sent M.A. sweeping off the stage in high dudgeon, and Miller, not to be outdone in temperament, "thundered that the opening was cancelled and *The Great Divide* would never again be played" (*BWHM*, 31). Or, as Maurice Brown has it,

> Miller then seized one of the huge Indian jars Moody had brought from New Mexico and smashed it on the stage, shouting one of his lines, "'Smashed to hell is smashed to hell!'—There will be no 'Great Divide.'" (*ED*, 211)

And everyone concerned, including the author, dismally and silently packed up and left the theatre.

The next day the stage manager, Bertram Harrison, was seeing to some last minute staging details when a forlorn, hangdog Moody appeared, and, as Harrison tells it,

> asked in sepulchral tones, "Have you heard from Mr. Miller?"
>
> "Yes, I've just talked to him on the telephone," was my cheery response. "He hasn't been around today, but Miss Anglin just left. She came to check some production details with me."
>
> Moody looked at me with utter bewilderment written on his face. "You don't mean you're going to open tonight," he exclaimed.
>
> "Why not?" I asked, honestly amazed by the question. "Oh—you mean—about last night? Why, that's nothing to worry about! Of course, they'll open."
>
> Moody threw up his hands, turned abruptly and tottered down the steps. "I call it absolute madness," he muttered to himself as he disappeared down Broadway. (*BWHM*, 32)

The opening of *The Great Divide* (3.10.06) at the Princess drew wall-to-wall rave reviews from the New York papers. The *Sun* (4.10.06) went so far as to assert that Moody's play was quite possibly "the best product of the American drama thus far," and that it surely stood preeminent among American plays "in striking true and deep into the wells of human impulse and passion." J.M. Handley of the *American* (4.10.06) was moved to declare that "in her stage creation of Ruth Jordan Miss Anglin has emblazoned one of the most brilliant pages in our theatrical annals." And Edward McKay of the *Evening Mail* was glowingly gratified on all counts:

> Not since Bartley Campbell's *My Partner* has a Western play of such breadth of plan and trenchant context been brought to Broadway. Miss Anglin's *Zira* was a *tour de force*, a burst of frenzy; her Ruth is a wonderfully adroit, flexible and fervid exhibition of acting—running through every phase from grave to gay—in speech, gesture and movement remarkable for naturalness and pulsating with primal emotions. Never has Mr. Miller been seen to better advantage. Dignity, restraint and pathos were equally manifest in his illustration of the reformed miner.

The next day "the line-up for tickets stretched all the way down to the corner of Twenty-eighth Street and half way round the block to Sixth Avenue. . . . The house was sold out continuously for over two hundred consecutive performances" (*BWHM*, 33).

Fairly early in the New York run, which ran to 238 performances, M.A. received a letter from James O'Donnell Bennett, drama critic of the *Chicago Record-Herald*, which not only demonstrates how much the Anglin voice meant to the Moody play but is quite remarkably prescient of the Anglin future:

> I cannot describe [says Bennett]—I could only feel—the astonishing effects of beauty and poignancy you produced upon me. I could not follow the facial play at all, being so remote; it was all vocal and such shading, I seldom have heard in a theatre. It was like delicious music, and yet it was altogether the voice of a human being—not mere lyricism, I mean; I went away awed and wondering. Later I thought what a deplorable thing it is that we do not hear you in Shakespeare—Queen Catherine—Lady Macbeth—Juliet. In gratitude to heaven for your great gifts you ought not to let the years run away from you—or with you—before you take up these roles—and Imogen too. Electra, of course, was written for you of all living women.
> (J, 47)

That Electra clarion call was to echo down the years—and indeed Queen Katharine (as a reading), Lady Macbeth and Juliet all subsequently did find a place in M.A.'s repertoire. Bennett's dulcet words, of course, resonate with those of James O'Neill about the Anglin voice, Shakespeare, and the Irish Sea;

she would inevitably remember them with pleasure and a sense of noblesse oblige.

She may also have remembered with pleasure (and with thoughts of Electra) the last words of John Webber's review of *The Great Divide*:

> Miss Anglin's Ruth Jordan marks the most important step in her upward career. There are no bursts of frenzy, such as characterize *Zira*, to dazzle us with their brightness, but a difficult sustained performance such as only an artist in the fullest sense of the term could carry through convincingly. No severer test, unless it be the *Electra* of Euripides, could be imposed on an actress, perhaps, than the prolonged note of the second act, that runs almost the entire scale of human emotion. It is all the more difficult from the fact that the action is almost entirely psychological. Yet Miss Anglin not only carries the action successfully, but holds her audience in thrall. (*Canadian Magazine*, 12.06)

At the very height of the heady success of *The Great Divide*, the British star Lena Ashwell (in *The Shulamite*) and playwright Henry Arthur Jones (on business) arrived in New York more or less together, and together they got in touch with Margaret Anglin. And against all probability (or even feasibility) M.A. agreed to their proposition of a friendly contest of performances of the title role in Jones's *Mrs. Dane's Defence*, a play in which "both actresses had scored heavily." Frank Morse gives a concise account of M.A.'s feat in *Backstage with Henry Miller*:

> On Wednesday and Saturday afternoon, regular matinees of *The Great Divide* were given. On Thursday and Friday afternoons Margaret Anglin staged two recrudescences of *Mrs. Dane's Defence* at the Lyric Theater and played two contrasting roles in the revivals.
> . . . Miss Ashwell appeared first in the big role. She played Mrs. Dane on Thursday afternoon, November 15 and Miss Anglin, as Lady Eastney, was just a member of the supporting company. On Friday afternoon, Miss Anglin played Mrs. Dane and Miss Ashwell appeared as Lady Eastney. Thus New York saw two fine performances of the Jones play, while the Anglin and Ashwell followers remained entirely unshaken in their respective opinions about the greatness of their favorite actress in a role that brought fame to both women. (p. 67)

It must be admitted, however, that the *Theatre* (Jan. 1907) critic gave the palm to Miss Ashwell for her more "understated," "intimate," "inside the skin" performance, which he preferred to Miss Anglin's more flamboyant "artful," "theatrical" one.   And in this opinion he is supported by Miss Ashwell herself, who allows that she was "the winner" in the Mrs. Dane contest because of the restraint of her performance.   She was a good winner, though, and had only sweet things to say about "that charming actress, Margaret Anglin," who was "always angelic to me" (*MAP*, 121-22).

But it was precisely Miss Anglin's "theatricality" (as well as her relatively unexploited flair for high comedy) which allowed her to bear away the bell in the character part:

> As Lady Eastney, Miss Anglin scored such a triumph as brought the house to its feet in cheers. One must revert to the palmiest days of Ada Rehan, Rose Coghlan, Fanny Davenport, Mrs. John Drew and the greatest of our comediennes, Agnes Booth, to find a parallel for Miss Anglin's Lady Eastney. It was delicious. It fairly crackled with humor, good-heartedness and shrewdness, the kind of shrewdness that springs from a big heart and a keen intellect. Miss Ashwell was dire in the same part. (*Theatre Magazine*, Jan. 1907)

The fact that this bravura performance was got up for a single matinee, in the midst of full-time work on another play, surely makes it the more astonishing.

One would hardly, at this time, associate the idea of Margaret Anglin with the idea of "free afternoons," but the *Bohemian* magazine of May 1907 reports that "Miss Anglin has taken to spending so many of her free afternoons [taking part in] settlement work on the lower east side of New York [that] she has become a familiar figure in Rivington Street and East Broadway."   On these impromptu appearances as Lady Bountiful she would show up in Rivington Street in her chauffeur-driven Pierce-Arrow with a great load of groceries which she would exchange with the "settlement people" for half a dozen ragamuffins who would be treated to a high style drive uptown "through Central Park and out Riverside Drive" and across to the Saint Regis ("my hotel"), with its "twenty towering stories." When M.A. asked one wide-eyed black child if she would like to live there, she said: "No, ma'am."

"No?" queried Miss Anglin in surprise. "And why not?"

"Look how high I'd have to climb to hang out de wash," was the sensible reply.

The record-breaking run was interrupted in March of 1907 by one of Henry Miller's (not infrequent) ego-boosting whimsicalities.

On Monday 25 February the Belasco Theatre (of unhappy memory) issued the following bulletin:

> Henry Miller will break the run of his big success in New York, cancel a single performance at the Princess Theatre, and on Monday night, March 4, 1907, will present Margaret Anglin and himself in *The Great Divide* at the Belasco Theatre for a single performance of the Moody play.

President Theodore Roosevelt had to absent himself at the last moment due to his son Archie's contracting diphtheria, but the house was otherwise all that Miller could have wished. The ambassadors of Britain (Dr. James Bryce), Russia (Baron Rosen) and Germany (Baron von Sternburg) were there. So were the ambassadors of Spain (Pastor), Argentina (Partela), Haiti (Léger), and Costa Rica (Calvo). The *N.Y. Herald* (5.3.07) list also includes twelve senators, ten representatives, three generals, three admirals, Speaker Joseph Gurney Cannon, Secretary of State Elihu Root, Secretary of the Interior Ethan Hitchcock, Controller of the Currency Allan Ridgley, four under-secretaries, and last, but presumably not least, "the Count and Countess of Hatzfeldt."
"The play was received with enthusiasm" by this august gathering in a house in which "there was not a vacant seat," and "Mr. Miller and Miss Anglin received many curtain calls" (*N.Y. Herald*, 5.3.07). The best and brightest had approved and applauded. And so the Washington critics were compelled to eat humble pie, and a vindicated Miller sat tall in the saddle.

In March of the following year Miller took the play back to the Nixon in Pittsburgh, the scene of another early hostile reception, but here, though he again had a large and well-disposed house, the Pittsburgh jinx continued as the triumphal course of the play was halted in mid-stream by what Miller later described as "an act of the guardian Devil of Pittsburgh." The incident was later retailed by Billy Rose in his syndicated column "Pitching Horseshoes":

> When Henry Miller opened in *The Great Divide*, one of the first tryouts was in Pittsburgh, and Henry got plenty sore when the critics panned the play and accused him of hamming it up. In New York, however, the play was a smash and ran for two seasons. When the show went on tour, the first stand was a repeat in Pittsburgh. This time the critics reversed themselves and said both Miller and the play were fine.
> One night, in the middle of his big love scene with Margaret Anglin, Henry noticed that several customers were sneaking up the aisle and making for the exit. "Get back to your seats," he

yelled. "The last time I played in this oversized smudgepot I was insulted, and I don't propose to let it happen again!"

The people went back to their seats and the play went on, but a few seconds later another bunch got up and began to leave. This time Miller almost threw a fit.

"Knaves and varlets," he screamed, "back to your seats!"

Margaret Anglin grabbed him by the sleeve. "Stop acting like a jackass, Henry," she said. "The theatre's on fire." (Rpt. *Reader's Digest*, 7.4.27)

But this is to get a little ahead of ourselves. The fact is, the thunderingly successful 1908 tour very nearly never happened. As the triumphant New York run entered its seventh month, relations between M.A. and H.M. became increasingly frigid, so that when Miller's lease on the Princess expired in April 1907 it was rather louringly agreed to break the run of *The Great Divide*, and a well-heeled but ill-tempered M.A. packed up and left (with mother) for England. "There had been long stretches in the last weeks of the run," says Frank Morse, "during which the co-stars, off stage, were not on speaking terms" (BWHM, 49).

It was in fact quite generally speculated in show-biz circles at the time that the tense angry silence between the stars was sexually charged and was the product of a love affair gone sour, probably because of M.A.'s "imperious" nature. M.A. was thirty-one in 1907 and at the top of her physical form, Miller, a robust forty-eight, was not far off the top of his. Indeed, sister Eileen, who was still living with Margaret at the time (and playing with the Lancers), was apparently more distressed by the persistent gossip than was Margaret herself. M.A. always insisted that her relationship with Miller, in good times and bad, whether harmonious or discordant, was based purely on things theatrical. But her frankness on this point may well be doubted.

Sad and miffed as she may have been at the outset, M.A. seems to have been a busy bee on her European junket. While buzzing through Brussels she improved the shining hour by dining with "Maurice Maeterlinck, the celebrated Belgian poet, dramatist and mystic" (*Toledo Blade*, 3.8.07), and while in Milan she had a memorable luncheon with Giacomo Puccini. According to the *Blade*:

Puccini, while in New York last winter, saw Miss Anglin and Henry Miller in *The Great Divide*, and was so impressed with the power, picturesqueness and subtlety of the Moody drama that its influence will be felt in the American grand opera which he is soon to write. Puccini considers Miss Anglin the greatest English speaking actress and says if she were French or Italian [like Bernhardt or Duse] she would undoubtedly hold a position of world-wide fame second to no living actress.

Puccini's *The Girl of the Golden West* (*La Fanciulla del West*), which was first performed in New York on the 10th of December 1910, though of course based on David Belasco's play of the same name, was clearly originally inspired by his vivid impressions of the Anglin-Miller western, and thus *La Fanciulla* may be considered, at least in part, as the Maestro's tribute to Margaret Anglin of whom he so willingly declared himself to be a fan.

While in Italy she also spent a conscientious week studying the ruins of Imperial Rome in preparation for a production of J.L. Long's *The Temple of Vesta*, which unhappily, in spite of the best will in the world on M.A.'s part, never quite came off. She also tells of a hair-raising motor trip from Rome to Siena, at breakneck speed, by way of "tortuous mountain roads, most of which skirted sheer precipices which dropped straight down into gaping chasms," with a wild-looking daredevil chauffeur who was "apprehended by the authorities in Siena" who informed M.A. that her demon driver was well known to them and was "quite insane" (*EWW4*). We shall find this fatal, or near-fatal attraction of insane persons to Miss Anglin recurring throughout her story like a spooky leit-motif.

Back in England she met and was regaled by Robert Brindle, M.C., the soldier-Bishop (R.C.) of Nottingham, who had wonderful stories to tell of the siege of Khartoum and the battles of Tel-el-Kebir, Atbara and Omdurman. She also visited the Anglo-American novelist Frances Hodgson Burnett (*Little Lord Fauntleroy*, *The Secret Garden*) at her place in Kent "and there reveled in the most wonderful garden I have ever seen" (*H7*). She was herself, at this time, the mistress of a splendid rose garden on her fifteen-acre estate at White Plains. An interesting note on M.A.'s previous two summers appears in the *Chicago Tribune* (25.5.06):

Margaret Anglin spends three months of summer vacation life in a houseboat on the great south bay of Long Island off Freeport, a typical seafaring town about twenty miles from New York city. The floating domicile is of most novel construction. Miss Anglin's house-

boat—she calls it *The Green Heron*—has a broad prom-
enade on all sides, and this is shaded by a covering of
cedar shingles.   There are three living rooms, a library
and an interior and exterior dining apartment.   The
actress has aboard her favorite books, wall sketches of
marine landscapes and many watercolors of native bird
and fish life.   The lounging room has a piano and
numerous smaller musical instruments and the furniture
of all the rooms is of mission type.   *The Green Heron* has
no motive power, the tides alone affording the means by
which the little craft is directed here and there according
to its owner's fancy.

At the end of the summer of '07, Miller followed M.A.
to England and there managed to smooth her ruffled
feathers and to work out the terms of a new and
presumably rather cool working relationship.   Oddly
enough, one of the flies in the Miller-Anglin ointment was
the stunning success of the Russian actress Alla Nazimova,
whom M.A. had discovered at Orleneff's Russian Lyceum
(in the Bowery) and introduced to Miller.   Miller took
some persuading, but then, to M.A.'s chagrin, became
completely engrossed in engineering Nazimova's huge
successes in *Hedda Gabler* and *A Doll's House*.   But the real
problem, in theatrical terms, after all, may have been quite
simply that *The Great Divide* was a ship with two captains.
In any event, Frank Morse recalls:

> A truce, at least a temporary one, was worked out.   *The
> Great Divide* re-opened in August, 1907, at Daly's Theater,
> with Miller and Anglin in their original roles.   The play
> immediately recaptured capacity business and continued
> triumphantly on Broadway until the early weeks of 1908,
> when a tour of the entire country was inaugurated.   The
> big success it had scored in New York was duplicated in
> every American city.   The Moody drama was presented
> to capacity audiences during 1908 and 1909, with a
> summer run in San Francisco sandwiched between
> regular seasons.   Miss Anglin did not, however, share all
> this success.   Soon after the transcontinental tour was
> begun she relinquished the role of Ruth Jordan and
> sailed for Australia and fresh stage triumphs. (*BWHM*, 49)

And so H.M. and M.A. split professionally for good in
the spring of '08.   There can be little doubt that the
success of *The Great Divide* coincided with the failure of the
Anglin-Miller friendship, and thus, ironically, constituted a
feeling loss to the American theatre.   It behoves us,

however, before taking our leave of Henry Miller, "fine actor and finished gentlemen," to glance at Frank Morse's last words on the Miller-Anglin relationship:

> It will give their old associates sincere pleasure to know that [twenty years after their sad falling out over The Great Divide] Henry Miller and Margaret Anglin, shortly before his death, again became friendly. On several occasions in his last months [in 1926] he spent quiet evenings with his former co-star and her husband, Howard Hull, talking over the good old days in the theater. It was peculiarly fitting that these two fine artists, who had given so much to the American stage, should prove great enough to forget their differences and resume the cordial friendship of their earlier years. (*BWHM*, 277)

The Canadian critic John Webber took the occasion of M.A.'s departure for Australia to make a very fair estimate of her professional stature and scope as she entered her thirty-third year:

> Miss Anglin is now touring Australia in a laudable ambition to extend her reputation to that sister colony, geographically so remote, but near to us by a hundred ties of kinship and still deeper ties of social and spiritual aspiration. Her brilliant achievements and assured position on the American stage certainly warrant the ambition, while no other artist could more worthily represent Canada and the stage of this country than she. Her work is always characterized by high purpose, loftiness of tone and genuine artistic refinement. The quality is distinctly poetic, in the larger sense, and spiritual, in the broadest understanding of that term. If one may venture a criticism, it is that she has been too long identified with emotional characterization for the complete rounding out of her art. An excursion or two in comedy we hope to see follow on her return to America. (*Canadian Magazine*, Nov. 1908)

Photo courtesy of Basile Anglin

Exuberant Australian hospitality met M.A. at every turn of her 1908-1909 tour; posters for *The Truth* and *The Thief*.

Chapter V

Australia—*The Thief, The Truth*: 1908-1909

> Will your grace command me any service to the world's
> end?
> I will go on the slightest errand now to the Antipodes,
> . . . rather than hold three words' conference with this
> harpy.
> (Shakespeare, *Much Ado about Nothing*, 2.1.273)

M.A. begins her description of her Australian tour with an
oblique suggestion that by the beginning of 1908 she was
more than ready to see the back of Mr. Miller for a goodish
while, and of Ruth Jordan, too, for that matter; despite the
financial rewards associated with both of those personages.
She had had enough, for the nonce, she says, "of conventional
American theatrical lines," and "it had come to seem to me,"
she continues,

> that the role of Ruth Jordan, while it was picturesque and
> significant in the development of American character, did not
> afford me all the emotional and spiritual opportunities I
> desired. (*H7*)

As far as Miller was concerned, Jerome Collamore recalls (C,
16.8.85) that

> Mary told me the reason she took the Australian tour was to
> get away from Henry Miller. . . . Once [summer of '07?]
> when she was settling down to watch a play in Paris, she
> was flabbergasted to find Miller blandly settling in beside
> her. . . . But when we were doing *Woman of No Importance* in
> '16 and needed a cyc. [cyclorama], I told her that Miller had
> one and she said, "I can have anything he has." . . . There is
> even a story, of some currency, of M.A. wandering around
> Central Park [in 1908?] with a revolver, contemplating
> suicide, connected with the Miller affair.

And so when the Americo-Australian impresario, J.C.
Williamson, appeared in February 1908 with a lucrative offer
to sponsor a Margaret Anglin tour of Australia, she accepted
with alacrity, and quickly terminated her contract with Henry
Miller and Lee Shubert.

Just before Williamson's arrival on the scene, she recalls,
she was dickering with Henry Arthur Jones over the rights
(which he wished her to take up) to his new drama *The Sword*

of Gideon. Indeed Mr. Jones almost won her over with a tête-
à-tête reading of the script, but her "partners" told her it
would not "go" in America. At the same time she was also
negotiating with Maurice Maeterlinck for the American rights
to both *La Mort de Tintagiles* and *Soeur Béatrice.* In this case,
her old friend and trusted adviser, Wm. F. Connor, assured
her that the latter piece, which she was especially keen to do,
"would be a failure from the very start. He had occasion to
change his mind when he became in after years the manager
of Madame Sarah Bernhardt." However, these abortive
negotiations resulted in "a correspondence of much interest
between the great Belgian author and myself" (H7). She was
also at this time considering an urgent offer from the highly
successful actor-manager (and matinee-idol) James K. Hackett,
to play the lead part of the boy, Tyltyl, in *The Bluebird* (1907),
to which he had just secured the American rights:

> Miss Anglin [said Hackett] is the only woman in America
> who can play the principal role, and I shan't produce the
> piece until she is in a position to appear in it. (*N.Y. Telegraph,*
> 24.3.07)

A Washington newspaper had earlier announced "that Miss
Anglin would shortly be leaving Henry Miller to become J.K.
Hackett's leading woman." That report elicited this telegram,
quoted "verbatim" by the N.Y. Telegraph (20.3.07):

> Hear I am to manage you next season. Is this true?
> Seriously, I have a splendid play for you. Regards to you
> and Henry. JKH.

Another factor which prompted M.A. to jump at the
chance of disappearing into the antipodes for a while was the
ongoing bizarre involvement with a distraught and obsessed
lady, one Mrs. James Stevenson of Brookline, Mass., who
claimed that M.A. was "her long-lost daughter who had [as
M.A. understood it] mysteriously disappeared in 1907" (H7).
Actually, according to the *Cleveland News* (17.10.07), Grace had
disappeared in 1897, and Mrs. Stevenson had been "round the
world" in quest of the lost girl, "and now she says she
recognizes her child in the person of Miss Margaret Anglin,
the actress." The resemblance between Margaret and Grace
was indeed "startling" (M.A.'s word), and at least one Boston
paper ran pictures of the lost girl and the actress side by side.
The fact that the bereft woman first saw M.A. in the title
role of *Zira* (*alias* Hester Trent, *alias* Ruth Wilding), the story
of a confidence-trick change of identity, might well have had

something to do with the establishment of her unshakable delusion. "It availed me nothing," says M.A., "to tell the poor deluded woman that I had a perfectly good mother of my own." She continued to insist that Margaret was "her own Grace," "and," had added reproachfully, "in your present position you could do everything for me and your sister" *(H7)*. M.A.'s affluence, however, could not have been a very significant part of the "everything" she had to offer, for the *Cleveland News* tells us that Mrs. Stevenson was "the widow of a millionaire real-estate dealer," and that Miss Anglin by admitting her claim "could become an heiress to her alleged father's estate."

In the midst of the harrowing Stevenson campaign, M.A. was cornered in her dressing room one night by a mad "mesmerist" who claimed to be in contact with "the real Margaret Anglin," at present immured in "a sanitarium, in Connecticut." This wild-eyed "seer" then offered to hypnotize her so that she might reveal her "true identity" (as Grace Stevenson). True identity, forsooth! M.A. got rid of him by promising to submit to the test "on the morrow" and then called the police *(Wha)*.

After having spent several weeks dodging Mrs. Stevenson's persistent attempts to invade her dressing room (sometimes with "sister" in tow), Margaret fled to Europe for the summer of '07. When she returned to New York in the fall so did the reproachful disowned "mother". And so Margaret was glad to go under in order to let things blow over. As it happened, Mrs. Stevenson was still lying in ambush when she returned from Australia, and M.A. went the length of having herself declared legally dead in Boston (gone under for good), in order to escape Mother Stevenson's prosecution (and allow Mr. Stevenson's estate to be settled); but she did have a respite of nearly a year under the liberal auspices of J.C. Williamson & Co.

Just prior to, and indeed overlapping the Stevenson trouble, another ongoing personally harassing non-relationship was taking its toll. It came to be known to the press as "the Anglin-Friend affair." That was before M.A.'s dogged devotee, first identified as the "amorous [would-be] playwright, Harry Friend," was correctly identified as Alfred Freund. This psychotic pursuer was also rich. He was the son of a St. Louis department-store magnate called, with grim appropriateness, Sigmund Freund.

Young Alfred (mid twenties—"long hair, glasses, mysterious look") began his campaign in the summer of 1905 by attending M.A.'s plays night after night, always in the same seat ("second row, aisle seat") and fixing her with an unwavering Svengali stare. This proved to be disconcerting. "Miss Anglin had him barred from the theatres in which she was playing." He then began to deluge her with letters, photographs and love poems: Miss Anglin gave them to Samuel Weller [sic] of Shubert Security. "He took to camping on the steps" to the stage door of the Princess:—Miss Anglin had Shubert Security "give him the gate." At last "he became impossible when he took to camping out on the stone wall of Central Park opposite Miss Anglin's residence at 34 W. 59th St." He was finally arrested on M.A.'s charge of "haunting and besetting"—"That face:" she said, "it has followed me so long, I see it in my dreams" (*N.Y. World*, 10.10.06). He was subsequently tried, found guilty, and committed to Bellevue Hospital for psychiatric treatment.

The *N.Y. Telegraph* (14.10.06) concluded its coverage of the case with this distinctly wry report:

HE STILL SIGHS FOR MISS ANGLIN

But Being in the Psychopathic Ward at Bellevue His Sighs Do Not Disturb Anybody

ALFRED FREUND AT THE BAR

Perish the thought that admiration for Miss Margaret Anglin is presumptive evidence of insanity. There are many of us who have admired the accomplished actress and who have managed to avoid Dr. Gregory and his little psychoscope in Bellevue Hospital.

But only a few of us wish to marry her, many even in this class realizing that there is a "Great Divide" between the ambition and the possibility of accomplishing our heart's desire.

Alfred Freund, of St. Louis, coming from the "show me" State, would like to know why he isn't licensed to pay court to the charming actress.

And a cruel judge has sent him over to Dr. Gregory and to the company of those who see many things that are not there. He is to be examined.

Freund, who is said to be the scion of a very opulent grocery store in the Mound City, has been trying for a long time, according to printed reports, to convince Miss Anglin that they were intended for each other, and at last she had to have him arrested.

Hereupon Henry Miller, a low-browed intriguer, from the make-up of Mr. Freund's mind, enters. Mr. Miller also entered the Jefferson Market Court yesterday morning, accompanied by

Miss Anglin, Miss Anglin's maid, and enough reporters to start a campaign daily.

Freund was there and had counsel. Mark Alter was the counsel.

Mark hasn't a proper respect for the [theatrical] profession. He actually treats representatives of it the same as he would ordinary mortals, and he told the Magistrate that his client thought Mr. Miller had come between him and his inamorata in a legitimate love affair. Mr. Alter did not undertake to say that his client thought logically, but [that] he thought.

If Mr. Miller could show the anger in a stage play that he showed then and there he would make the hit of his life.

"How dare you, sir! How dare you!" he shouted to Mr. Alter, but the latter continued to dare.

Freund insisted before the court that until a week ago he received frequent encouragements from Miss Anglin, "and many signs from the stage." He also said that it was his belief that Mr. Miller had interfered in behalf of a friend of his own, but he didn't name the friend Mr. Miller, from his viewpoint, had been recommending.

Miss Anglin said she didn't wish to see the young man punished. She felt that charity should be extended to him.

And he got Dr. Gregory—who is charity incarnate—but he uses a psychoscope and is likely to send Alfred back to where he has to bathe in Mississippi water. What!

At this time, too, M.A. was in litigation with the New York, New Haven and Hartford Railroad Co. for compensation for a broken collarbone sustained when an engine backing down a siding grade caused her horses to rear and throw her from her gig. She eventually got a $5,000 settlement (a tenth of what she was asking) by answering a question about how far she was from the steps of the Swift packing plant when she first saw the descending engine:

> The distance in question [she said] is the distance from the steps to the railway, minus the distance between the horses' noses and the engine. (*N.Y. Telegraph*, 24.10.06)

"'Exactly,' replied the lawyer." And that *eclaircissement* apparently did for the defendant.

So much for the trials and tribulations of 1906-07. "Revenons à nos moutons d'Australie," as Miss Anglin would have it. "On the 20th of May, 1908," she recalls, "I took train for Vancouver, and thence set sail for the South Seas" (*H7*). In the party were her sister Eileen, her manager, Louis Nethersole, and her four principal actors, Henry Kolker, Susie Vaughan (Mrs. K.), Sydney Stirling and Harry Overton.

A day ashore in Honolulu left M.A. "with the impression that it was the most beautiful place [she] had ever seen." Ceylon, though splendidly exotic and languorous with its "perfume laden hills," was, she thought, not a patch on Hawaii—especially Hawaii in the evening:

> The most enchanted hour of my whole life was spent with [the actress] Ada Dwyer in Honolulu. *There* is a fairyland to dream of. Never have I imagined that anything in this world could be so bewilderingly lovely as the marvel of ocean and blue sky, of liquid stars so big and so near to the earth that you fancy you could reach up and touch them; of a golden moon, not a common little silver orb like ours, swimming in that wonderful sapphire sky; of breezes spicy with strange southern odors and heavy with the breath of strange, sweet flowers. (*N.Y. Post*, 20.05.09)

On the twenty-four hour stopover at Fiji M.A. holed up at the hotel during the day and kept an apprehensive eye on the thermometer, which eventually "levelled off at 118°." Her maid, who did brave the elements, told her that the Fijian restaurateurs did not consider it warm enough to make it worth their while to manufacture ice-cream.

> I shall never forget that hotel [says M.A.]. It was spotlessly clean, with white curtains and mosquito nets at every window. The presiding angel was a Mrs. MacDonald, a perfect autocrat in her way. At dinner our wonderfully attentive waiter looked as though he were tricked out for some fantastic comic opera. He served us in all his grandeur of white evening shirt, dress coat, and high white collar, beneath which flared a red and green striped tie. Otherwise his costume consisted of a loin-cloth and bare legs. The solemn face that looked out from a shock of bushy hair was almost more than our gravity could withstand. (*H7*)

At Fanning Island the total white population of twenty-five scrambled aboard "and welcomed the ship like drowning men"; and one of them vociferously assured the wide-eyed actress that he remembered her quite vividly:

> "I saw you play in Vancouver as Mrs. Wiggs of the Cabbage Patch. I know it was you," he said in his most complimentary manner, "for I recognize your hoarse voice." (*H7*)

It was, in fact, the above-mentioned Ada Dwyer who had played Mrs. Wiggs in Vancouver and would be playing her in Australia in July.

A final adventure consisted of a proposal of marriage to her piquant little sister from "a long-bearded Greek ex-priest who, we were told, had bought an island somewhere in the Pacific, and was on his way there to be crowned king." Eileen, however (with a little help from M.A.) was proof against the dubious attractions of the *défroqué* and his coconut crown:

> So when we reached his watery cross-roads the old man set off in a boat, and the last we saw of him, he was bobbing up and down in a tropical blue sea, as he was rowed to his island possession. *(H7)*

At last, after twenty-eight days in transit, the Anglin entourage arrived in Sydney on 17 June. "It was Australian mid-winter and very cold." But after a warm welcome at dockside from the Williamsons and the highly regarded Australo-American actor George S. Titheradge ("who had played with me in California"), M.A. arrived at her hotel suite to find it a veritable "bower of flowers"—typical, she says, of that "exuberant Australian hospitality" which met her everywhere *(H7)*.

Williamson, incidentally, had been careful to have M.A. proclaimed everywhere as "the celebrated *American* actress," and went to some lengths to get the adjective "Canadian" deleted from several notices—it would destroy "the big-time effect," he told the offending scribes. M.A. made a humorous mouth about it afterwards, but raised no objection at the time *(Pittsburgh Leader, 5.1.10)*.

She set to work immediately upon Henri Bernstein's *The Thief*, for which production she devised her own script from the three extant versions (French, English and American), having been "given *carte blanche*" by the author. After nine days of rehearsal, the company opened on Saturday 27 June at Her Majesty's Theatre:

> In Sydney [she remarks] the opening night for a new play is always Saturday; that is the convention there, and I feel it has great advantages—a day of rest for the reviewers, instead of the mad rush to press, and a rest for the players after the inevitable strain. *(H7)*

Thus the *Sydney Times* reviewer had ample time to form the considered opinion that M.A. was an actress of "superb presence and extraordinary resourcefulness," though indeed the Bernstein play might be thought a little "lacking in substance." The *Telegraph* reviewer was most impressed with M.A.'s "flawless transition" from the high-comedy manner of Act 2 to the big, emotional, conjugal confrontation scene of Act 3:

> The distinguished young actress, tall and slight in form and of expressive face, has all the nervous impetuosity requisite for such a big scene, where strenuous emotion is keyed to a high pitch. Her voice, well modulated, silvery in quality and of singular carrying power, is capable of all the fine shades of meaning; and it is curious to note that in moments of excitement it assumes an altered tone, with a piquant touch of the brogue. Miss Anglin's methods were so sure and well judged that the scene was never overweighted.

M.A. owned to being disconcerted by "the perfectly enormous size" of Her Majesty's with its "odd acoustics and sight lines," and by the outspoken nature of the audience, given to shouting "Shut up" to coughing fellow auditors, and "Speak up" or "Come out of hiding" to players of obscure diction or position, or, more particularly and respectfully to her as *sotto voce* star, "Cough it up ma'am, cough it up." The *Chicago Record* (31.1.09) gives this record of M.A.'s first experience of Australian audiences:

> At the close of the second act there was a tremendous demonstration in honor of Miss Anglin, and a member of her business staff, going to her behind the scenes, said: "It's a triumph—you've conquered them absolutely."
>
> "Don't speak to me," she responded. "These people are barbarians. Haven't you heard the remarks from the gallery?"
>
> Later in the evening she was able to estimate the audience from a different point of view and to realize that what at first had seemed insolence was a manifestation of the intense eagerness and interest with which the Australian theatre-goer sits down to the observation of plays and play-acting.

And if she had qualms and pique at mid-play, at the end she had a perfect "deluge of flowers"—all but two violets of which she gave away to "memento-of-the-occasion seekers" at the stage door.

Despite this display of enthusiasm, however, Williamson, an old-school actor-manager was disappointed by the new "quiet method" adopted by Miss Anglin. "It would never have done at Wallack's!" he remonstrated:

> He had not realized [M.A. allows] that acting in the days of which he spoke was more florid, more external, less repressed and selective than it is today, . . . and he

Theatre Magazine

M.A.'s portrayal of Shakespeare's heroines Katherine and Viola "swept the Australians off their feet." (1908)

> [naturally wished] our presentment of *The Thief* to be
> heightened. I simply replied that we must go on as we had
> begun and leave it to the public. *(H7)*

As it happened, *The Thief* ran for five weeks to large and
enthusiastic houses. And Williamson was further chagrined
when his favorite, the much more highfalutin and "external"
Zira, was coolly received by the public and dismissed by the
critics as "old-fashioned melodrama."

The quiet method reasserted itself with M.A.'s production
of Clyde Fitch's *The Truth,* and this well-made and strong-
finishing problem-comedy "met with great success" until
"toward the end of the engagement a street car strike and
incessant rain dampened everyone's spirits." *The Truth* was
beginning to acquire the reputation of a jinx play, for just six
months earlier the brilliant young American actress, Clara
Bloodgood, committed suicide during a highly successful run
of the Fitch comedy. But according to Louis Nethersole
(M.A.'s business manager), it was not *The Truth* that
precipitated the disastrous streetcar strike (which reduced
theatre attendance by 75 percent), it was a conductor called
Groucher who was fired for stealing tuppence from his own
fare-box. "You may imagine how I felt about it," said
Nethersole. "I could not understand why Groucher had
chosen the very time we were in Sydney to put into effect his
get-rich-quick scheme" *(N.Y. Telegraph, 5.9.08).*

Before the fates conspired against her, the *Sydney Times*
had long since paid this tribute to M.A.'s work in *The Truth:*

> The part of Becky Warder, which Miss Anglin assumes, is a
> comedy one in the highest sense, not essentially farcical or
> frivolous, but full of lights and shades, of which the clever
> actress made ample use, and created a fine impression; in
> fact the house was in an almost continual titter all the
> evening.

But this piece also contains a big, emotional, conjugal confrontation scene, and once again it was Miss Anglin's meat:

> This scene is in the second act, and in it Miss Anglin proved
> herself the consummate actress that she is. Driven to bay by her
> husband's upbraiding, she is by turns defiant and pleading,
> remorseful and reckless; her sustained force in this scene is truly
> admirable, her naturalness throughout adding to the effect.

The same article gives us a fleeting non-committal glimpse of
sister Eileen: "A newcomer was Eileen Warren, sister of the star.
She did justice to the small part of Laura Fraser."

In Melbourne October meant April, and the warm weather came on apace, and M.A.'s "huge bungalow in the shape of a cross" was bedizened by brilliant camellia blossoms, and serenaded by troops of strange birds, most "persistently and startlingly" by the kookaburra or "laughing jackass." On 10 October Miss Anglin and her inner circle were splendidly entertained in Melbourne harbor by Admiral Emery and his fellow officers in the wardroom of the U.S. battleship *Louisiana*, and on the 11th Miss Anglin returned the compliment by giving a luncheon at the Imperial Hotel. On both occasions Eileen was captivated by the dashing young Lieutenant Charles T. Hutchins, Jr. (himself an admiral's son), whom she was to marry exactly twenty-one months later in St. Patrick's Cathedral.

At the theatre, things were going along swimmingly with the Sydney repertoire of *Zira*, *The Thief* and *The Truth* (along with a couple of performances each of *Camille* and *Helena Richie*), when M.A. suddenly decided it was time for Shakespeare, and immediately began work on *The Taming of the Shrew*. Again Williamson and Co. demurred ("Australians hate Shakespeare"), but M.A. was adamant:

> And so they allowed me one week for Shakespeare. But it met with such a splendid reception that the management completely succumbed and begged me to prepare another Shakespeare production for them. By this time I was pretty well worn out, having been responsible for almost all aspects of all productions, but I consented to play Viola if Mr. Titheradge would conduct rehearsals. (H7)

And so a victorious Viola succeeded a conquering Kate, and the Anglin Company was doing land-office business; but with the American fleet in the harbor and "Cup Week" at hand, Melbourne management wanted the Anglin company out and their own company in for the really plummy part of the season, and so it was off (in November) for the smaller and less lucrative but still warmly appreciative houses of Adelaide (two weeks) and Ballarat (one week).

On 3 November 1908, Louis Nethersole sent this communication to Locke Robinson, editor of the *Cleveland Plain Dealer*:

> Miss Anglin's Melbourne season closed gloriously last Thursday night, when she played *Twelfth Night* before an audience that overflowed the theatre. Of all the plays that Miss Anglin presented in Melbourne, *The Taming of the Shrew* and *Twelfth Night* were far and away the most appreciated

and yielded 30% greater receipts than any of the others. . . .
Miss Anglin opened her season here [Adelaide] last Saturday
night with *The Thief* and enjoyed the same flattering
reception as in Melbourne and Sydney.

In another letter to Locke Robinson, dated 13.10.08, Nethersole
told the story of M.A. and the blackfellows (the Australian
aborigines):

A few days ago she paid a visit to a Reservation a dozen
miles from Melbourne. She spent some hours there and
bought lots of boomerangs and native basket work and
besides she distributed a good deal of money among the
men and youths who gave exhibitions of boomerang casting,
racing, etc. As we were leaving the Settlement Miss Anglin
told me to ask one or two of the blackfellows whether they
would like to go to Melbourne and see her play and to
invite them. They did not enthusiastically accept but nodded
their heads and some of them would go to the theatre. The
next night *forty* of them turned up having walked the entire
distance from the Settlement. After a good deal of
protesting from the local manager I succeeded in getting him
to see the humor of the situation and he agreed to let them
in away up in the gallery where they witnessed a
performance of *The Awakening of Helena Richie.* When the
play was finished the coloured "gemmen" came to the stage
door and enquired for me. I asked them how they liked the
play. Some of them grunted, the others remained silent.
Then the spokesman for the party tipped his hand by
demanding one shilling for each man. Naturally I was
astonished and asked what for. The answer came
sullenly—"Well, we have been mighty good to that white
woman in there" (meaning Miss Anglin). I replied that I
thought it was the other way about, remembering the money
she had spent at their camp and the treat she had given
them at the theatre. "What did they mean?" I asked. "Well,
we have been upstairs there and listened to her yabber
yabber for three hours and we never said a word and it's
worth a shilling each man for coming all that way and
wasting our time." And they would not go away until I
had split up ten dollars among them. Miss Anglin for the
future intends to keep away from native villages.

Of the "blackfellows," M.A. was later to remark: "Their
intelligence is nearly the lowest in the human family. I
believe the Bushmen of South Africa are below them, but not
far. . . . Still, they have a remarkable sense of humor, and
may be recommended for their invariable good nature" (*Green
Book*, July 1909).

A somewhat similar story is told of her visiting a gold mine near Ballarat, being rigged out in "overalls, cap and torch," and descending to the "minus 2500 feet" level. After the tour she invited the foreman to come to the theatre to see her play, and to bring along his mate (the official guide). The foreman must have heard plural for he showed up at the theatre the next night with a regular mob of miners in tow. "How many are there?" asked the flummoxed manager. "Fifty," said the foreman. "Is that all?" said Nethersole. "It's all that could get away, sir," said the foreman, "the rest is on the night-shift" (*Cleveland Plain Dealer*, 3.12.11).

In the last week of November 1908, M.A. returned (for a concluding engagement of four weeks) to Her Majesty's in Sydney:

> And there I met Mr. Jack London who had just gone through the terrors of a shipwreck, told by him afterward in such graphic manner in his *Cruise of the Snark*. He came to see the play and was in such a weak condition from his recent experiences that he had almost to be lifted into the theatre. I shall never forget those adventures as he told them to me that evening. (H7)

As the Sydney engagement was winding down towards mid-December (corresponding to our mid-June), James Williamson approached M.A. with a lucrative offer to take the company to New Zealand:

> But by this time the heat was so appalling that I could scarcely get through the day's work. My vitality was entirely in shreds and patches, and because of the heat and the strain, I had collapsed at one of the matinees. (H7)

She was clearly very near the end of her tether; and so she wisely declined Williamson's offer. But the slightly Mephistophelian impresario was both persistent and imaginative:

> One evening he came into my room with a huge bag of sovereigns. In a melodramatic manner he opened the bag and poured the gold onto the floor. "I'll give you all of that if you will go to New Zealand," he cooed, with his arms spread like the wings of some dark dove. (H7)

But prudence prevailed over pelf, and M.A. pronounced a silent "Retro me, Sathana" and the antipodean tour was over. In twenty-five weeks M.A. had played the lead 166 times in seven plays.

It is interesting to note that while in her article, "My Australian Tour," M.A. represents the Shakespeare as something of an afterthought (opposed by Williamson), she later told Morgan Powell that it was, for her, the central element of the tour:

> Miss Anglin told me once that what had decided her to make the Australian venture was the fact that it offered her an opportunity she had long awaited to play Shakespearean heroines. . . . The outcome was sensational. . . . Her portrayal of Katherine and Viola simply swept the Australians off their feet.   Williamson, who had seen the best English speaking actresses in these roles was astonished at the outbursts of applause, "quite exceptional in Australia," he said. (*Montreal Star*, 8.1.58)

The *Melbourne Argus* (15.10.08) reacted to the first night of M.A.'s *Twelfth Night* in this wise:

> Viola was understood in every grace by Miss Margaret Anglin. With all the dexterous touches at her command she made Viola live and move and have her being full of agility, wit and pathos. . . . The duel with Sir Andrew Aguecheek was managed with perfect comic tact. The interviews with the lovesick Orsino, her strange impulses, depth of conviction, and sincerity were noted by an actress thoroughly sure of herself, developing and unfolding the psychology of the character charmingly, and will remain as permanent records of the art which dominated the whole performance.

And the *Sydney Times* (18.11.08) had this to say about her Shrew:

> Miss Anglin shows the noble imperious gentlewoman behind the vixenish shrew. In the early scenes she is tempestuous and ill-tempered. When the necessity demands she snaps out the spitfire lines with a veritable venom. But what a change towards the end of the piece, when, as the loving and subdued wife, she acts with delicacy, charm, and much pathos.

And last, but assuredly not least, "Professor A. Nugent Robertson of Sydney University, said to be the greatest living authority on the works of the Immortal Bard in the Antipodes," having witnessed M.A.'s performance of Katharina and Viola, was moved to declare that

> Miss Anglin hereby proves her right to be placed in the very limited class of actresses of the first rank; and again shows that the aristocrats of art are born to their place and do not merely achieve it. Style of this quality is something above and beyond [the technique gained from] accumulated stage

experience. This is one of those rare moments [in dramatic art] when we may say, "The style is the woman." (*N.Y. Times*, 27.3.09)

In one of the last of his ever-ebullient letters to the American press, Louis Nethersole enthused:

> Our *Twelfth Night* pleased all classes of playgoers. During the fencing scene they roared as at a farce, though Miss Anglin's Viola never receded from the mood and manner of pensive delicacy. The fun of the *Taming of the Shrew* they declared they liked better than anything they had seen in the musical comedies, and the galleries were packed with rough men of the streets. (*Chicago Record*, 31.1.09)

Indeed, the *Shrew* was so successful that M.A. authorized Nethersole to announce (*N.Y. Dramatic Mirror*, 10.10.08) that she planned a 1909 double-bill production of *The Taming of the Shrew* and John Fletcher's all-but-forgotten sequel *The Tamer Tamed* in which she would play Kate as tamed and tamer on alternate nights. Unfortunately this interesting project was never realized.

On 19 December 1908, the vigil of Doubting Thomas, the apostle of the Indies, a weary but victorious M.A. set sail for Calcutta, but not before she had been accorded a triumphal procession to quayside—"crowds following me to the steamer and throwing flowers in my way" (*H7*). At Calcutta she received a gilt-edged invitation to bring the Shakespearean faith to India in 1909—an invitation which she cherished but eventually declined.

And so from Calcutta (not without its seamy side) to steamy Colombo where "one seems to be constantly attended . . . by a horde of beggars, filthy and noisy, who shout and gesticulate and implore alms" (*Green Book*, July 1909). Still she was prevailed upon to stay long enough "to visit a native seer, who recalled many incidents in her past life and made a number of flattering predictions as to her future." From Colombo, Margaret and Eileen set out (with renewed optimism) by car (with a "Cingalee chauffeur") to Kandy, 150 miles to the northeast. On the way they had a run-in with a highly disrespectful "herd of [six] elephants" which squashed the car, leaving Margaret and Eileen pale, shaken and infra dig, but otherwise unscathed. Ultimately the bad elephants were made to tow the disabled vehicle (with the sonsy sisters still in it) into Kandy (*N.Y. Review*, 9.1.10).

In that pleasant and ancient plateau city Margaret and Eileen were presented by the Governor of Ceylon (to whom they had a letter of introduction) to the Maharajah of Rhodipore ("one of the most powerful native princes on the island") at the Maharajah's palace. On the following day the Maharajah paid an official visit to the Misses Anglin at their hotel in Kandy:

Margaret Anglin, Tearologist, Didn't Make Sphinx Cry

Cleveland Leader Nov. 7-1909

While on their world trip, M.A. and her sister Eileen absorbed the atmosphere in Egypt, a "land of theatrical effectiveness." (1909)

Now, the etiquette of the natives is that when a prince pays a call he must be asked by his host to retire at the conclusion of the visit.   But the Governor of Ceylon omitted to advise Miss Anglin of this important point, and after his highness, who spoke English fluently, had exhausted his small talk concerning India and America, an awkward pause ensued.   Presently he began to wriggle about in his chair and his secretary, who accompanied him, seemed extremely uncomfortable.   The conversation became desultory and ultimately lapsed into a depressing silence, until the Maharajah surprised his hostesses by suddenly springing to his feet and imploring permission to take his departure.

It was not until Miss Anglin went to say goodbye to the Governor that she understood the innocent breach of court manners that she had perpetrated. (*Milwaukee Clarion*, 12.1.10)

Miss Anglin, taking her new epithet, "celebrated American," very seriously, was conscientious in her commentaries on her grand tour to compare all things British somewhat unfavourably to all things American.   Thus British Ceylon sank in comparison to American Hawaii; and, indeed, one of the first things she remarked on her return was that American gentlemen were the most agreeable of all she had encountered (*N.Y. Post*, 3.10.10). Something of this spirit is apparent in her next journal entry:

Aden was our next stop in sailing up the Indian Ocean into the Red Sea.   This is a place where it only rains once a year and where the British maintain a garrison. The regiments have to be changed every year, because it has been found impossible for white men to live more than a year on the rock, for that is all it is, without drifting perilously near to insanity.   I think Aden is the most frightful place I have ever visited for heat, dirt, squalor and depression.   Aden is another part of Great Britain's wonderful Dominions! (*Green Book*, July 1909)

The voyage to Egypt was enlivened by "a collision with a mail steamer" and by "running aground in the Suez Canal," which last "I confess I enjoyed, for it allowed me to catch my first glimpse of the limitless desert—a thin sunset skein of flying flamingoes and a single ant-like Arab in all that vastness.   I never knew anyone better able to catch that immensity than Livingston Platt when he came to make the scenery for my production of *Antony and Cleopatra*" (*H7*).   And so on to "that treasure city of Alexandria" which she ransacked, in vain, "for traces of

Cleopatra." And thence to Cairo where she met and talked turkey with Beerbohm Tree (the actor-manager) and Louis Parker (the playwright).

Margaret and Eileen settled down in Cairo for a lazy fortnight of wallowing in orientalism and absorbing atmosphere:

> Here in Egypt [says M.A.] we were in a land of theatrical effectiveness. The streets were a mass of color, rugs of priceless design hanging from the windows of many houses in the old town. . . . We retired at night to those strange evening sounds which emanate from an oriental street; in the morning we were awakened by the hee-hawing of asses, and we would look out of our window upon a motley assemblage below, amid which towered the stately forms of camels. (H7)

And then were was that "never-to-be-forgotten trip up the Nile in a dahabeah," and then there were "the pyramids, the temples, the avenues of Sphinxes," and then there was that most palpable form of orientalism, camel-back riding in the full blaze of the desert sun. In for a penny, in for a pound was Miss Anglin's motto, always.

From Cairo the sisters travelled to Bremer-Haven, thence to Berlin, Paris, Rome, Nice (where they joined forces with mother), London, Paris again, and London again. April in Paris in 1909 found M.A. "leas[ing] an apartment on the Champs Élysées, which she intends to retain permanently as her European home" (*N.Y. Telegraph*, 23.4.09). Perhaps the highlights of her six or so weeks in Paris—which included "delicious little half-hours with Maeterlinck, Rostand and Réjane"—were her two cordial meetings with Sarah Bernhardt:

> I had two memorable breakfasts with Madame Bernhardt in that wonderful house of hers where every curio you touch has a history, and where huge cases hold countless treasures given to her during her long and wonderful career. She sits at the head of her table in a throne-like chair and is a wonderful hostess. It was then that I was asked to play *Madame X*, which I had seen Jane Hading play, and Madame Bernhardt advised me strongly not to undertake the role. She said it was *unbeautiful!* though she afterward played it herself. (H7)

At this time the charming Margaret was just short of thirty-two, while the divine Sarah was just past sixty-two. "But," says M.A., "you'd never think she was over forty. Her complexion is wonderful. I expected to see a few wrinkles or a crow's foot or two, but Madame Bernhardt is amazingly minus both." Bernhardt, an inveterate and outspoken motor-phobic, had just been prevailed upon to acquire, against her better judgement, a motor-car, and had immediately become, like Toad of Toad Hall, an addicted enthusiast. "I never walk any more," said S.B., "motoring is too delightful. Come, let us have a ride." "So," says M.A., "we went for a delightful spin in her motor" (*Chicago Tribune*, 30.1.10). This "delightful" exchange took place some seven years before the amputation of S.B.'s right leg.

In view of the instant rapport the two prima donnas appear to have discovered, it is interesting to note Mlle. Manhattan's summing up of M.A.'s Australian tour:

> For a solid five months Miss Anglin leaped from triumph to triumph in Australia, achieving a popularity even exceeding that of Sarah Bernhardt, previously the idol of the Antipodes. (*N.Y. Sun*, 20.5.09)

Margaret also took time in Paris to give "a special performance of *Helena Richie* for the purpose of securing the French copyright of the play. . . . She was assisted in this event [at the Theatre Antoine] by a brilliant company including the distinguished players Le Bargy, Guitry, Madame Rejane and [Henri] Lavedan, the dramatist." After the performance Margaret and Eileen "entertained at luncheon" these celebrities "and about forty others" (*N.Y. Telegraph*, 23.4.09). They then left for London where M.A. had scheduled a conference with Charles Frohman about a possible London season for her in the fall of '09. During this London fortnight she also kept herself busy with a series of working luncheons with H.A. Jones, A.W. Pinero, A.E.W. Mason, W.J. Locke (re. *Septimus*) and H.A. Vachell (re. *Her Son*).

Mlle. Manhattan, who wants to know "if it is true that she capitulated to Cupid while the big stars of the southern hemisphere were getting in their fine sentimental work during the wonderful Australian nights," tells us that "after her very pleasant dalliance with Dame Fashion in Paris," M.A. went to Rome and spent "Easter" and the following "brilliant week in the Eternal City" (*N.Y. Sun*, 8.4.09). *The Telegraph* (7.4.09), however, printed this announcement:

> Margaret Anglin leaves London this afternoon for Rome. She is to be blessed by the Pope [Saint Pius X], both Miss Anglin and her sister, Eileen, are ardent Catholics. Margaret Anglin has been in London discussing with Horace Annesley Vachell a new romantic play he has written.

M.A. arrived at New York (aboard the *Kaiser Wilhelm* II) on 25 May 1909, and almost immediately departed for her "delightful new summer place . . . in Manchester-by-the-sea, Mass., . . . one of the most exclusive summer resorts in the country" (*N.Y. Telegraph,* 26.5.09).   When she entertained the actresses Alice Kauser and Ada Dwyer and the reporter Mlle. Manhattan, "the rare, pale Margaret Anglin" impressed the latter as "quite the nicest girl I know" and as looking all of "sweet seventeen." She had lost twenty pounds on her grand tour, and at 5'6" and 112 lbs., was "so slender that really one had to look twice to see if there was anyone there when she threw herself into one of the big stuffed chairs in her little drawing room" (*N.Y. Sun,* 30.5.09).

Later that summer M.A. joined the novelist Margaret Deland at her picturesque summer residence at Kennebunkport, Maine:

> And there we put the script of *The Awakening of Helena Richie* through the third degree, Mrs. Deland criticising it from the standpoint of the old Chester atmosphere of which she herself was the delightful creator. I never spent a pleasanter time than I did while Mrs. Deland and I chugged up and down the little Kennbunkport River in a boat, talking over the future of *Helena Richie.* (H7)

Helena had, as we have seen, already been given quite well received performances in Melbourne and Paris, and also in New Haven and Philadelphia in April of 1908, but M.A. was convinced that the piece had to be substantially rewritten in order that it might reintroduce her to Broadway with suitable panache, and justify the Ceylonese seer's rose-coloured projections.

Chapter VI

Helena, Antigone, Marriage, and Green Stockings: 1909-1912

Look, leaders of Thebes,
I am the last of your royal line.
(Sophocles, *Antigone*, ll. 940-41)

M.A.'s return from Australia and the grand tour was not, therefore, as John Webber had hoped, to be marked by a bold excursion into comedy, but by a return to melodrama and the tear-jerking trade. Tear-jerking is, however, too crude a phrase for the "restrained" and "refined" melodrama of *The Awakening of Helena Richie*, a tale of a woman of fine sensibility who deserts her brutal, dipsomaniac husband (whom she accuses of killing their child), cohabits, as "sister," with a weak and selfish lover, adopts an orphan boy-child who becomes the apple of her eye, and then, upon the death of her husband, confesses her adultery, loses her lover, and offers to give up her doted-on little David. And all this waywardness and weeping takes place in prim and proper "Old [1860] Chester [Pa.]" amid the hoop-skirts, frock-coats and antimacassars. The play ends with a contrived happy ending, but indeed asks some tears in the true performing of it. "Margaret Anglin," says the *Telegram* critic, "made a living, glowing Helena Richie, good to look at, sincerely acted and pathetically appealing. The handkerchiefs of the fair sex at the Savoy are likely to be wet with sympathetic tears over Helena's story for some weeks to come." And indeed *Helena* was to have 120 New York performances—a very good run for that time of high play turnover.

Most of the reviewers were impressed with the high moral tone of this play about adultery, and stressed the fact that the sweet, self-indulgent Helena's awakening is to the higher claims of "unreflecting love," "the marriage of true minds," and "truth's simplicity":

> It is a clean, sweet, wholesome play, because it rings true to the environments of right living as the old town recognized it. It needed only one act to stamp the great calibre of the work, and the next act brought more strength, but the third act produced one of the greatest curtain scenes that this town has ever seen. Call after call did Miss Anglin answer, only to be brought forth again, and at the fifteenth response she appeared leading the

Photo courtesy of Basile Anglin

The handsome young journalist Howard Hull became M.A.'s stage lover, as Haemon in *Antigone*. (1910)

author [Margaret Deland] and the stage-writer [Charlotte Thompson] to the stage. Too embarrassed to speak, they tried to bow into the sheltering scenery, but again Miss Anglin brought them forth, and again they were mute. Then followed a siege. The audience determined to have something and finally, after twenty minutes of applause that never wavered, Miss Anglin told how happy and grateful she felt over the great welcome after her two years' absence. (N.Y. *Commercial*, 21.9.09)

The same reviewer goes on to say that M.A.'s performance of Helena Richie "can be classed as one of the finest examples of emotional acting ever seen on a New York stage." And even the crapulous Alan Dale, who hated the play, remarked, by way of conciliation, at the end of his excoriations:

> The real interest of the evening lay in the return of Miss Margaret Anglin to our desolate hearts. Miss Anglin loves to weep, and has made a special study of it, I believe. She is even to be relied upon for real tears, which are as nice as real rain or a real steam-engine. Last night she did many things remarkably well and with a good deal of repression. In fact, for Miss Anglin, it may be said that her expressions of distress were [mercifully moderate] and that she [took some pains] to be as undisagreeable as possible. Many will think that in the third act she was not nearly as noisy as she might have been. This was a great relief to me. Miss Anglin got all she could out of such a tiresome story. (N.Y. *American*, 21.9.09)

The *Brooklyn Eagle* critic (21.9.09), also slightly tongue in cheek, is otherwise poles apart from Dale and begins thus exuberantly:

> Cheer up, you lovers of acting who were brought up on Clara Morris and Bernhardt and who cherish your memories of Mrs. Fiske's girlish Tess! Your long fast is ended. Margaret Anglin is back, and last night at the Savoy, in *The Awakening of Helena Richie*, she gave such a performance as Bernhardt might have given thirty or forty years ago, but the like of which none but Miss Anglin could give today.

And he concludes with this historically interesting comment:

> For the young theater-goers the performance offers a fine example of the style of play and of acting which ruled much of the last quarter of the nineteenth century.

While on tour with *Helena*, M.A. gave a young curate at the Harrisburg Pa. Cathedral a memorable ecclesiastical moment. The curate remembers it this way:

> It was about 9 o'clock when an automobile dashed up to the church and a bizarre-looking woman got out. She wore an

immense wig of coarse black hair, a very old-fashioned dress, earrings as big as chandeliers, and her eyes were heavily jetted. "I want to go to confession at once," she explained breathlessly. "Tomorrow is First Friday and I have never missed. The first act of my play has just ended and I must be back at the theater for the second." In less than ten minutes the auto dashed away, carrying Miss Margaret Anglin on to the second act of *The Awakening of Helena Richie*. (*Catholic Universe*, Sept. 1912)

Catholic readers will not need to be told that the mystical anchoress, St. Margaret-Mary Alacoque (1647-90), for whom Margaret-Mary Anglin was *not* named, was the originator of the First Friday devotion (conceived of as an extension of the Good Friday veneration).

It was also while touring with *Helena* that M.A., that childless doter upon children, brought a circus to her brother Arthur's two-acre backyard in Grosvenor Street in Toronto to bring joy to the hearts of six small children and 194 of their (mostly small) friends and admirers. Herbert Whittaker concludes his "The Canadian Who Became America's Top Leading Lady" with this account of the event:

> But perhaps Toronto has the happiest memory of Margaret Anglin from a summer's day long ago. It was in June [1909] when a slim, 33-year old actress with red-gold hair and a thrilling voice arrived to visit her brother's large family on Grosvenor Street. To the ecstatic delight of all those nephews and nieces, she phoned all the way to New York and commanded her manager, Louis Nethersole, to bring a small circus immediately. He obeyed and turned up himself to act as ringmaster. And there, in the big yard, in the middle of a circus, stood the beautiful young actress, laughing—laughing in that thrilling voice. (*Globe Magazine*, 7.9.57)

The dashing Aunt Margaret was doubtless a cynosure figure, made even more thrilling by carrying a brilliant Australian parrot on either slim shoulder, but the real star of the show was "a decrepit old lion," shabby, forsooth, but lovable, who, at the height of the excitement "fainted in the ringmaster's arms." The circus company included "two clowns, a comic juggler, a ventriloquist, a Punch and Judy show," a couple of performing dogs, a couple of chimpanzees, the aforementioned parrots, and a "hoot-owl." The sunshiny Louis Nethersole brought the whole thing off in apple-pie order, and, as the *N.Y. Telegraph* (11.6.09) says, "he handled his monocle well."

The circus scene gives us a domesticized version of "Miss Anglin, the complete outdoorswoman"—owner of two country estates, erstwhile huntress and fisherwoman, now something of a naturalist, and always an avid horsewoman: "any day you might see her riding in Central Park on her splendid bay mare, Clytemnestra." She had in 1895, at the age of nineteen (in the company of "her brothers" at Rice Lake, Ont.) exulted in "landing many a six pound muskalonge" and, more alarmingly, in "killing with a single shot through the heart a thousand pound bull moose." "She keeps the trophy head in the hallway of her home" (N.Y. *American*, 28.7.01). Having thus signally qualified as an Amazon, she apparently never killed another animal of any size (Howard was left to deal with the rats), and became a dedicated conservationist whose favorite (and lavishly supported) charity was the A.S.P.C.A.

But the other, the boudoir or salon, the *précieuse* Miss Anglin, who *did* now grant interviews, if assiduously cajoled, was wont to present this type of appearance, as "the charming center of a charming scene," in her "hotel suite":

> Miss Anglin, swathed in the softest of sea-shell pink negligees, over which foamed filmy laces, reclined on a couch amid drifts of pink satin cushions and eiderdown coverings. Her hair, in that condition best known as "artistic disarray," was surmounted by a quaint little cap of sheer muslin, touched here and there with little knots of lace and wee pink French flowers.
> The room was a hotel room no longer. Plants bloomed in the windows and palms banked the fireplace. A few late books lay invitingly on the table, and the writing desk held an open box of stationery, and pens, ink, sealing wax and tapers. Vases of roses and violets were scattered here and there on tables and mantelpiece, and on a little stand directly behind the couch where Miss Anglin's pretty head nestled stood a huge jar of deep pink carnations and a slender silver vase holding a handful of lilies of the valley. The scenic arrangement would have done credit to any stage manager in the land. (*Chicago Tribune*, 20.1.10)

At the same time as she was refurbishing *Helena*, M.A. was taking her first steps towards the production of Greek tragedy, generally considered her most noteworthy contribution to the life of the American theatre. Arnold Johnson, whose dissertation, "The Greek Productions of Margaret Anglin" (1971), is the major source-book for this part of her work, informs us that:

> When she returned to America in the summer of 1909, she began an intensive study of the Greek plays "under the guidance and inspiration of Alice Kauser." *Antigone* was selected as a suitable role for Miss Anglin's first Greek

endeavor. In the spring of 1910, arrangements were formulated
with the Hearst Greek Theatre [in Berkeley, California], and on
June 30, 1910, Miss Anglin made her premier appearance in
Greek tragedy. To Miss Anglin, the experience of acting in a
Greek classic in an outdoor theatre was exhilarating: "I believe I
was happier than I had ever been before in my work."(J, 48)

Her devotion to the cause of bringing the classics to the
people, always financially marginal, at best, resulted, in this
instance, in a substantial fiscal loss. Johnson says that M.A. lost
about $5,000 on the *Antigone* production, for despite the
reported attendance of 8,000, there seems to have been only
$4,000 paid and a take of a little over $4,500, as against a little
over $9,500 in expenses—and when one thinks of the work
involved, the mind boggles. Johnson gives us a fair idea of the
rigors of M.A.'s schedule for the summer and spring of 1910:

During the spring, Miss Anglin began her westward tour across
the United States in her regular attraction, *The Awakening of
Helena Richie.* Along the tour route she conducted rehearsals for
Antigone. In Denver, Professor George Riddle joined the Anglin
company and gave instruction in the finer points of Greek play
production. The company finally arrived in San Francisco on
June 19. On June 20, Miss Anglin opened at the Columbia
Theatre in *Helena Richie* and began preparations for *Mrs. Dane's
Defence.* During the day, she would make the twenty mile
journey by motor car and ferry boat from San Francisco to
Berkeley to organize her Greek production. Before the evening's
performance of *Helena Richie,* she would return to San Francisco.
When she had matinee and evening performances at the
Columbia, she would leave for Berkeley after the evening
performance. Rehearsals would last from twelve until three
o'clock in the morning. (J, 158)

In order to clear June 30 for *Antigone,* M.A. had to schedule
two additional matinees—two more straws for the camel's back.
As Arnold Johnson observes:

Such arrangements must have been extremely difficult for her
supporting company, but for Miss Anglin, the leading actress
and supervising manager of *Antigone,* the effort must have been
exhausting. Miss Anglin was, however, indefatigable in her
energy and drive. Immediately after *Antigone,* she was again
touring her commercial vehicles northward. This was the typical
plan for most of her productions at the Hearst Greek Theatre. (J,
158-59)

Given its lack of precedents, both in the American theatre and
in M.A.'s experience, the success of her *Antigone* was truly

remarkable.   Critics were generally impressed by the spare
stateliness and austere grandeur of the production, centred
upon and dominated by M.A.'s "cold-fiery" Antigone.   She
was, says Burns Mantle, at once perfectly Greek and perfectly
human:

> It seemed as though a figure had stepped out of one of
> those old Greek bas reliefs. . . . The success was positively
> impressive. No other player of my time has ever extracted
> from spoken lines the very essence of heart-wrung grief, or
> launched the bitter curses of deep anger or risen to the
> supreme height of joyous gratitude for one beloved, as
> Margaret Anglin did yesterday. (*N.Y. Evening Post*, 1.7.10)

In the same vein James Bennett speaks of hearing that night

> the most melodious voice that utters the language on our
> stage today [producing] the most wonderful declamation of
> tragic poetry that any woman of our stage has risen to in
> many and many a year. (*Chicago Record-Tribune*, 3.7.10)

For him, the performance cast "a spell of ancient, consecrated
loveliness," while to the *Theatre* (Aug. 1910) critic,

> Miss Anglin showed complete mastery of "the grand
> manner" without for a moment losing her sense of reality.
> Twenty-five centuries sweep lightly across the woman soul
> and leave it as it was. *Antigone* is immortal, and Miss
> Anglin's interpretation was conceived in large unhurried and
> majestic conviction of this truth.

Clayton Hamilton recalls especially the long moment of
breathless silence which greeted the stark and sombre
conclusion of the play:

> A friend standing in the wings heard Miss Anglin say to
> herself, "I've failed, I've failed!" Then, after an appreciable
> pause, there came a noise that sounded like the rushing of
> the tide. . . . Louder and louder grew the acclamation until
> it seemed to shake the skies; then, suddenly, the stage itself
> was assaulted by hundreds of clamorous spectators. One old
> man whose face was bathed in tears tore his hat into shreds
> and tossed the pieces high into the air. (*Vogue*, Aug. 1910)

The single objective, single-mindedly pursued in all of her
Greek productions, was "to present a beautiful play in the
most beautiful way I can" (J, 94), and, as Arnold Johnson
observes, she was consistently successful in achieving this
objective, taking full and artful advantage of all the "highly
conducive" elements which the Hearst Theatre had to offer:

the calm night, the listening throng, the trees and the starlit
sky, the antiphonal roll of the verse, the lazing colors massed
on the stage. (J, 94)

The Hearst Theatre, which is a scaled-down model of the
ancient (5th c. B.C.) theatre in Epidaurus, in the Pelo-
ponnesus, was considered by M.A., who was something of a
connoisseuse of theatres ancient and modern, to be "the most
beautiful theatre in the world" (J, 93). "Its setting, amidst an
encircling sweep of hills," says Ada Patterson (*Cosmopolitan*, Aug.
1915), "is quite idyllic"—in such a setting, she avers, "such a
performance of a Greek tragedy becomes almost a religious
experience of great beauty."   And M.A. herself was moved to
remark:

> The air was so still and so heavy with perfume, and the
> stars so bright and so near the earth, with one radiant planet
> hanging just above the altar, that it was no great task to
> span the centuries and believe oneself beneath attic skies.
> (*Harpers*, 6.9.13)

In spite of this resounding success, M.A. never produced
the *Antigone* again, although she often seemed on the point of
doing so.   Indeed, the very next year both Harvard and Yale
invited her to produce it in their theatres under the auspices
of their redoubtable classics departments, but she backed off
because of the looming incubus of academic interference which
she quite justifiably feared.   She did, however, play *Antigone*
again: at Berkeley in 1928 under the direction of Charles von
Neumayer, and in a run of nine performances in 1930 at Ann
Arbor under the direction of Robert Henderson.

One very important spinoff from the *Antigone* production
was her discovery of the acting and amatory abilities of the
handsome   young   journalist,   Howard   Hull,   who   had
accompanied   (as   assistant)   Professor   George   Riddle   of
Harvard,   M.A.'s   academic   adviser   on   the   technicalities   of
Greek drama.   Apparently Margaret had no sooner been
introduced to the fawn-haired and faunish Howard than she
knew she had found her stage lover, and immediately
conferred upon him the role of Haemon which, in the event,
he delivered with *éclat*.   Whether or not Howard played the
part of the lover offstage as well as on is a moot point, but
this perhaps impious question might serve to lead us into a
brief digression into the matter of the romantic involvements
of one of America's outstanding romantic actresses.   One's
guess would be that her love affairs with a number of

M.A. with Howard Hull shortly after their wedding in 1911: the genial, self-effacing husband of a celebrity for twenty-six years.

attractive theatrical men during her long career were pretty strictly wine and roses affairs, verging occasionally upon sexual brinksmanship.

She was certainly sweet on the darkly handsome William Faversham, her leading man in her early days of stardom (and still a valued associate twenty years later), but nobody suggested that the affair went beyond mutual admiration and fondness. She was also definitely very fond of the playwright Paul Kester, the "darling Paul" of the voluminous correspondence. But even such phrases as "a case of pure passion to see you" (16.3.19) and "The very moment there is a place for you to lay your precious head you will get a telegram from me" (30.6.19) sound sisterly enough in context. The Miller affair, as we have seen, was more problematical in more ways than one. And it must be conceded that rumor also made her the mistress of the composer-conductor Walter Damrosch. The rather dashing, bearded Damrosch, we are told, came to be known at mid-career as something of a tomcat, and not surprisingly, says his biographer, George Martin, for

> he was away from home and wife for long periods when he was still young, charming, handsome, and full of energy that would normally find some release in bed, and was closely related with others in the same condition. Throughout his life gossip would link his name with various artists, primarily Isadora Duncan and the actress Margaret Anglin. (DD, 183)

Dr. Damrosch, fourteen years Margaret's senior, would have been a youthful fifty-three in 1915, Margaret a spritely thirty-nine.

Maurice Zolotow, speaking of a greater age discrepancy in the other direction (also in 1915?), makes this surprising remark about Alfred Lunt (another M.A. discovery):

> Laura Hope Crews [to whom M.A. had recommended him], like Miss Anglin, was at once taken with Alfred's looks and charm. At this phase of his life he was irresistible to aging actresses. Miss Anglin was twenty years older than he. Miss Crews twenty-four years older, and Lily Langtree, to whom Miss Crews tenderly bequeathed her vaudeville partner, was forty-four years older than Alfred, . . . but she took it for granted—as had Margaret Anglin and Laura Hope Crews—that Alfred would be her lover as well as her leading man. The legitimate theatre was really a far more immoral place in those days, though the plays themselves were more innocent than contemporary plays. (S, 43-44)

Against this suggestion of sexual liberation (or even license) one might wish to set a little piece on stage kissing which appeared in *Theatre Magazine* in August 1908. After assuring us that the lovely Maude Adams always fakes her stage kisses (the lips of the principals remaining half an inch apart), the reporter continues:

Margaret Anglin, on the other hand, believes in the genuine kiss. In her opinion, if it is essential for an actor to put his arm around her, he should be able to do so without causing any shrinking on her part, and the same holds good with the kiss. Reality and not illusion is her creed. The kiss, when finally won in *The Great Divide*, was a genuine breaking down of all the false barriers which nature (and the playwright) had put up between her and her virile lover. Despite Miss Anglin's boldness in defence of stage realism on this point, there has been a minimum of kissing in her stage life. Her theory is strong and bold, but her practice pretty nearly puritanical.

Whether or not she strayed occasionally from the straight and narrow, "puritan" is not a bad word for her, as it was not a bad one for her puritan Catholic father and elder brothers. When she was asked to write an article on "The Star Idea" for *Theatre Magazine* (Dec. 1920), these phrases were at the centre of it:

There is no deeper significance to our lives than spiritual growth, and to each one of us, our "star" is a hidden light, rather than an electric sign. . . . To the artist, there is only one standard of virtue in art, and that is the ethical value.

And perhaps, as a final gloss on these somewhat idle speculations, her thoughts on the subject uttered in December 1916 should be recorded:

So far as concerns the temptations and pitfalls which so continuously and conspicuously are insisted upon as an ever-present element of the theatrical world, it can be said without reservation that any and all such temptations and pitfalls insistently have refused to exhibit themselves, either for my delectation or my downfall. (EWWI)

In any case, however one cares to speculate about M.A.'s playing of the mating game, she did marry Howard Hull, with all due form and reverence, a little less than a year after their portrayal of the stage fiancés in *Antigone*. Through June of 1910 the nightly drives from San Francisco to Berkeley were usually made up of a foursome: M.A.'s chauffeur up front, and a congenial crowd of George Riddle, Howard and Margaret in the back.   The rehearsals (says the *Atlanta Constitution*, 11.6.11), far from being the usual wearisome grind, "seemed to Miss Anglin and Mr. Hull the most divine poetry":

> But rehearsals and performance were all too soon over. The fragrant California days and mellow California nights ended. "It has all been so beautiful. I am sorry to leave it, "said Miss Anglin, and her eyes were sad. "I have never been so happy in my life," said Mr. Hull.

Then, in January of 1911 (according to the same article), *Green Stockings* needed revision and M.A. thought of Howard, a self-styled, unpublished "playwright."   Howard came, revised, helped out backstage, took bit parts, and generally made himself very agreeable:

> Presently, the season being near its end, both began talking of their vacations. Miss Anglin said, "I think I shall go abroad." Mr. Hull said, "I should like to." A look, a few words that are really none of our business, and it was settled. They would go abroad. They would go together. Their vacation would be a honeymoon.

M.A. concluded her tour of *Green Stockings* on Saturday 6 May 1911 in Wilkesbarre, Pa., and married Howard on Monday 8 May in New York. Her reputation of being "a very private person" offstage suffered no diminution in the circumstances of the wedding, which took place virtually *in camera* in the Lady Chapel of St. Patrick's Cathedral, with the bride's mother (according to the *N.Y. Times*, 9.5.11) as "the only guest."   The ceremony was performed by "her old friend, Father Gleason" (assisted by the Rev. Dr. Sinnott).   "The bride is thirty-five years old, the groom about twenty-eight" (actually thirty). "After the ceremony Mr. and Mrs. Hull had a quiet supper in the home of the bride's mother in West 58th Street." And the next morning they set sail on the *Kronprinz Wilhelm* for a honeymoon motor trip "through the south of France" (or, according to another account, "the Austrian Tyrol").

M.A. herself tells us (Str) that the honeymoon tour took her and Howard to the famous ruined theatres in Carthage ("where I played Dido all day") and Timgad ("where we walked in snow up to our knees!") in North Africa, and Syracuse, Messina ("where we picked our way through wreckage from the earthquake"), and Taormina in Sicily. In Taormina, she recalls, "We slept in a monk's cell in the old Dominican monastery, . . . [and] rose at daybreak to see the sun rise over the ruined stage of the ancient theatre, with Aetna faintly vaporous in the distance," and, no doubt, the ghosts of the fifth-century Greek players even more faintly vaporous on stage.

The notice in *Vanity Fair* (27.5.11) tells us that "Margaret Anglin's literary husband is, naturally enough, a Bostonian," but the *Toronto Star* (7.12.13) sets the record reasonably straight on Howard:

> Mr. Hull comes from an old Kentucky family, his father [Wm. E. Hull] having been for many years an editorial writer and dramatic editor of the *Louisville Courier-Journal*. Young Hull, after a short experience on the stage, followed in the steps of his father and joined the staff of *Everybody's Magazine*. He visited London and the Continent for that publication, and was connected with the Home Office for some time. . . . Since their happy union Mr. Hull has toured with Miss Anglin as her personal representative. The Hulls make their home in New York when not on tour. They also have a summer place in the Adirondacks where the Anglin lodge is situated in one of the most secluded and picturesque spots in the historic hills.

The *Times* article on the marriage remarks that "Mr. Hull made his first stage appearance [at the age of twenty] in the chorus of Hall and Stuart's musical comedy *Floradora*" (and indeed persuaded his sixteen-year-old brother Shelley to join him when the tour reached Louisville), and had his last bit part in *Green Stockings*. "He will," said Miss Anglin, "in future devote his time to writing." (Verb. sat.) "He has," the *Times* reporter adds, "written a book of verse that will be published in the autumn." Unhappily, Howard's book was not published in that or any other autumn; its faded leaves are now sadly scattered and lost. It is perhaps worth noting that M.A.'s decision to ban Howard from the boards was received with mild surprise by many who tended to share Howard's good opinion of himself as a player.

In the fullness of time both Howard's ten-years-younger brother, Henry, and his sister-in-law, Josephine (Shelley's wife), would take part in M.A. productions. His five-years-younger brother, Shelley, was, at twenty-six, an established Broadway supporting actor in 1911. In the following year he starred with Mrs. Fiske in *Lady Alice*, and in 1913 he hit the jack-pot with Billie Burke in Maugham's *The Land of Promise* and Pinero's *The Amazons*. Shelley, however, never collaborated with M.A.—a pity, for their high degree of professionalism and stage elegance were highly uncommon

common qualities. It might summarily be said, at this point, that for the next twenty-six years Howard did very well as the genial, self-effacing husband of a celebrity, and only his taste for tippling in his later years spoiled the effect at all.

But one word more remains to be said about the marriage, and that a never-published one, for if the St. Patrick's marriage, as sketchily recorded by the New York press, seems almost clandestine, the earlier marriage, which it ratified, was completely so. Howard, in fact, remained with Margaret for most of the period between the wrapping up of the *Antigone* production in July of 1910 and the St. Patrick's marriage of May 1911, and, as a matter of record, they were married in Waukegan on 24 September 1910 by Father William Gavins in St. Mary's Church (ICBVM), so that the intimacy of their relationship in the course of their tour of the south had (as they supposed) the blessing of the Church. However, one of M.A.'s clerical friends apparently informed her that since Mr. Hull, a notorious agnostic, and son of an even more notorious one, had never received any form of Christian baptism, her Waukegan marriage was invalid—hence the St. Patrick's re-run (after Howard's baptism which, as he said, meant nothing to him).

Howard's letter (28.6.10) to his mother (Elinor), just before the performance of *Antigone* tells that he had been engaged to play Lionel (M.A.'s lover) in *Mrs. Dane's Defence*, and a pleased M.A. had told him, "'You are not the best, you are the *only* Lal.'" "Miss Anglin says [he continues] my depth of passion is equalled only by Irving, and you know she is a cold, isolated, chary person who calls on God to kill all bad actors." After *Antigone* (2.7.10) he finds himself rendered almost speechless by his own brilliance in the "stupendous success":

> To hear 7,000 people give you the biggest round in the play, save Anglin, is too much for my nerves. . . . God, but she was indescribable; matchless, elate and imperishable. . . . Riddle says I'm the best actor since Booth; ah, it's all crazy, and so am I.

A week later (10.7.10) he writes from Seattle to his mother and his brother ("dear boy"), the just-turned-twenty Henry (Hank), and he breathlessly imparts to them "a secret":

> I am engaged.
> I would have you believe it, as it should be. This time it's real, and I love her with all the truth and honor and deepness and tenderness that is in me. I love her *greatly* and *for ever*. Now you have it.

I didn't suppose that it would ever happen to me, but it did, and please wish me the happiness I know I will have. The name is Mary Anglin, sometimes Margaret. . . .

Mother dear, you shan't lose me, we've been too close for nearly thirty years. I won't say you'll have another daughter like J[osephine]—'cause she's different—and maybe you won't like her that way, but you'll love her. She is everything I always dreamed of and wished a woman might be if ever I fell in love, and God knows I am in love.

I never thought I'd choke and nearly die, and then ask a woman to marry me.

And she loves me, that's all. Of course this is the most terrible important secret—it is vital that no one ever suspect it. Please understand, this is not a secret like Shelley's at all. Big issues are involved, and it must be kept a secret until September, and you shall come to London if we are to be married there, as it now looks as if we would have to be.

Now this is not sentiment. Ormonde fell down awfully in *Mrs. Dane* and nearly ruined *Shifting Sands*, so he was let out, and I take his place in two weeks as leading man at 100 per.

On the back of the envelope of this carefully preserved letter one finds this pencilled protest (apparently in Elinor's hand) against the fates and against Howard's feckless character: "1910—Triumph!; 1933—committing slow suicide: Fool!" The dashing poet, player and lover had dwindled into the soppy country "caretaker." But this is to get rather considerably ahead of the game, and after all the decline and fall of Howard was not only a "slow" process, but one beset with a goodly number of alarms and excursions and diversions.

Oddly enough, it was in the midst of her first assault on the formidable bastion of Greek tragedy that M.A. announced (with some fanfare) to the New York press that "she was through with tearful roles. She wanted to do comedy." She told Colgate Baker of the *N.Y. Post* (3.10.11) that it was quite true that she could produce real tears at will on stage, "but I never cry off stage, . . . in fact I am one of the most cheerful individuals in the world. My sense of humor is so keen it's positively embarrassing. Why, I even laugh at the comic supplements." What she wanted, as a serious actress concerned with the projection of the sympathetic imagination, was as wide an emotional scope as possible. "I don't mind at all being called an 'emotional actress,'" she told the *Chicago Tribune* (5.2.11), "—all acting that has the breath of life in it is emotional. . . . But it is the art of acting characters that appeals to me, rather than the particular natures of the characters acted."   She was obsessively interested in *embodying* characters, not in *identifying with* them.   To that extent she was content to remain outside her characters.   "I don't take Mrs. Dane home with me."

The result of this "Tired of Tears" manifesto, with its open invitation to the playwrights of America to supply her with a bright, fresh, new American comedy, was a veritable flood of 420 manuscripts—none of which was chosen to be the vehicle of her new comedic departure.   The play she chose was *Colonel Smith*, a light English farce by A.E.W. Mason, of *Witness for the Defence* and *Four Feathers* fame; M.A. herself (with Howard's help) substantially revised the script and, with Mason's approval, renamed it *Green Stockings*.   That title alludes to the old English custom which required an unmarried woman to wear green stockings at the marriage of a younger sister.   With two such ordeals behind her, and with a third impending, Celia Faraday invents a mythical Colonel John Smith, in Somaliland, to whom she is engaged.   Having thus established her marriageability, she dispatches the good Colonel with an obit in the *Times*.   One of the letters she so ostentatiously wrote to him is found and posted by her well-meaning sister and actually reaches a Colonel John Smith in Somaliland who, just after his fictitious death, arrives in London (under a pseudonym) to confront his fair dispatcher. The exchange between the sly Smith and the cagey Celia, says the *Theatre* reviewer, was "simply delicious in its whimsical and amusing value."   The same reviewer gives somewhat qualified praise to both the play, "a distinct success," and to the leading lady:

> In forsaking the emotional for the comic, Miss Anglin has made a bold leap, but she has accomplished the jump with success if not brilliancy.   Her methods are sure and expert, but a little more seriousness at times would improve the performance, . . . which is, nevertheless, a creation of vital force and humor. (*Theatre*, Nov. 1911)

An earlier reviewer was not much impressed with the play but was still pleased to pay homage to the star:

> Despite her departure from the familiar path of emotionalism, Miss Anglin is delightful and reveals a personality little suspected before.   Indeed at times her vehicle might be harshly criticized were it in the hands of a less capable comedienne, and, seemingly without effort, she causes sustained ripples of laughter. (*Pittsburgh Leader*, 17.1.11)

An even earlier performance produced "a frothy, exhilarating evening's entertainment . . . for President and Mrs. Taft and a capacity audience . . . at the Columbia Theater" (*Washington Post*, 9.1.11).

Green Stockings had a forty-eight performance run in New York, and then took to the road again, but during the stand in Cleveland, M.A. came to loggerheads with her sponsors, Liebler & Co. It is all rather complicated, since at least some part of the falling out had to do with her flat refusal to do the part of the heroine of Milton Royle's new play *The Snare*, which he had written especially for her, and which he had scheduled as part of the tour. The heroine in question is deserted by her no-good husband, murders her no-good bigamous, surrogate husband, escapes the just consequences of that act, and is finally reunited to her repentant, no-good real husband. "I will *not*," averred Miss Anglin, "play a part which involves the commission of a serious crime or sin without some justification and for mere dramatic effect." And that, according to the *N.Y. Times* (19.12.11) was the cause of the breakdown of the Anglin-Liebler relationship. But the *Cleveland Plain Dealer* (11.12.11) has a different tale to tell, and it tells it in doggerel:

> O, where's the show when a show goes wrong?
> When a prima donna can't sing her song
> To the grief
> And the brief
> That is filed in court
> And is brought to bear at the last resort. . . .
> Yester eve, or some such time
> Margaret Anglin, whose art's sublime,
> Filed a suit in the Federal Court,
> The only port
> Where she could anchor in case of storm.
> She asked relief
> From all her grief,
> And promised to make it warm
> For Liebler & Co.
> Who owned the show, . . .

In more conventional terms the article goes on to say that M.A. had brought suit against Liebler for $1,703.72 which she claimed as her share of author's royalties, since she (and Howard) had substantially revised the script—"Yesterday she had the box office receipts attached upon the filing of her suit":

> Liebler & Co., the defendants, deny that the money is due the actress and maintain that they had neglected to pay her claim because she had had her dressmaker's bills, in that sum, charged to the box-office.

Nuff said, perhaps.   In any case, M.A. assumed complete control of the *Green Stockings* production, and after another forty-two weeks of touring (including appearances in her three home-towns of Ottawa, Saint John and Toronto) she triumphantly announced a clear profit for the show of $57,000 (J, 62)—a veritable bonanza in those days.   Her performance of *Green Stockings* in Ottawa was attended by "a large and brilliant gathering, including Governor General Earl Grey and Countess Grey, and Sir Wilfrid and Lady Laurier" (N.Y. *Herald*, 18.4.12).   In her subsequent week in Toronto "The Royal Alexandra Theatre was filled at every performance by her devoted and enthusiastic admirers" (N.Y. *Review*, 25.4.11); while in Saint John

> several hundred people gathered at the station June 30 to welcome her. The Governor of New Brunswick [Josiah Wood] and party and the Mayor of Saint John and party occupied boxes at the performance of *Green Stockings*. Miss Anglin was serenaded at her hotel by the City Cornet Band, one of whose selections was "When You and I Were Young, Maggie." (N.Y. *Mirror*, 10.7.12)

"A name to which I have never answered," says M.A. (Str), "—still, in my exhausted condition, I was touched to tears by this spirited performance by a greybeard band of old friends of my father. I was thankful for the concealment offered by my heavy veil."

The following intriguing dispatch appeared in the *Louisville Times*, perhaps appropriately, on April Fool's day, 1911:

> Count Leo Tolstoi [the novelist's son] saw Margaret Anglin play *Green Stockings* in Boston the other night and waxed enthusiastic. In addition to his other accomplishments, he is a playwright and one of his plays is now holding the boards at a theatre in Paris. He asked to be presented to Miss Anglin and complimented her upon her work. The next day he submitted to her the scenario for a play on Russian political life. It appealed to her so strongly that a contract was immediately entered into and the Count has undertaken to deliver the completed manuscript by the middle of July. It will be produced this fall under the Liebler ensign. Miss Anglin's role will be that of a nihilist student, and the story will treat of certain events that took place in Moscow just prior to the "Bloody Sunday" massacres of a few years ago.

Perhaps fortunately for all concerned, the manuscript never materialized, and the conservative and circumspect Miss Anglin was never actually required to wave a red flag to the rabble from the barricades.

It might well be remarked at this point that by 1911 Miss Anglin had become a fairly substantial capitalist. One of her most appealing business enterprises was her ten-acre "violet farm" at Glencoe, Illinois, from which she was able "to take care of the entire violet market of Chicago throughout the winter." It seems a wonderfully appropriate business for one of the finest Violas of stage history. In striking contrast she was also co-owner ("with one of her elder brothers") of "a big brewery in central New York." She also owned a farm in the foothills of the Adirondacks upon which she was endeavoring to establish a profitable dairy herd. The *Pittsburgh Post*, (1.12.11) correspondent adds: "Miss Anglin's investments of her surplus profits are made largely in Canadian land, under the advice of her brother Arthur, who is a King's Counsel in Toronto," and, he might have added, a notoriously over-cautious investor.

The *New York Mirror* (12.2.12) gives this description of the house she bought in 1911:

> There is a quaint English air about Margaret Anglin's new home at 67 East Ninety-third Street. A stone's throw from Central Park, it has the quietude that the region east of the Park affords. The exterior is of red bricks cemented with white. One mounts by a flight of steps to reach the white mullioned, grille-fronted door. Within there are high-ceilinged rooms with straight high wainscotting and light coming from high, many-paned windows, a wide staircase, a drawing room, dining room and library, with the genial glow, yet gentle severity of the English home in their mahogany furnishings and old paintings. The star herself gathers strength for her taxing work in a sleeping chamber of grey walls bordered by garlands of pink roses, the low dressing table draped in white lace caught up with pink ribbons, the chairs and divan and even the rugs being of pink and white.

Not much Bolshevik red here; and the hammers and sickles are in their proper place, out at the farm.

Two other plays of this period loomed large in M.A.'s plans to finance her productions of the classics. The raising and dashing of her hopes are described by Arnold Johnson:

> To finance a prospective tour of Shakespeare, Miss Anglin in February of 1912 invested huge sums of money in *Lydia Gilmore*, an "emotional drama" which Henry Arthur Jones had written especially for her. The funds she hoped to obtain on a year-long tour of the Jones play were to be used for her Shakespearian tour in 1913 and 1914. When *Lydia Gilmore* proved to be a financial disaster, she invested

additional capital in *Egypt*, a play by Edward Sheldon, whose writing usually guaranteed box-office success. Sheldon's play which was produced in September of 1912 was also an unexpected failure. With these two options destroyed, she had to revert to another tour of *Green Stockings* in a different area of the country. Fortunately, by the spring of 1913, she had amassed enough money to prepare for her Shakespearian repertory. (J, 62)

While her liaison with Jones was unfortunate in view of *Lydia's* box-office belly-flop, it was pleasant in terms of H.A.J.'s well-publicized high esteem for his American leading lady. In an interview he accorded to *Theatre Magazine* (Apr. 1912) Jones had this to say about his new play and its star:

One of the chief reasons I had for giving *Lydia* Gilmore an American premiere was to have Miss Anglin create the title part. I cannot say that I had her definitely in mind when I conceived the role—or anybody else, for that matter. But when the story had taken definite shape, and before I had begun to write it, in casting about for an actress, I thought of Miss Anglin. By happy chance she was in England at the time, and when she heard the outline of the story she was delighted, and accepted it at once. Then, too, she had done such excellent work as Mrs. Dane that I felt especially grateful and knew that we might expect her interpretation of Lydia would be a fine one. Indeed, I am very happy to be associated with Miss Anglin; she is a charming woman, very sympathetic and sincere, while as an actress, in her equally able rendering of either tragedy or comedy, I put her beside our Mrs. Kendal.

Margaret Kendal (1845-1915), by the way, was the daughter of the dramatist T.W. Robertson, and was "very big in Britain" in the seventies and eighties in many of the roles (Ophelia, Rosalind, Galatea, Dora) that Margaret Anglin was to star in a generation later in America.

Lydia Gilmore is a quadrangle in which Lydia's lawyer-lover pins a murder rap on Lydia's two-timing doctor-husband whom Lydia was shielding out of love for her son. In the end the bad doctor commits suicide and the good lawyer gets Lydia and little Neddy. The *N.Y. Telegraph's* critic went to the last night of *Lydia* (12.3.12) which had run two weeks less a day at the Lyceum, and spoke feelingly of the "dead weight of gloom and morbidity" under which M.A. had chosen to labor in the disagreeable Jones play. Nevertheless, he believed that the conscientious craftsmanship of M.A.'s performance, "playing Lydia faithfully and flawlessly as it was written," tended to add appreciably to the cumulative dismalness of the overall effect. "Indeed, in the last act, her rendition was exquisite. It had poetry and charm, convincing emotionalism and almost uncanny intelligence. . . . Still, it seems a pity that so much perfected art should be squandered on such unworthy material."

Egypt actually fared moderately well in the provinces, but came to grief in Chicago and never reached New York. M.A. was so incensed over the treatment of *Egypt* at the hands of the Chicago critics that she announced her intention of boycotting Chicago until "the present tribe of Yahoo reviewers" had been replaced. James Bennett, the dean of Chicago critics, first asks Miss Anglin ("too good an actress for any but the best material") to reconsider, and then proceeds to this not unbarbed conclusion:

> Mr. Sheldon's *Egypt*, over which Miss Anglin still is grieving, was a silly, half-baked, mawkish, tedious fabric of juvenile sentiment which was not killed by reviewers. It lasted a few evenings only. Reviews cannot so quickly slay. *Egypt* killed itself. It died in this town and Miss Anglin was not so pitiless as to drag the remains to New York for an autopsy. We marvel that a woman with so bonnie a sense of humor and an artist of such long experience should sulk in so poor a cause. Is she going to shut herself out of New York because the reviewers of that city raked fore and aft the play of *Lydia Gilmore* when she produced it? *Lydia*, we believe lasted a week.
> (*Chicago Record-Herald*, 21.12.13)

Egypt Smith-Komello is a runaway child who is adopted by the gypsies and later (at sweet seventeen) reclaimed by her upper-middle-class father, spruced up and married to a youth of fashion, but when her gypsy lover, young Faro Black, comes whistling up the back alley, she is, not too surprisingly, off again to the raggle-taggle gypsies O. While James Bennett declares that Sheldon had produced an absurd farrago "preposterous in movement and meaningless in effect," *The Pittsburgh Leader* (24.9.12) assures us that

> Edward Sheldon has produced a strong play replete with all the romanticism, the brutality, the lax morality, the positive passions, the undeviating love and hate, the superstition of the gypsy, his allegiance to and belief in signs and charms, enchantments and incantations. Elaborate staging and gorgeous costuming with detailed attention to minor particulars make *Egypt* a very

enthralling drama with a problem that is worked out excellently. . . .

As the gypsy, at times coarse and vulgar, passionate and clever, primitive in spirit, but veneered with the polish of a few years in board school, yet in every fibre of her being the Romany child, with the call of the fields—a nomad in the blood—Miss Anglin is wonderfully convincing in her various moods.

Between the *Antigone* of June 1910 and the return to Shakespeare (and Greek) production in the spring of 1913, M.A. tried to make a commercial go of at least six new (or relatively new) plays—three melodramas, *The Rival* (Kistemaecker), *The Child* (McFadden) and *Shifting Sands* (Ingersoll); and three comedies, *The Backslider* (Egerton), *Pomander Walk* (Parker) and *The New Religion* (Zangwill). The first two won M.A. cool commendation for her lead performances in brief, unremunerative runs; the last two failed to reach production. No histrionic or fiscal joy for M.A. in this hodge-podge. It is worth noting, however, that *The Rival*, a loser in 1911, was destined (in its 1920 revision as *The Woman of Bronze*) to become M.A.'s greatest and longest-running money-maker.

It was in this period of uncertain roads and shaky vehicles that M.A. told the *Pittsburgh Leader* (16.3.11) interviewer that she most certainly *did* not mean "to devote her whole life to the stage," and added her own paraphrase of "The Lake Isle of Innisfree":

I shall retire when I'm forty and go to live in Ireland. I want a home near the sea—where I'll hear nothing but the sound of it, and where assistant electricians, who *will* whistle, will cease from troubling—and I can be at rest.

At this fidgety time too, however, M.A. had the solid satisfaction of seeing a theatrical labour of love come to fine fruition. This was her production of *Hippolytus*, not the Euripides play (which M.A. was to produce in 1923 in the Gilbert Murray translation), but a recognizably Victorian blank-verse drama by Julia Ward Howe, owing more to Racine than Euripides, and, happily for M.A., with the part of Phaedra writ large. This play had been created for Charlotte Cushman, Edwin Booth and E.L. Davenport in 1858, but never acted or published. As a tribute to the poetess of "The Battle Hymn of the Republic," and in aid of the philanthropic J.W.H. memorial fund, M.A. was asked to mount a production of the long-forgotten drama, and she did so with suitable pomp and circumstance on 24 March 1911 at the Tremont Theatre in Boston, just five months after the poet's death in that city on 17 November 1910. The single "excellently produced" performance, which played to a "packed house," in addition to its memorial and charitable purposes, doubtless also served the more personal ends of whetting M.A.'s appetite for Greek drama, and of allowing her to spread herself vocally in the florid diction. "The lines," she avowed, "are not only highly poetical, but speakable—something not always found in plays written by persons without direct knowledge of the stage" (*Boston Herald*, 19.3.11).

M.A.'s undertaking to produce this *Hippolytus* with the Liebler Company was the happy result of a delectable afternoon tea taken virtually *tête-à-tête* with the eighty-year-old poetess and social-justice crusader eleven months before her death. And this is how M.A. recalls J.W.H. (a woman whose "quiet courage" seemed to deny "the rigor of the committed life"):

> She was quite the most beautiful old lady I'd ever met. . . . She sat in a big armchair like a queen on her throne in the soft, mellow candlelight; behind her was a Christmas tree. She wore an exquisite lavender gown that fell in soft, simple folds, and on her white hair was a little lace cap. . . . Her presence was redolent of graciousness rich and rare, graciousness of appearance and of imagination, and the more full for the power lying behind it. Somehow it made me think of those elms you see in meadows, strong but tender, graced by twining tendrils and lavish leaves. (*Boston Herald*, 19.3.11)

Miss Anglin was apparently still tossing off such verbal glissandos at will to open-mouthed interviewers. And so she left that memorable taking of a toast and tea with a copy of the *Hippolytus* under one arm and Charlotte Cushman's long letter about it under the other.

And so this tribute was paid and this play was played—"and so far as Miss Anglin was concerned, her acting was in the true spirit of tragedy, dignified and deeply impressive" (*Cleveland Leader*, 28.3.11). The grave poetical lines were given full and resonant value—but it was, as we have already observed, the featherweight lines of the crassly commercial *Green Stockings* that were to be the springboard to the plateau of full-scale Shakespeare.

Theatre Magazine

M.A.'s "Year as a Producer" was launched in September, 1913 at Berkeley, California with the *Electra* of Sophocles.

Chapter VII

Sophocles, Shakespeare and Wilde: 1913-1914

Electra, betrayed, alone,
down in the waves of sorrow,
bewailing her father's fate,
like the nightingale lamenting.
(Sophocles, *Electra*, ll. 1075-8)

In June of 1913, upon their return from Munich where they had been looking at German productions of Greek tragedy, M.A. and Howard settled down in New York to start work on *Electra* and Shakespeare. At this time they were living in East Ninety-third Street (number 67) in an old brownstone three-storey house completely refurbished to M.A.'s specifications (including a fake red-brick facade). The *Dramatic Mirror* (Sept. 1913) was particularly impressed by the chinoiserie dining-room, with its "cunningly accommodated, . . . exquisite series of Fragonard prints," and by the lounge, with its "furniture of inlaid ebony upholstered in red brocade," its "specially designed Adams piano," and its "striking Ivanowski portrait of Miss Anglin as Helena Richie."

It was against the dining-room background of "window curtains of Chinese embroideries in black and blue" and "tall mantel vases which carry out the design and tell their story of ancient romance," on 25 June 1913 that Howard Hull told the *Philadelphia Times* (26.6.13) interviewer that:

> There may be an actress or two who can play Electra as well as Miss Anglin. There may be one or more who can play Rosalind as well, or Lady Macbeth and the rest, but I affirm without fear of successful contradiction that . . . no actress living is her equal for versatility of talent and breadth of interpretive instinct.

This credo was, of course, pronounced *before* Howard had actually seen Margaret in any of these roles—and it is perhaps the more touching for that reason.

And "it was in her Chinese dining-room in blues and blacks, at a dinner served with the silent perfection of an automaton," that M.A. talked in May of 1914 with the *Theatre Magazine* (June 1914) critic of her 1913-14 season.

It all began at the conclusion of the last *Green Stockings* tour in mid-February at which point Margaret and Howard "sailed for Europe. After visiting the principal cities of the continent, they toured through Sicily, Egypt and Italy for the purpose of gathering material for her Shakespeare revival." Then came a summer of arduous rehearsal, and then "Margaret Anglin's Year as a Producer" was formally launched on 6 September 1913 at Berkeley with the *Electra* of Sophocles. "I was preparing for three years to produce *Electra*," she said, "—three years' study for one night and it was well worth it, for it was one of those perfect nights that come to us seldom in our lives."

It was indeed all she could wish it: a soft, starlit, sweet-scented California night, a hushed, reverential audience of near seven thousand, a well-tuned company of forty and a splendid set and setting. "It was [says the *S.F. Bulletin*, 9.9.13] an achievement never to be forgotten by those who saw it, for its earnestness, its impressiveness, and its beauty." To which the *Theatre* (June 1914) critic adds:

> Demonstrating that she was no mere dreamer translated to another period and manner of life she gave the Greek play an American climax, furnishing it by leaping upward, sword in hand, exultant, ferocious, unwomaned by her triumph over fate. Characteristic of the perfect night was the appearance before her in the starlight of a venerable officer, saying "Here is my classpin. I would give it to none but you." He thought he had pinned it into Electra's ragged robe. Miss Anglin found that he had pinned it into the flesh of her arm. That there was neither wound nor blood showed how in moments of intense exaltation there is a self-hypnosis that defies external circumstances.

The *California Advertiser* (13.9.13) reviewer remarks of Miss Anglin's "splendid characterization" of Electra that it was "illuminated by the radiance of humanity." Audiences and critics alike were struck by the vivid immediacy and nowness of her recreation of the classic roles, as Arnold Johnson puts it:

> She was able to convince the audience that her Electra was a complete human being who was filled with a multitude of human complexities: her love of her father, her love of her brother, her resentment at injustice, her hatred of her stepfather, her love of her mother perverted into hatred by her mother's crimes, and above all her fierce love of piety and justice. (J, 100)

What she carried intact across the centuries (and across the language barrier), says Clayton Hamilton, was "the wonder and the sting" of Greek tragedy (*SOS*, 216).

"She reached back across the centuries," says the *S.F. Examiner* (8.9.13) critic, "and lifted out of a vanished civilization the great work of the greatest Greek tragic poet and placed it before a vast audience in exquisite perfection. It seemed almost like the working of a miracle, and yet it was done through the ambition and studious labor of Margaret Anglin." "With this performance," adds the same reviewer, "she asserted her right to rank among America's greatest tragic actresses."

The poet-professor Charles Phillips of Notre Dame University composed, under "the self-same stars" that "gazed on Argos and the maiden's grief," a high-flown sonnet, which concludes thus stirringly:

> How like a wounded bird that beats its wings
> Against the crowding fates, with tender wail
> Telling in cadenced sorrow all her woes
> To the deaf heavens, sad Electra goes!—
> Then sudden, till the shaken stars grow pale,
> Up through the night her cry of triumph rings!

The "beautiful diction" of Fuller Mellish in the role of the Guardian came in for equal praise (*Oakland Tribune*, 7.9.13) with the "rich vocalization" of M.A.'s Electra. The Gluck-cum-Debussy music, composed and conducted by William Furst, was also commended (J, 145) as movingly "sensual, sinister and majestic." And Livingston Platt was lauded for the highly effective stark simplicity of his set and the counterbalancing flair of his lighting and costume effects:

> Mr. Platt [says the *S.F. Examiner*, 7.9.13] has a lyric nature, and he works out his dreams in terms of drapery. . . . Because his dreams have been successfully wrought into silk, *Electra* last night was a thing of exquisite costumery. Rose hues and apple greens and lavenders floated airily across the stage—costume colors that caressed the senses like a perfume.

Along with the resounding artistic success of the '13 *Electra* went a modest financial success—declared expenses of $4,107 being well covered by a net take of $8,500—though, given the arduous weeks of preparation, one could hardly consider the one-night's-wonder a genuine money-maker. Johnson, incidentally (J, 177), tells us that the demand for seats was so brisk that scalpers were getting seven times the marked price for tickets on the day of the performance.

"From that perfect night," writes the *Theatre* (June 1914) interviewer, "Miss Anglin passed to the production of three Shakespearean comedies and the tragedy of a queen's unhappy love."

> Weeks of laborious rehearsals [he continues], painstaking and painful in the heat of August in New York had preceded them, and years of deep study and absorption of Shakespearean plays and authorities on them had gone before her San Francisco premiere as a producer of the bard.   She had read her Mrs. Jameson's *Heroines of Shakespeare*, and she knew her Furness.   Moreover, she had her own convictions, distinct and unalterable.   To the production of each of the quartette of plays she brought research plus conviction.
>   "It amuses me to hear symbolism read into the Shrew," she expostulated, "when Katherine is the most obvious of all his characters and the comedy the most obvious of all his plays.   When I run gaily in to do my lord's bidding in the last act I do it with a twinkle in my eye.   I don't play it as Shakespeare wrote that last scene, but if he were living I believe he would approve it."

Solid Scholarship, she maintained, should *underlie* the production, but should not *appear* in it:

> The function of art [she insisted] should be to entertain. If instruction comes, then so much the better, but first of all let entertainment with a waggish nod and merry mien lead the van, and instruction, philosophy or what not follow. (*Vancouver World*, 1.11.13)

"I have tried," she told *Drama Magazine* (8.3.14), "to reach the happy medium between the traditional reading of Shakespeare and the colloquial."   And most critics agreed that she succeeded admirably in doing just that.

The Shakespeare tour opened in San Francisco on 22 September 1913, and at least one critic, William Winter, decried M.A.'s performance both for obviousness ("blatancy") and for deviousness, in her delivering of the final contrition-submission speech with just that wicked "twinkle" in her eye which she speaks of above—"as if," says the indignant Winter, "it were mere mockery, implying that it is hypocritical, a jest secretly understood between Petruchio and his wife."   This sounds like Winter wanting to have it both ways in his wholesale demolition

of M.A. as a Shakespeare actor-producer. "Miss Anglin," he
concedes, "no doubt understands and admires the poetic
heroines of Shakespeare, but she is radically unsuited to them
in personality and style" (*SOS*, 315).   But this is the same
William Winter who devotes twenty pages of his *Richard
Mansfield* to Mansfield's production of *Cyrano* without deigning
to mention the name of his highly acclaimed Roxane.   There
may well be a missing Anglin-Winter feud chapter that is by
now irrecoverable.

Notwithstanding Winter's remark that "Miss Anglin's
assumption of Katherine was the worst embodiment of hers
that I have seen" (*SOS*, 537), the *Shrew* seems to have been the
most generally approved of the Anglin Shakespeare
productions.   It was, indeed, generally, perhaps unflatteringly,
felt that a truculent, wildcat character was right up her
psychosomatic alley.   "Miss Anglin," says J.R. Towse (*N.Y. Times*,
20.3.14) "played Katharina along the broadest lines of
shrewishness.   She was ever Kate the Curst, and embodied
that character with abundant spirit and vigor.   But . . . ."
The objection, for most critics, was that M.A.'s Kate (and as a
result her whole production) was too continuously pitched
high and strident.   The whole thing lacked "shading."   This
this fairly common perception one might wish to pit against
the wholly laudatory *S.F. Chronicle* (23.9.13) review:

> The fine art of Miss Anglin, evidenced this many a year in
> many sorts of plays, brings changing shades of pure delight
> to the role of Katharina. . . . From every production angle
> Miss Anglin has gone the best of the latter-day Shakespeare
> producers one better.   By that I do not mean merely that she
> has outdistanced the stars of tradition (that would be a
> simple feat), but that all of the most sumptuous recent
> productions must take second place. . . . The succession of
> scenes in *The Taming of the Shrew* is a succession of beautiful
> pictures toned to a natural nicety.   This is not only with
> regard to the painted canvas itself, but to the grouping of
> the playerfolk on the stage and the costumes they wear and
> the relation of the groupings to the costumes and costumes
> to scenery.   This, as well as the acting part, has been the
> work of Miss Anglin.

"The performance," says the *N.Y. Telegraph* (20.3.14), as though
answering Winter, "was brilliant":

> In her angry moments Miss Anglin was superbly furious—a
> beautiful devil, with furnaces well stoked. . . . And while
> she scored most notably in the stormy rages, she was also
> tellingly effective in the lighter, tamer moods that followed,

as she alternated sweet appealing gentleness with some slight mockery. In her concluding scene while describing the duties of a wife to her husband she added a touch of gay raillery that gave the interpretation especial finish and charm.

Eric Blind brought high-spirited rambunctiousness, "the power of a great voice," and a somewhat awkward delivery to the role of Petruchio.

But perhaps the sedate and judicious Towse should be allowed the last word:

> Miss Anglin, who is credited with the arrangement and production of the piece, elected to play it in a mood of the wildest farce, and from this point of view the performance undoubtedly was a good one. There was incessant action on the stage and the fun was fast and furious. But this effect was gained at the cost of some radical compression of the text and virtual disregard of the finer qualities of the play.

The second production to be staged was *Twelfth Night*, and here again critical opinion was fairly sharply divided, though most found M.A.'s Viola lively and charming enough and most gave high entertainment marks to the production as a whole. One of the most remarkable divergences of opinion had to do with the speaking or "reading" of the lines. The devil's advocate, William Winter, hears in the fabled Anglin voice not only "little feeling for poetry," and more than a touch of harshness, but "a slight impediment in articulation." And the *Boston Globe* (4.3.14) reviewer flatly states that the text of *Twelfth Night* was "beyond the vocal resources of her company." But the *Boston Evening Transcript* (4.3.14) reviewer has a nearly opposite opinion:

> Most of the company handled the text with a clear grasp of its meaning and a clear feeling for its rhythm, for the shape and colors of its phrasing, for its fancy or beauty or saliency of image. It will be objected that in so doing they spoke it, and Miss Anglin in particular, a little manneredly, a little ornately. True, but thereby they escaped the twin pitfalls of Shakespeare performances nowadays. They were not conversational at the one extreme; they did not mouth at the other. They comprehended that they were speaking a speech of fantasy, and so were bound to glamor it.

The *Toronto Star* (29.12.13) critic is convinced that "there could scarcely be a more beautiful delivery" of the celebrated passages beginning "Make me a willow cabin" and "She never told her love"; while the *Toronto Globe* review of the same day declares that "Never was the wit of the masquerading damsel dropped with more telling effect."

The *Rochester Democrat* (6.1.14) reviewer, though he thinks Miss Anglin's Viola "somewhat underplayed," is altogether favorably impressed by the note of "sweet melancholy" which she so effortlessly transposes into the "subdued humor" elicited by the disguise-and-discovery motif. He is much taken, too (*pace* Winter), with her "charming voice" which "delights in varying cadences." "She plays the role [he concludes] always in the right key, ever with its sentiment and its wit bearing this subtly pervasive strain of melancholy."

To advert once more to William Winter, his final word on M.A.'s Viola is "mechanical," while his considered judgement on Sidney Greenstreet runs as follows:

> Mr. Greenstreet's proceedings as Sir Toby were clownish, vulgar, displaying no sense of the character, not a particle of humor, exceedingly boisterous, and physically and vocally repellent. A worse performance of the part, —more completely mistaken as to its meaning, and more grossly common has not been given (*SOS*, 102).

With the foregoing we may contrast these lines from the *N.Y. Tribune* (23.3.14) reviewer:

> Miss Anglin's Viola . . . was at once gracefully boyish to the eye and warm and ardently womanlike in the feeling revealed, and played over and lightened constantly with a really delightful lightheartedness and girlish fun.
> No less successful was Mr. Greenstreet's Sir Toby—altogether the most authoritative and richly amusing of the three somewhat similar parts he has played. The ease and evenness of his work, the way in which he constantly contrived to give Sir Toby's smoky humor the air of belonging to our own day—or to carry the spectator back into his own—was as rare as it was uproariously funny.

The *N.Y. Times* saved most of its praise for Livingston Platt:

> As for the setting . . . it is impossible to speak with anything but the greatest enthusiasm. More than Arden or fair Padua, this Illyria, this land of Shakespeare's fancy, gives rich opportunity to Livingston Platt in his designing of the costumes and sets.
> He has realized it in beauty. There is oriental splendor in the palace of Orsino; and in the garden of Olivia, the loveliness of rose-tinted blossoms, green cypresses, and tawny walls rising against a far and hazy sky. . . .

On 2 October 1913, M.A.'s *As You Like It* was unveiled to the same generally favorable but mixed response. Sidney

Greenstreet, generally considered a creditable Touchstone, was, according to William Winter, "silly, vacuous, vulgar and offensive, and beneath criticism." As for Miss Anglin, "her Rosalind, while radically defective, is the best of her Shakespearean impersonations" (*SOS*, 315). Surprisingly, however, Winter finds himself almost bereft of words in the face of a "superb Jacques" by Fuller Mellish—"a work of art, and indeed the only memorable feature of this revival."

A more balanced, but nonetheless ambivalent, appraisal appeared in the *N.Y. Herald* (17.3.14):

> Last night's gathering seemed to find no little enjoyment in the work of Miss Anglin and her company, for when she first appeared she was welcomed with applause, and she had curtain calls after each important scene. Yet it cannot be said that Miss Anglin was a contagiously merry or roguish Rosalind. She spoke her lines well, she acted with considerable freedom, as indeed one would expect of an actress with her training and experience; but, save for occasional flashes, . . . her Rosalind did not reveal extraordinary poetic, romantic or comedic charm. She looked pretty, though, clad as a shepherd youth.

The *Life* (26.3.14) review is equally ambivalent. It begins with the lines: "Margaret Anglin gave us a delightfully joyous Rosalind. It is difficult, yes, impossible, to recall a Rosalind so attractive in looks." But it then goes on to accuse her of having a very uneven and insecure vocal line, and adds that "this was a defect of the whole company, and therefore it seems it must have been, in part at least, the result of vicious or negligent coaching." This, also, is a kind of viciousness not often attributed to M.A.

To finish on a more typical note, we might choose (almost at random from the host of favorable reviews) this from the *Dramatic Mirror* (18.3.14):

> Miss Anglin has presented us with a bright new Rosalind—a spirited, playful, teasing, wholesomely garrulous wench, with a swashing exterior, a nimble tongue, a ringing laugh, devilment in her eye, and a cock-a-whoop bearing, just the sort of a girl to make her way in the woods, inspire love-madrigals, and turn the head of a bold, love-lorn swain like Orlando. Less orotund of measured speech, perhaps, than Julia Mar-

lowe, but withal poetic and gallant, with just the proper dash of vivacious raillery and devil-may-care abandon in her movements.

Otherwise the performance was rather heavy. . . .

Except, of course, when Fuller Mellish was on—"Mr. Mellish's Jacques is delightful." Mr. Mellish, it may be added, also scored as Malvolio.

S. Morgan-Powell's pondering of M.A.'s Shakespeare productions raised again for him the moot question as to whether her greater talent lay in tragedy or comedy:

> Perhaps, all things considered, there is a slight balance in favor of comedy. Her Viola is an adorable figure of the most fragrant romantic quality. Her Rosalind is the very spirit of Romance walking in the Arden forest paths, pure woman, and pure fascination, all through. Yet her Cleopatra is of the very essence of tragedy, a figure so fraught with the atmosphere of impending doom one hesitates to say the woman who can thus portray her is a better comedienne than she is an interpreter of the spirit of tragedy in drama. (*Montreal Star*, 21.7.23)

The show-stealer in *Antony and Cleopatra* was Livingston Platt, who produced a superb set which combined simplicity of design with richness of evocation. The roof of Cleopatra's palace came in for especial praise, as in this description by Walter Eaton:

> There is nothing at the sides except two tall screens. The roof goes off indefinitely into shadow. At the back is a low wall, rising on the right to a ledge six or seven feet high. Behind the wall is the blue night sky. The effect of height and space is the first impression. On the wall sits Cleopatra, her jewels dimly sparkling in the moonlight making purple pools of color on her streaming robe. Above her, on the higher part of the wall lies a silent figure, silhouetted like a sphinx. The eunuch, Mardian, shines naked ebony in the moonlight. Out of this atmosphere, dripping tropic languor, rises the voice of Cleopatra: "Charmian! . . . Give me to drink mandragora." (*American Magazine*, April 1914)

Indeed, Clayton Hamilton (*Vogue*, 15.5.14) thought that the Reinhardt-Craig-inspired Platt, an impressionist painter "with an unusually gentle palette," was the real star of the Anglin Shakespeare season:

> His sets [says Hamilton] are very beautiful and very simple. . . . In the *Shrew*, for example, he suggests the gorgeous richness of the Renaissance in scenery so light in structure it

M.A. as Medea (1915): the production of Greek tragedy is generally considered her most noteworthy contribution to the life of the American theatre.

may be shifted in ten seconds and packed without damage in a traveling trunk.

Add to all that that he was handsome, suave and debonair, and it is not surprising that Miss Anglin was wont to call him "my Good Angel."

Winthrop Chamberlain's commentary is fairly typical of the guarded approval M.A. generally got for her Cleopatra: "satisfying if not impressive," is his word:

> Physically, it must be confessed, she does not quite look the part, though not without a certain opulence of charm. But that is soon forgotten in the revelation she makes of the essential femininity of the character. Cleopatra's wiles, her changing moods, her vanities and tempers, her passion—these things Miss Anglin interprets with an assured artistry. And the lamentations of the queen over the dead Antony, followed by the climax of her own picturesque suicide, are nobly done. (*Minneapolis Journal*, 2.12.13)

Walter Eaton, however, while conceding that the production of *Antony and Cleopatra* (first staged in Winnipeg in November 1913) as a whole was "hauntingly beautiful," found M.A. "least successful" in her big "emotional" part of Cleopatra, for, he observes:

> When all is said, Cleopatra was the supreme harlot, and so far as the play is a love tragedy, it is the tragedy of harlotry—though glorified by immortal verse and pageanted with armies and empires. Miss Anglin, however, does not so play it. She keeps her vision fixed on Cleopatra, the queen. (*American Magazine*, May 1914)

She captures the stateliness, says Eaton, and "loses the haste, the hectic heat, the race of passion, the mad alternation of moods of the royal strumpet." And thus, he says, she loses "the swiftness" of the tragedy, and her production falls prey to "slowness." Indeed, he concludes

> The queen is as long a-dying as poor Tristan in the opera, and Miss Anglin falls frequently into an error which we would never have predicted—the error of intoning verse, the ancient trick of "elocution."

It appears that M.A. was simply too high-toned for the part, and that leads one to revert to the conclusion of the Morgan-Powell article just cited:

> Margaret Anglin is a close student of dramatic art, a
> woman of strong character, authoritative but quiet
> personality, rare distinction in style, and unfailing
> personal charm. Happily married into a noted family of
> actors, she leads a life of retirement when away from the
> stage. But she is still in the prime of womanhood, and
> there are heights still to be climbed. I believe that if she
> could ever fling off for a brief space the atmosphere of
> ultra-refinement that surrounds her, she might achieve
> the greatest artistic achievement of her life. (*Montreal Star*,
> 21.7.23)

The *Harper's* (7.2.14) review of her Shakespeare productions
begins where Powell's leaves off:

> Miss Anglin is a cultivated gentlewoman; she lacks that
> quality of the histrionic temperament which makes the
> possessor eager to hide everybody's light, except his own,
> under a bushel . . . —her company is an all-round
> company of capable actors.

Her gentility was clearly, occasionally, in a very smooth
and gentlemanly way, held against her by her gentleman
critics. However, Margaret Bell, writing in *Maclean's* (April
1914), displayed no such gentlemanly niggardliness of
accolade:

> Here [she proclaims] was the regal Cleopatra in all her
> splendor and majesty, all her petulance and
> intellectuality, the acting of which showed how mean had
> been all previous performances. It remained for Margaret
> Anglin to show the theatregoing public that the great
> courtesan could be played.

The *comme-il-faut* gentleman critic, John Colton of the
Minneapolis News (6.12.13), very much liked the looks of
M.A.'s "Dante Gabriel Rossetti Cleopatra," but he was less
interested in her performance of the Serpent of old Nile
than in the "poised and gracious" lady he met after the
performance:

> A graceful figure, wrapped in a coat of plush and fur,
> wearing a hat swung from her face and a discreet
> enveloping veil. The veil was a very jealous affair but
> the clear, glad depths of her eyes showed will-o'-the-wisp
> glints through spot effects and meshes which failed to
> conceal a characteristically untidy mop of spun-bronze
> hair. A woman of the medicinal-benignant type is
> Anglin, muscled and strong but not stout. Her eyes are
> gray and meaningful; a lovely luminance lives in their

corners as though perpetually awakening from the fringe of a dream. She has a firm chin and a sweet tense mouth. She holds her head high and patricianly. She meets you squarely and serenely. There are depths of reserve in her face. Her voice is cool and restful, and in speaking she "paints her words," that is, each word is chiaroscuro, shaded, ornamented, jewelled.

Colton was also impressed by the account "an actress in her company" gave of Miss Anglin, as producer-director and co-worker:

She is a model of patience. She never finds fault, never scolds, never harries her people. She never has tantruns or rages. She is never unjust or rude. If she cannot praise she is silent. If she cannot laugh she is still. I have never seen her lose her temper.

The eight-month Shakespeare tour (which included the single performance of *Electra* and a dozen of *Lady Windermere's Fan*) concluded in New York's Hudson Theatre in a run lasting from March 16 to April 6. The road trip had included sixty-five cities and covered over eleven thousand miles; M.A. was proud and happy but more than a little way-worn at the end of it:

At any rate [she confessed] I exceeded my physical limitations by my season's work. I proved that to myself when I was too tired to continue with *Antony and Cleopatra*. I was sorry, but the strength was not left in me to play it again this season, and I am resting in *Lady Windermere's Fan*. Mrs. Erlynne is so easy a part that it can hardly be said to be work. (*Theatre*, June 1914)

The *Theatre* critic ends his account of his interview thus cosily:

We were lingering over the last taste of sweets when the maid announced that the chauffeur had brought the car around. Rising, Miss Anglin said: "The greatest lesson this year has taught me is that you must go into a big venture with blind courage. If you stop to think of the difficulties in the way your heart will fail you. . . . I am glad to have done it all, glad to have survived, glad to have given this demonstration of the value of blind courage."

The "easy part" of Mrs. Erlynne was used most effectively to ease M.A. out of the rigors of the big tour; and, indeed, not only did she run it through April and May in New York, she toured it (along with the occasional revival of *Green Stockings*) through the end of 1914 and the beginning of 1915, at which time she discovered Paul Kester and *Beverly's Balance*.

The *Chicago Record-Herald* (12.4.14) tells us that

> Miss Anglin rehearsed and mounted this production in two weeks while acting in three Shakespearean dramas at night and at two matinees.

With a few minor and temporary exceptions the Wilde company was the Shakespeare company. One would have supposed the transition to be a difficult one, but the women apparently emulated Miss Anglin in the effortlessness of her transformation,

> And how well the men—some of them, as Sydney Greenstreet, appearing all last winter in the garb of Shakespearean clowns—don evening dress and utter epigrams! They do not labor over those epigrams; they drawl them out as natural speech. They point them not by rote but with artistry. There is an air of breeding over the whole production (which is beautifully set), and the distinctive tone of high comedy is not lacking.

Again the gentlewomanliness of Miss Anglin was at or near the centre of most of the critical appraisals. The *Indianapolis News* (16.1.15) reviewer, for instance, remarks that

> a person of Miss Anglin's social and theatrical background is able (as few of our actors are) to understand that it takes ladies and gentlemen in spirit and in manner to make the roles of ladies and gentlemen convincing.
>
> It is in just this matter of culture and breeding and distinction of manner that Miss Anglin is better fitted than almost any other American actress for the embodiment of such characters as Oscar Wilde has put into his plays.

The *News* reviewer is also impressed by M.A.'s deft use of the "touch-and-go" style, with her "fine lead-crystal voice," with her "wonderfully expressive face," especially that characteristic "curl of her lip, which she can turn either to the appearance of scorn or pleasant wit. Call it a mannerism if you will, but she certainly makes eloquent use of it."

Clayton Hamilton (*Vogue*, 15.5.14) remarks that M.A. (in collusion with Howard) "has taken some liberties" with the text:

> In preparing her acting version of *Lady Windermere's Fan*, Miss Anglin has obliterated most of the soliloquies and asides and has considerably cut down the more rhetorical passages of the original text. . . . Moreover, she has elected to do her own big speech ("It is the woman who pays") not in the traditional

manner as a front and center declamation, but in a natural, conversational style, so that the flow of the piece is not broken.

Everything, he says, is done in the interests of "simplicity and naturalness" of production.

The *Chicago Record-Herald* (12.4.14) likewise praises M.A.'s spare, understated style, and her skilful avoidance of "maudlin emotionalism" and "sentimental mushiness," and goes on to describe her "big scene" in this way:

> The great moment in this comedy comes in the third act, when the mother rediscovers her heart and persuades her daughter to go back to Windermere. At this point Miss Anglin was very splendid. Just a catch of the breath, a darting forward of the head to kiss the girl, a quick heart-breaking withdrawal from the temptation—and it was over. The audience had scarce time to find itself misty in the eyes—and the men were on the scene. Yet in that brief moment the tale was told, the revelation made, with a sharpness, a precision only possible to players of great skill.

This commendable, and much-commended production clearly deserved to do well, and it did well. This "old play" by an out-of-favor author was, surprisingly, easily the hit of the New York spring season. The *N.Y. Review* (18.4.14) tells us that

> A very good indication of how *Lady Windermere's Fan* has caught the town is the fact that all the book shops report an extraordinary demand for the Wilde literature since Miss Anglin's revival of the brilliant comedy.

The production also broke the Hudson Theatre record for a single performance take:

> Miss Anglin's engagement at the Hudson has boomed since she changed the bill to the Wilde comedy, and on Saturday night the patronage exceeded the biggest previous receipts at the Hudson by $17. Until the arrival of *Lady Windermere's Fan* the house record was held by Otis Skinner in *The Duel*.

Just as Lady W's triumphant progress was beginning to relegate the Bard to mere oblivion, M.A. received the following telegram (dated San Francisco, 7 April 1914) from the west-coast impresario Charles Towie:

> Will you accept an invitation to be present in Stratford-on-Avon in August? Mr. Flower [chairman of the Shake-

speare Theatre] is here, and again wishes to make place for you in any Shakespearian play in which you choose to appear. (*N.Y. Telegraph*, 8.4.14)

M.A., with more than crocodile tears, regretted that "unbreakable [and lucrative] American engagements [would] not permit her to appear." Her English jinx continued to work, and her old friend, the British-born-and-educated William Faversham, took her place as the token American star at the 1914 Stratford Festival.

As the first words of this chapter (in praise of sublimity) belonged to Howard so do the last and they are of the nature of what theatre-folk call bathos—the art of sinking from the sublime to the ridiculous. And of all his sad words, the saddest to Howard was "bankruptcy." "Not a word to throw to a dog," as Rosalind would say. And yet wealthy Meg let him say it, so that he might extricate himself from the toils of a suit for damages of $2,878 resulting from the injury of one Mary Cooper, a black woman, who was run down by M.A.'s chauffeur-driven car which, for some reason, had Howard's name on the ownership papers.

It was the contention of Howard and Margaret that Mrs. Cooper stepped in front of their lawfully proceeding vehicle without looking, and that they, as owners of the vehicle, were in no way responsible for her catastrophe. The following account of the court-room proceedings appeared in the *N.Y. Telegraph* of 8 April 1914:

> "How far away from the car was Mrs. Cooper when you first became aware of the impending disaster?" asked the counsel for the plaintiff.
> "About a yard," replied Miss Anglin.
> "Ah, but what would you say was your best judgement of a yard?"
> "Thirty-six inches," replied the actress, just like that.
> Would she measure the distance with her hands for the benefit of the jury? Indeed, she would. With one hand suspended suspiciously near her nose, Miss Anglin stretched the other about two feet, and said she thought that was about right.

The original suit was for damages of $25,000 brought by Mrs. Cooper in respect of injuries including a broken leg and collarbone, and $2,500 brought by Mr. Cooper "for the loss of his wife's services":

The jury went out and wavered for about an hour, and then sliced ninety per cent off Mrs. Cooper's demands, and gave her a verdict of $2,500 and her husband $250.

That set the stage for the second episode of the Hull-Cooper melodrama, which was introduced by the *N.Y. Telegraph* (13.5.14) in this wise:

> Howard Hull, dramatist, author, and husband of Margaret Anglin . . . filed a voluntary petition in bankruptcy in the United States District court yesterday, scheduling liabilities of $2,878 and assets of only $200, representing the value of his personal wearing apparel, which is exempt under the statutes.

The *Philadelphia Telegraph* (14.7.14) adds that

> Further testimony revealed that Mr. Hull has been supported by his wife since the time of their marriage three years ago.
>
> Mr. Hull admitted frankly and without hesitation that Miss Anglin furnished their house, paid his car fare, bought his clothing, and provided all his spending money. He also admitted that he did not work, and had at the present time no means of livelihood except that provided by his wife.
>
> The examination before William H. Willis, referee, was to determine the ability of Mr. Hull to pay a judgement for $2,828.50 [sic] obtained against him several months ago by Katherine [sic] Cooper, colored, who suffered permanent injuries when she was knocked down at Fifth Avenue and Thirty-third Street, on September 4, 1912, by an automobile owned by Mr. Hull.

The earlier report, in addition to naming a different sum, had called Mrs. Cooper "Mary," and had said "Sixth Avenue" and not Fifth; but what is of real interest in the case is Howard's easy surrender of his sovereign personhood, and the complaisant, nonchalant manner of that surrender—a manner typical of the man.

M.A. as Iphigenia: the lavish production featured fifty instrumentalists and thirty singers, plus 500 student extras. (1915)

Chapter VIII

Beverly, *Iphigenia*, *Medea*, *Caroline*: 1915-1916

Her performance of Mrs. Arbuthnot, like her performance of Mrs. Erlynne, reminds us that here we have the last of the great emotional actresses. (Channing Pollock, *Green Book*, June 1916)

> . . . and still dispensing round
> Her magnanimities of sound.
> (W.B. Yeats, "A Prayer for My Daughter")

What M.A. needed after the exhausting ardors of the Shakespearean tour was an easy lightweight money-maker, and just such a vehicle was provided for her by the Bostonian-Virginian novelist-playwright Paul Kester, who was to become one of M.A.'s most faithful friends from this time onwards—the "little comedy" was entitled *Beverly's Balance*. Beverly Dinwiddie, an impoverished young gentlewoman of Virginia, has come to New York to become a star on the musical stage—she fails not only as a dramatic soprano but as a twittering chorus-girl. As a last resort (under the auspices of her hare-brained lawyer-cousin) she agrees to act as (purely Platonic) co-respondent in a divorce suit proposed by the vain and silly wife of a young millionaire, so that she may wed a British Lord. Beverly, however, by her sweet empathic ways, although often comically misunderstood, manages to reconcile the jarring couple and to get an agreeable husband for herself in the person of the inane but handsome cousin. It's just a bit of sophisticated froth, says the *Chicago News* (17.4.15),

> but it's just enough in the way of a play to suit the requirements of that considerable element among New York playgoers who want just a little theatrical entertainment between the time when they finish their dinners and the going on to the inevitable dancing, without which no night's amusement is complete.

The *N.Y. Review* (17.4.15) critic was "delighted" by M.A.'s "feathery" way with the "arch little role" of Beverly—a part which "in less sympathetic hands" might remain "an insipid little nothing":

> Miss Anglin laughs into the role, she dances into it, she smiles and coos into it, and hands it to you as a delicate and joyous souffle with a flavor and zest to delight the most jaded dramatic

palate. And the wonderful Anglin voice that runs over with tears in *Helena Richie*, the voice that sings to you and charms you in the verse of Shakespeare, that thrills you and chills you in the Greek tragedies, that lovely haunting voice laughs and teases through the three acts of *Beverly's Balance* in continuous ripples of joy.

The Hattons (*Chicago Herald*, 6.6.15), in an article entitled "Miss Anglin Our First Comedienne," echo the *Review* critic's enthusiasm about the diction, and go on to this somewhat didactic effect:

> Clayton Hamilton remarked recently that Miss Anglin was the one actress in America who speaks the English language perfectly. "It is always a luxury to listen to Miss Anglin," he said, "and it would be a good thing if all the schoolchildren in America and England could learn from listening to her how the English language really sounds." Miss Anglin was born in Ottawa and brought up in one of the leading families of the Canadian capital; and this is probably the reason why her speech is neither British nor American, but absolutely English. Her speech is fully as superior to that of most of the noted actresses who come to us from London as it is to that of most of the popular actresses who have grown up in New York. Not only is her reading perfect in pronunciation, it is also faultless in enunciation; there are no local tricks, no mannerisms in the handling of her voice. If all our actresses and actors could be taught to speak as beautifully as Miss Anglin there would be no need to fear for the continuance of a noble standard in our English speech.

No hint in this encomium of what another critic calls "her fickle flirtation with a southern accent"; instead the Hattons go on to praise her flawless timing—"she plays pauses, timed, as it were, to the hundredth of a second"—and the mellow mode of her comic art:

> Her understanding of human nature is deep and genial; she knows our deficiencies, but she forgives gracefully. Her mirth lacks the snappy cutting nervousness of Mrs. Fiske's; she is too big to exercise that tart, acidulous wit which marked the excellent acting of Grace George; she is above the farcical antics of her little sisters of the musical comedies.

Oddly enough it was M.A.'s apparently effortless performance in Kester's feather-weight piece which led to the happily memorable between-acts exchange with the impresario William Harris, "dean of New York's stage aficionados," recorded in the *N.Y. Sun* (28.4.15):

"I know that some persons say that you are the best actress in the United States, but they are mistaken," said the dean to the actress. Margaret Anglin lifted eyes large, grave and reproachful to those of the dean. "Because," he continued slowly and with emphasis, "you are the best actress in the world."

M.A. herself, at this time, considered success in comedy to be as high a theatrical goal as success in tragedy:

> I am a firm believer [she declared] in the theory that the primal purpose of acting is entertainment. If a dramatist has a text, let him preach it if he must, by all means, but those who act his characters are concerned only with making them true to life, and thus best please the audience.
>
> It makes no essential difference to me whether a play be emotional or humorous, all I ask is that it be "real." But, taking the two broad fields of pathos and humor, I can say that I am just as well pleased to play a role in comedy as one that offers opportunities for emotion. I cannot agree with the doctrine that playing on the emotions is the only organ of the theatre, while playing on the risibilities is mere buffoonery, for it is, in fact, harder to make people laugh than to make them cry.
>
> With only the fundamentals of dramatic training, any number of women can carry a so-called "big" situation, tense with emotion, and be heralded a success, but the woman who can handle a really humorous situation is a rarity. Emotional acting is easier because it is generally merely an expression of the natural passions. True comic acting is an acquired art that demands perfect technique and a true knowledge of life. (*Cleveland Plain Dealer*, 13.5.15)

However strongly she may have felt, in the heat of the interview, that she was herself just such a "rarity" as she had described, a true comic actress, the call of Greek tragedy was still her most insistent inner voice. But it was, after all, the consistent success of *Beverly*, both in New York and on tour, that allowed M.A. to indulge her obsession with the big Greek productions and to return triumphantly to the Greek Theater at Berkeley in August of 1915.

Through June and July of 1915 she conducted a westward tour of *Beverly* which brought her to San Francisco on 21 July, at which point (while still playing *Beverly*) she immediately began rehearsals for the *Iphigenia in Aulis* and *Medea* of Euripides and the *Electra* of Sophocles. After the concluding performance of *Iphigenia* on 4 September she resumed her tour of *Beverly* in Los Angeles and eventually toured the production back east. The series of four performances at the Greek Theater also began with *Iphigenia* on 14 August.

The *Iphigenia* was a very lavish and very expensive ($20,000) production. Walter Damrosch, the celebrated conductor of the New York Symphony Orchestra, was engaged to compose an original score which fifty instrumentalists and thirty singers performed under his direction. The instrumentalists were concealed from the audience by a line of evergreens especially planted for that purpose. Miss Anglin worked very closely with Dr. Damrosch in devising the general shape and tonal quality of the score and setting the choral odes. There can be little doubt that the Damrosch music added considerably to the pomp and circumstance of the occasion, but critical opinion was divided as to its dramatic rightness, and the *N.Y. Evening Journal* (8.4.21), speaking of the Met performance, damns it with faint praise:

> There was nothing archaic in the music, it was simple, effective and smoothly made, with some grandiose portions; but it was not exceptionally good. (J, 142)

However, the *N.Y. Times* (29.8.15) reviewer considered that it was "strikingly symbolic in the tragic scenes preceding the departure of Iphigenia," and that it had just the right kind of "dissonantal excitement" when it "supported the marching soldiers, the chariot arrivals and the shouting Greeks."

This last remark is indicative of the grandiose proportions of the *Iphigenia*, which employed some five hundred student extras:

> The production [says Johnson] was described by Charles Phillips as one of the most memorable spectacles in the history of art in America. Walter Anthony called it epoch-making theatre, and the *New York Times* described the production as a magnificent spectacle in the proportions of a mighty pageant. The marching soldiers, the panoplied chariot arrivals, the furious shouting Greeks, the lavish bridal procession, the musical flourishes, all contributed to the theatrical thrills. (J, 105-06)

M.A. thought of *Iphigenia* as "the least tragic of the tragedies," and she was more than content to treat it as "melodrama" with a marked tendency towards "spectacle and pageantry" (J, 91). The Iphigenia story—sacrificing the silver girl to the Moon in exchange for safe sea passage to Troy—is, after all, the prelude to the poetical pyrotechnics of the Trojan War.

There was scarcely a critic who did not find M.A.'s blonde-tressed Iphigenia wonderfully sweet, pathetic and moving, or even inspiring and/or "spiritually exalted" (J, 121). A few, to be sure, wondered where the "classical starkness" had gone, but it was not until the Met performance of '21 that the charge of anti-classicism was made censoriously explicit:

> All this lavish embellishment [said Maida Castellan in 1921], all this overblown spectacle and pageantry in Margaret Anglin's production of *Iphigenia in Aulis* distorts the classical style. No student of the drama should be allowed to accept this incongruous production as authentic. The whole tragedy is presented in a romantic manner and in a modern way, instead of in the proper austere and economical classical manner. (*N.Y. Call*, 9.4.21)

One of the tour-de-force aspects of the *Iphigenia* was that M.A., pushing forty and none too sylph-like in figure, was able convincingly and movingly to impersonate a teen-age heroine—as Arnold Johnson puts it: "Miss Anglin portrayed Iphigenia as a young, tender, trusting, palpitant and self-sacrificing girl; a particularly difficult feat for a mature woman of thirty-five" (J, 101). Even more difficult for the stoutish woman of thirty-nine, which she in fact was. But if M.A.'s Iphigenia was a stout sylph, Alfred Lunt's Achilles (her champion and prospective husband) was a very slender stout fellow. This is Howard Lindsay's irreverent recollection of the twenty-two-year-old Alfred's first big moment on the classical stage:

> The stage was 140 feet long. As Achilles, Alfred, who was extremely skinny, was loaded down with heavy armor. I shall never forget his grand entrance. He looked like a conquering hero, about eight feet tall, but as he crossed that vast stage, with the armor weighing him down, he sagged more and more, so that by the time he got to the position for his first speech he resembled a midget. (*S*, 45)

Incidentally, we have Alfred Lunt's word for the exhaustiveness and rigor of the Anglin rehearsal methods, but also of her generous concern for each member of the cast as an individual artist. "With her amazing capacity for work and drive for perfection," says Arnold Johnson, Miss Anglin was wont to "exhaust the cast with incessant repetitions of troublesome scenes. Although rehearsals were often hectic, a rigorous discipline was still maintained. Off-stage con-versation was not permitted, and actors were expected to be

fully prepared and ready to perform" (J, 250).   Fifty-six years
later Lunt remembered his apprenticeship with the formidable
directrix in these terms:

> She put me through hours and hours of rehearsals, but
> didn't exactly frighten me as much as exhaust me. She was
> determined that she would make a better actor of me, and
> for that I shall be everlastingly grateful. (J, 250)

The *S.F. Call* (8.9.15), incidentally, describes Lunt's glittering
Achilles (*pace* Howard Lindsay) as "a splendid foil" to M.A.'s
"tender, wistful" Iphigenia. That the preparatory "rigors" had
ultimately the desired effect may be gathered from the
opening lines of the *Boston Evening Transcript* (26.8.15) review:

> The occasion was wonderfully impressive. When the lights
> went out before the start of the performance, through the
> darkness one could see great masses of people in the circular
> tiers of seats, the eucalyptus trees standing in the
> background and the stars shining overhead.   Out of the
> darkness came a woman's voice, a dramatic soprano, singing
> strange music, beautiful and sad. When the music subsided
> a soft light gradually disclosed the walls back of the stage,
> ornamented with trees and shrubbery. The hangings in the
> centre opened and revealed, seated at a table, Agamemnon
> the king . . . like a knight in silver armor clad. . . .

The second Greek production of this season was the *Medea*
of Euripides.   Whereas M.A. had used a heavily reworked
pre-Romantic (1781) translation by one Robert Potter for
Iphigenia, for the *Medea* she was content to use, almost without
alteration, the elegant new (1910) translation by Gilbert
Murray.   It may have been this modern, clean and "crisply
vernacular" text that made the audiences feel that the *Medea*
was the most "modern" in feeling of all M.A.'s productions,
or it may simply be that the bloodthirstiness accorded with
the prevailing sense of impending world war.   In any case,
"modern" was a word that appeared in many critiques; and
Miss Anglin herself was heard to say: "Medea is typical of the
jealous woman of any time" (J, 77), by which we may take her
to mean that the character is the embodiment of the fury of a
woman scorned—which is not quite the same thing. She is,
that is to say, the personification of a burning spirit of
vengeance born of a sense of bitter injustice.   But the
modernity of feeling was, so to speak, counterpointed against
high-style delivery—what one critic called "a declamatory
tour-de-force" (J, 124). The audience was simply swept away by
her vocal verve and panache:

The grand manner [says Arnold Johnson] which was so much a part of her personality and acting style enabled her to exhibit a Parthenon grandeur in all her Greek roles. Even as the barbaric queen of Euripides' *Medea*, she was able to invest the role with [what Walter Anthony called] "the majesty of the human soul even in tempestuous moments when passions sweep its vastness." (J, 120)

To express the barbarism and orientalism of Medea, Miss Anglin was costumed in a green robe and blood-red scarf. A tiger-skin crossed her body and was attached over one shoulder. One broad frontal lock of her long raven hair was grey, and she was decorated with ear-rings, high jewelled sandals, and wrist and arm bracelets. Her *Medea* chorus was dressed in russet and yellow costumes. . . . To indicate the innocent and child-like character of Iphigenia, Miss Anglin appeared in a close-fitting pure white garment surrounded with loose draperies; in contrast, the chorus was swathed in lavenders, greens, pinks and blues. (J, 246)

The costumes were designed and created (to M.A.'s general specification) by the omnicompetent Livingston Platt. All the sets for the Berkeley productions were also of his devisal—that for *Medea* consisting essentially, in Johnson's words, of "a nobly solid and majestic facade of a Greek palace, with a flight of stone steps leading up to heavy bronze gates between the central towers of the palace" (J, 148). Platt also devised the very subtle and imaginative lighting effects.

The *S.F. Call* (23.8.15) begins its report on the *Medea* in this way:

The memory of Margaret Anglin's *Medea* has become part of the enduring stone of the Hearst Greek Theater to all of the vast audience who sat through those terror-swept hours last Saturday night . . .

Eleven thousand persons gained admission; and the space usually occupied by the orchestra had to be given over to the audience. Walter Damrosch, with his large number of players were moved to the space immediately in front of the stage.

Turbulent, terror-striking, Miss Anglin's Medea was positively sublime in her fearfulness. The Greeks of old hated Medea, as Euripides meant they should; but there was no hatred for the Medea who, in the gloom and gray of the Berkeley night, cried out her wrongs to the starless heavens.

Her scorn and noble rage when she recounted her injuries touched heights that are not found outside of *King Lear* when Robert Mantell gives them voice. And nothing finer has been seen in the Greek Theater than the scene

wherein Medea took leave of her children and revealed the
heart of the vacillating mother, now severe and vengeful,
now yielding and repentant and filled the cup of pity with
the line: "I am broken by the wings of evil."

The same sense of soul-stirring impressiveness is more
elaborately stated in George Sterling's sonnet "Medea: To
Margaret Anglin" (J, 313), which begins thus:

> She has heard mighty music from the Past,
>   And deathless trumpets from oblivion
>   And she has seen the blood of heroes run
> To stain the morning of a day forecast.
> How high, O Art, the ministry thou hast!
>   Behold! the magic of thy chosen one
>   Has called their shades from Lethe to the sun,
> And ghosts of gods from heavens that could not last.

Alfred Lunt, who was one of the supers in *Medea* retained
this vivid recollection:

> Miss Anglin's Medea was quite amazing. She had never
> during rehearsals "played up" fully. So when she came to
> the scene in which she dragged her two children off to be
> killed, using a great full and terrifying voice, the two
> children were literally so frightened she had difficulty
> dragging them off-stage.   This I doubt could ever be
> repeated. It was real. It was actual. (J, 306)

Lunt also recollected her sending an understudy (by
elevator) up to the top of the ramparts of Platt's set, whence
Medea was to hurl imprecations down upon the head of Jason
(Lawson Butt), so that she could study the effect from the
middle of the auditorium.   "The poor girl was forgotten up
there and not hauled down until well after midnight nearly
frozen to death" (J, 307).
Young Alfred was also a super in *Electra*, but with a
difference. He describes his part in this way:

> Miss Anglin added a procession preceding Clytemnestra's
> entrance. She wanted something decadent, almost obscene,
> and, not having a part in that play, she asked me if I would
> lead this procession and perhaps in some effective manner I
> might think of.

Lunt's first attempt was described by Miss Anglin as "just about
the most wholesome entrance I've ever seen in my life—a nice
normal American boy leading the family to church."   And so he
tried again, this time, according to Maurice Zolotow:

Alfred gilded his hair and his nipples, painted his fingernails and toenails red, and draped vineleaves in his hair. He got two members of the company to be assistant deviates. He painted *their* fingers, toes, hair and breasts. Now he came on, obviously drunk, and embracing two Grecian boys.

"I'm sure we shall all be arrested," Miss Anglin said, laughing. "But we will do it—though it is a bit more *fin de siècle* than I had in mind, Alfred." (S, 45)

As it happened, they were not arrested, and the *Electra* was a huge success, playing to an awestruck over-capacity crowd of some "eleven thousand" (seven thousand paid, according to the perhaps inaccurately kept books). Indeed, as Johnson tells us:

In 1915 there were so many people demanding tickets for *Electra* that the Hearst authorities urged the public to remain away from the playhouse since it was already in excess of capacity. One reporter said he passed thousands of people who were unable to get into the theatre. (J, 178)

Those who succeeded were certainly not disappointed, if we may trust the usually conservative voice of the *N.Y. Times*. John Corbin concludes his review (29.8.15) with these reflections:

Revenge as a religious duty does not easily command our sympathy but, like *Hamlet*, *Electra* has power to move us, and deeply, by the beauty of its language, the intensity of its characterizations, and the tragic force of the story. The audience yesterday was held breathless throughout and, at the climaxes, was swayed by the most powerful emotion. The performance left one stunned and limp, yet with the sense of having for once been privileged to live on the pinnacles of dramatic art.

"I remember," says M.A., that inveterate collector of the commendations of the great,

I remember, with a great deal of pleasure, the enthusiastic tribute paid me by ex-president Taft who witnessed the *Electra* and said that he thought the performance one of the greatest experiences of his life. (H 5)

But this well-nigh perfect *Electra* came within an ace of coming into this breathing world scarce half made up, as the fine atmospheric Furst score almost failed to sound—the orchestra having decided to go on strike at the eleventh hour. "But M.A. was having none of that nonsense. She told her stage manager, Howard Lindsay, to round up all the football players among her student extras and have them bear down upon the musicians like a human steam roller about to crush them and their precious instruments" (C, 14.7.85).   M.A. herself was "tremendously keyed up" by this exercise of rank intimidation, *and* by the music which duly arose for Maestro Damrosch, "religious, sensual, sinister and majestic" (J, 145).

But it was the music of the prima donna's voice that most impressed the fifteen-year-old actress Emily Kimbrough who "at that age of hyperbole worshipped Miss Anglin."   Fifty-six years later the sights and sounds of the 1915 productions were still fresh in her memory, and she was moved to observe that

> Judith Anderson's today is the voice nearest Miss Anglin's, and yet it has not the rich, the golden warmth of hers. Miss Anglin's Medea was a woman of savage love and hate, but Judith never gave the anguished love of her children with which Miss Anglin's voice was brimming. Miss Anglin as Iphigenia had a clear rather high voice of a young girl, totally without the organ-like vibrations of Medea.   As Electra her voice was strident, harsh in denunciation, tender, loving, yearning toward Orestes, yet quite different from the passionate voice of Medea.   Also she moved as a dancer moves, expressing character or emotion—the walk of an entranced young priestess as Iphigenia going toward her immolation, the slinking crouch of an animal in *Medea*, the heavy weighted walk of sorrow, despair, in *Electra*. (J, 304)

Miss Anglin, incidentally, saw Judith Anderson play *Medea* (the Jeffers version) in 1947, and remarked that Miss Anderson had got the barbarism all right but had lost the queenliness—a quality that Miss Anglin credited herself with having duly kept (J, 35).

After cataloguing his impressions of "the rare feast of beauty which Margaret Anglin has bestowed upon Southern California," the *Theatre* (Sept. 1915) critic concludes thus admiringly:

> It would satisfy the ambition of most actresses to play three roles as different and compelling as Iphigenia, Medea and Electra in a lifetime of stage endeavor. Miss Anglin packed these achievements within the space of three weeks. But with Miss Anglin it is not enough to play. She has the producer's instinct. To direct a finely balanced whole is to her as satisfying as to illuminate a character with all that is in the character and herself.
>
> To succeed is to lose yourself in your work. Wherefore Miss Anglin lost herself in that span of a woman's life comprehended by the soft yieldings of Iphigenia, the consecrated, filial vengeance of Electra, and the brooding,

bursting fury of Medea, and in the myriad of details that comprised the trinity of productions.

"The productions were triumphs," says Alfred Lunt quite simply, and apparently even the elements were subservient to Miss Anglin.

> For *Iphigenia* the night was clear and starry. For *Medea* it was threatening with storm clouds. For *Electra* it was dark and foggy. And then for the second production a week later of *Iphigenia* the night was again clear and starry. Extraordinary, wasn't it? (J, 206)

After the brief but arduous glory of the Greek festival, and before going back to the profitable frivolity of *Beverly*, M.A. indulged herself in a two-week run in San Francisco of Charles Phillips' blank verse drama *The Divine Friend*, a religio-emotional play about Mary Magdalen, a role M.A. had always wanted to play—unfortunately the piece was more emotional than dramatic, more florid than profound, and both critics and public generally perceived it as such, and it failed to "go." This was doubly unfortunate because M.A. was a personal friend of the poet, and because she had conceived high hopes on the basis of the *S.F. Call* (5.10.15) review, which expressed enthusiasm in such glowing terms as these:

> Miss Anglin's announcement while the production was in preparation that the role of Mary was one of the most powerful ever written for her proved abundantly true. There were moments when the audience, swept along by the vivid art of the actress, felt it must turn away and stop its ears unless the tension were relieved.
>
> As the woman steeped in degradation yet clinging to the memory of her one love, wracked by despair and self-abasement when that memory is quickened into reality by the appearance of the man she betrayed, Miss Anglin gave glimpses of power and genius far greater even than in the most poignant roles of the Greek tragedies.
>
> While never materializing on the stage, the spirit and influence of the Nazarene are upon the people of the drama at all times. His hand is on the latch-string, but he never enters.
>
> The production given *The Divine Friend* leaves nothing undone that could add to the impressiveness and beauty of the stage picture. High praise is due to Miss Anglin for her latest achievement as a producer.

Something of both the sweetness and the weakness of the play can be surmised from an excerpt from one of Mary's speeches quoted by the *Call*:

He is the Friend of Friends—
Friend of my very soul,
who took me in the hollow of His hand;
whose voice like music wrapped my spirit 'round,
enfolding me in sweet security;
whose loving eye flooded all my being over
with smiling light.
Why, when He walks in the sun, there is no shadow,
but a lovelier light!
He loosed the burden of my unwept tears,
unbound the silence of my muted soul,
made the stars sing again, the sun to smile,
the earth to blossom as the rose.

Before leaving San Francisco in the fall of '15, M.A. had occasion to reverse a stand she had taken on female suffrage ten years earlier. She was enlisted to address the local suffragettes ("delegates to Washington to petition President Wilson"). Surprisingly, she accepted. Surprisingly, she told them they were perfectly right in declaring that in being denied the vote women were being denied the fullness of their humanity. ("Do I contradict myself? Very well, then, I contradict myself.")

> You are the mouthpiece of the West [she told them], speaking to
> the government for the women of the nation, and in a most
> profoundly true sense, for the women of the world. (*N.Y. Telegraph*,
> 11.10.15)

In February of 1916, M.A. did indifferent business in Atlantic City and Pittsburgh with a new production of Rupert Hughes's melodrama entitled *The Vein of Gold*. In the following year the same play, slightly revamped, and rechristened *The Lioness*, did slightly better for her. In the story Gregory Compton is a literate Wyoming rancher with a sweet, unlettered wife called Ida. The culture-starved Gregory is easily seduced by a sly sophisticated easterner called (Mrs.) Ora Blake, but the dauntless Ida undertakes a rigorous course of self-education and soundly trounces Ora on the field of culture, and wins back the astounded Gregory. And thus she discovers the true vein of gold within her soul as well as her true lioness nature, which last is also discovered when her dissolute tutor tries to steal a kiss:

> Whereupon she yanks him bodily from his chair, and with all
> the force of that good Anglin arm she heaves him through the
> window. (*Pittsburgh Post*, 29.2.16)

What was for this critic "a lightly entertaining mixture of farce and emotionalism, . . . spotted with exaggerated effects making it both unreal and unconvincing," was for another "a vivid dramatic portrayal of a woman struggling to free herself of the dulling dross of her environment and breeding":

> And it is to this struggle that Miss Anglin brings all the deep resources of her incomparable genius, so that at the end the woman, the primitive animal, the lioness, has remained, even while the demands of a new civilization, of a new code of conduct, have striven to discard her from the scheme of things.
>
> Thus, of all the types of women which Miss Anglin has portrayed, of all those subtleties of womankind which her art has so enriched, this new one of Ida Compton, the lioness, gives her the greatest range, offers the richest possibilities and commands the warmest response. (*Buffalo News*, 6.2.17)

M.A. gave up on her unprofitable *Vein of Gold* in March of 1916 and went on to the Auditorium in Chicago to mount a big production of *Romeo and Juliet* in which the portly forty-year-old was to essay the part of the fourteen-year-old Juliet. This was, of course, another part she had always wanted to play, but her chance came rather late in the day, and, perhaps fortunately, this production, which was "rehearsed and staged but not performed" (J, 328), never went through the crucible of audience and critical response. She had arranged to get a forty-eight-year-old William Faversham, fresh from his big Iago, presumably for Mercutio and *not* Romeo. But Faversham, at the eleventh hour, opted for Henrietta Crosman and (Shaw's) *Getting Married* instead.

She did play both the *Shrew* and *As You Like It* during this period, but, as the *N.Y. Sun* (25.4.16) says, it was once again a case of (shades of *Lady Windermere*) "Wilde to the Aid of Shakespeare." On 24 April 1916 she returned triumphantly to New York with a brand new production of *A Woman of No Importance*:

> The Shakespearean overture to this revival [says the *Sun*] was acted not here but in Chicago. After the abandonment of the elaborate revival of *Romeo and Juliet* at the Auditorium, Miss Anglin played some of her Shakespearean repertoire. But as that was not for New York, she wisely selected the old Wilde [problem-comedy] as a substitute.

Margaret, of course, took the role of Rachel Arbuthnot, yet another high-minded fallen woman. A sort of irony-invested, grand-manner style was just what Wilde needed and just what Anglin gave him. As one impressed critic remarked, one wants a *real* lady to play Wilde:

> and it is just in this matter of culture and breeding and distinction of manner that Miss Anglin is better fitted than

Photo by Schweig, courtesy of Basile Anglin

M.A. and Sidney Greenstreet in an open-air *As You Like It*, produced for the St. Louis Pageant Drama Association to celebrate the tercentenary of Shakespeare's death. (1916)

almost any other American actress for the embodiment of such characters as Oscar Wilde has put in his plays. (*Indianapolis News*, 16.1.15)

It is, indeed, M.A.'s "deliciously" subtle and elusive ironic mode that is, a little tartly, singled out for praise by Louis Sherwin of the *N.Y. Telegraph*:

> Miss Anglin showed us last night that all that [creaky Wildean] artificiality and sentimentality can be transformed into irony by an actress with a sense of humor.
> . . . Of course, she can do the big emotional scene [when the expectations of her naive son and a naive audience demand it]. Being a born comedienne [sic], Miss Anglin can do the emotional bla-bla in her sleep. She aroused the usual round of silly applause when she produced it to order, whereas the inimitable touches of humor she invented passed unnoticed.

An incidental social note for the spring of '16 may be gleaned from the diary of Josephine Hull which has this to say of 30 April:

> Shelley and I to the Hippodrome, McCormack's concert, then to supper with the McCormacks, Howard and Mary, Schneiders, Ditrichsteins, Kreislers, et al.—delightful! (*DJ*, 133)

It looks as if the elder Hulls were sponsoring the younger at this event, since R.M. Winnans (*EWW* 5) recalls another evening in the spring of '16 when John McCormack was the guest of Howard and Mary at their 93rd St. (#61) town house. On that genial occasion (the great comedian Chauncey Olcott was there in fine feather), "the world-famous Irish tenor sang a number of Miss Anglin's particular sentimental favourites [perhaps to her accompaniment] with an expression and range of feeling known only to his most intimate friends."

Seventeen years later M.A., as a former medalist, was to be one of Count John McCormack's sponsors on the Laetare Medal committee and was at Notre Dame to favor the great tenor with a warm collegial embrace (and amused condolence) on the occasion of Governor Alfred Smith's forgetting to bring the medal to the ceremony (*W*, 16.10.85).

Incidentally, Winnans' article (dated May 1917) is largely taken up with the depiction of M.A. as "a lover of Nature, with whom she communes in intimate understanding." Up to 1914, he tells us, she usually managed "to spend part of the summer motoring through the British Isles and Europe." Otherwise she vacations on "a beautiful 170-acre tract near Lake Balford in the Adirondacks," or at her New England summer home "down

Cape Cod way" (i.e., Woods Hole, Mass.).   Sometimes she goes
camping in the wilderness where she "delights in the *frisson* of
the Big Dark" and "the dawn matins of the forest birds."   She
also delights in hill-country hiking, canoeing, "at which she is an
expert," and swimming, at which she is "strong," and for which
she demands sleek swimsuits, "without skirts."

> At her New England home [says Winnans] she maintains a most
> wonderful rose garden, which is a veritable riot of variegated
> colour and a combination of all the sweet fragrance of
> flowerland. She has not only the rose garden, but long arbours
> of roses, and the outer walls of her house are covered with
> trailing vines of climbing roses of every choice variety. It greatly
> delights her that all summer long the rose vines and bushes are
> alive with birds that fill the days with their silvery song. And
> no bird need go hungry or neglected away from her charming
> home by the sea. Not when she is there to feed and care for
> them.

In May of '16, M.A. accepted a commission from the St. Louis
Pageant Drama Association to produce a big open-air *As You Like
It* for the tercentenary of the death of the Immortal Bard. The site
of the event was to be a natural amphitheatre at a bend in the
River of the Fathers in Forest Park, discovered and designed by
the "Napoleonic" Miss Anglin herself in collaboration with the
Park Commissioner.   The "wide, gently sloping meadow blending
softly with the bank of the little river" provided a perfectly
situated space which was 150 ft. wide and 70 ft. deep, allowing
for the devising of a huge natural stage (under the arches of
ancient oaks), seating for 9,912 spectators, and tents for actors.

> "Fancy how those tents will look in moonlight," enthused
> the actress.
> "But the performances will be daylight ones," observed the
> Commissioner.
> "No," said Miss Anglin. "Night is so beautiful. It is full of
> charm and witchery and mystery. No daylight performance can
> compare with it. We must do all night performances I must ask
> you to let me have my way in this." (*Theatre*, June 1916)

"A supporting cast numbering no fewer than 1200 persons"
was engaged, and so were the services of C.J. Sharp of London
("the world's authority on English folk-songs and dances") as
chorus and choreography director (for the 400 who were to dance
and sing Elizabethanly, prior to Miss Anglin's speaking of an
epilogue).
The *N.Y. Times* correspondent reported on 8 June that after
two successive rainouts (on Sunday and Monday evenings) the

show finally went on, despite more rain, on Tuesday the 7th. With a gusty light rain sweeping the amphitheatre, Miss Anglin stepped to the front of the stage and asked for a voice-mandate to go ahead with the performance, and got it. And then, as the *Times* reviewer puts it:

> Fair Rosalind braved rain and a soggy stage, and Touchstone's legs shivered in a cold damp wind. . . . A crowd of between 8,000 and 9,000 attended, many coming while rain was falling. Repeated applause attested their enjoyment of the comedy in which 500 [sic] persons took part, headed by Miss Anglin as Rosalind.

The Jacques for this production was the famous English Shakespearean Robert B. Mantell, then in his sixty-second year. Alfred Lunt, in the minor part of Le Beau, "dared not speak to such an eminent actor" *(Toronto Star*, 1.11.49), and communicated with the great man through the gracious mediation of Miss Anglin. M.A. told Jerome Collamore that

> during rehearsal she had all the extras lounging around cracking and eating nuts during Mantell's "All the world's a stage" speech, and he seemed to accept that setting, but when it came to performance, he rose and strode down stage center and declaimed the speech to the audience. (C, 16.10.85)

"Naturalism be damned," he said, and Miss Anglin bit her tongue. Mrs. Mantell (Genevieve Hamper) played the shepherdess Phoebe, and Louis Calhern her lover Silvius. Sidney Greenstreet again presented a bumptious Touchstone, Frederick Lewis was a worthy but mildish Orlando, and Henry Hull was his wicked brother Oliver.

The *Times* reviewer also remarked on the excellence of the natural acoustics and the effectiveness of the natural background:—"the Arden stage was, most suitably, the natural sward and foliage, with but few embellishments." He was also happily able to report that half an hour after Orlando's opening "As I remember, Adam," and before the Duke's "Sweet are the uses of adversity," "the rain ceased, the stars came out, and the production was brilliant." The weather continued fair from this time forward, the following five performances were uniformly successful, St. Louis agreed that Miss Anglin was "captivating," her production "delightful," and her sylvan stage everything she said it would be as a romantic property *(St. Louis Star*, 14.6.16).

Speaking of "witchery and mystery," as M.A. just was, it was at this time that she told her true-life ghost-story to *Harper's Bazaar* (April 1916), which account may be marginally supplemented by the earlier version found in *H7*. "And, as I am not in the least superstitious, you make take this quite seriously":

> A few years ago [she confides] I was living in a fashionable uptown Fifth Avenue hotel. At about 12 o'clock one night I retired after eating a light supper. The maid switched off the lights, leaving the door between the bedroom and the living-room open, so that the electric light from the street filtered through the curtains. I did not fall asleep immediately but lay half dreaming. Presently I became aware of a draft. I sat bolt upright. To my amazement a figure in a smoking jacket rose from a corner, glided into the living-room and passed out a window. I sprang to my feet and turned on the light. The door was locked; so was every other opening but the window, eight storeys above the street.
>
> The next day on returning from rehearsal I found my maid, a strong, unexcitable Irish girl, in a state of panic. All afternoon the table in the sitting room had cracked, rapped and tapped and generally performed most disturbingly. I ordered an examination. It was solid and substantial.
>
> Shortly afterwards, while drinking tea with Charlotte Thompson and Alice Kauser, I was on the point of narrating this untoward happening when Charlotte jumped up exclaiming that something had tugged at her coat. I quieted her as well as I could, but soon she departed. Then Alice exclaimed, "Margaret, something did pull her coat—I saw it!"
>
> The next day another guest sitting in the same chair cried out in alarm when she felt a damp hand on the nape of her neck. Here was an atmosphere which would have made Poe happy. But it did not make me happy. I sent for the manager. He refused to believe anything of the kind could have happened. But his protests lacked fervor and I began investigations. Soon I learned that a former manager of the hotel had committed suicide a few months before. Whether the deed was done in my apartment was not disclosed, but I lost no time in moving.

After a good run in New York with *A Woman of No Importance*, M.A. went on to another comedy success in Somerset Maugham's *Caroline*. In the story, the witty solicitor Robert Oldham, Caroline Ashley's (Platonic?) lover of many years' standing, cannot bring himself to marry her when her chronically absent husband dies suddenly and unexpectedly. Caroline is glad that he cannot, but they both feel (and all their friends feel) that he *ought* to marry her. They are therefore both greatly relieved when the husband providentially (fictitiously?) comes back to life in the Antipodes. And eventually they can settle back into their comfy social routine of mildly naughty flirtation with no strings attached.

It is all pretty thin, flimsy stuff, and the New York *Globe* critic declares that "as a vehicle for Margaret Anglin it is quite inadequate." But such was not the reaction of the opening-night crowd, according to the *N.Y. Sun* (21.9.16).

> So favorably did the spectators receive the play that after many curtain calls at the close of the second act the author was unable to escape from Miss Anglin and timidly took one call with her, though nothing could induce him to attempt a speech.

Persons like the *Globe, Tribune* and *Post* reviewers (who were all bored) were all, apparently, simply "persons lacking subtlety and sophistication," for as the *Chicago Tribune* (31.10.16) says:

> *Caroline* demands a dainty appetite for its appreciation—a sense of well-bred whimsicality, of suave epigram, of well-mannered burlesque. . . . *Caroline* is light as gossamer and evanescent as the dust blown from butterflies' wings; . . . in it the rough spirit of travesty is purged of its gross humor and refined into an aristocratic fantasy.

The *N.Y. Times* (21.9.16) spoke for all "sensible" theatre-goers when it said, quite simply, that M.A.'s performance of Caroline was "a really memorable achievement in high comedy."

The Anglin production of *Caroline* was nominally under the direction of the author, but by Maugham's own admission he merely sat mumchance at rehearsals while M.A. told her players, in no uncertain terms, "Now look, this is what Mr. Maugham wants." Mr. Maugham's admiration of Miss Anglin as a producer knew no bounds:

> She has a keen humor [he observes], which enables her to see every implication of laughter that a situation or a repartee contains, and an imaginative gift which sees the play on paper as already a living thing. . . . Another quality of the ideal producer which Miss Anglin has in an eminent degree is good temper. I think I may say that the rehearsals of *Caroline* were conducted without an unkind word, and as one grows older it begins to dawn upon one that kindness is the most valuable of human qualities.

"This is the first time I have ever seen a play produced by a woman [he adds]; and I can quite honestly say that I have never seen a play produced more capably." As for her own histrionic gifts:

> It would be unbecoming to me to remark on the great talent of the actress, for her popularity, the high place she holds in the opinion of all qualified to judge, must make any words of mine otiose. (*N.Y. Times*, 1.10.16)

It is not very surprising, after all this, to find M.A., in a letter of 2 November 1916, commending the notably crusty Maugham to the fond regard of Paul Kester, as "a very charming gentleman." There appears, indeed, to have been something a good deal more genial than an armed truce between these two imperious personalities.

S. Morgan-Powell recalls that M.A. brought *Caroline* to Toronto in November of 1916. She appeared at the Grand Opera House, the Princess having recently burned down:

> Unfortunately, the late Ambrose Small had just undertaken to discipline the newspapers, and the press, which would not accept his dictates, was neglecting his theatre. So it happened that there was no mention of Miss Anglin's presence in the city, except in the Saturday page of the *Mail and Empire*, and not unnaturally, she was deeply hurt at such treatment in a city that she had regarded as her second home. (*Montreal Star*, 7.4.27)

This chilly reception of *Caroline* followed hard upon what she took to be a cool Toronto reception of her 1914 Shakespeare tour; and this unfortunate Canadian experience (or possibly some adverse comments she heard in Toronto about the American isolationist stance during the war) may have prompted her oddly jingoistic Christmas 1916 article for *Theatre Magazine*, "What Santa Ought to Put in Our Stockings." The answer to that question is: "a properly balanced and intelligently conducted repertoire theatre for every one of our larger cities"—with American players and playwrights given heavy preference:

> I believe in American plays by American authors for American people. . . . There is a great awakening in our country to the fact that we need America for the Americans, and it has extended to the professional stage. That is, the public wants more purely American plays, which is but natural . . . —America and American ways and American life should come first.
>
> If we are to have war plays, let them be of American wars. If we are to have plays of finance, let it be American finance. Americans understand the thrill of the stars and stripes, they know what the flag stands for, what their forefathers have suffered for it, and the American war play means more to them than any other war play could. Also they know all about the American dollar, almighty at times in what it will do, and at other times worthless to help in certain trials.

This does not sound much like the voice of Electra, or even Caroline, nor does it reflect that fact that in the previous three years M.A. had been connected with only one successful American play, the featherweight *Beverly's Balance*.

Speaking of Toronto, it is interesting to note that in May of 1916, while appearing in *Lady Windermere's Fan* in Toronto, she told a *Star* reporter that "after seven years as a producer-manager," she intended "to give up the nerve-wearing managerial duties." She would, however, allow herself one more shot at "Shakespearean production" (meaning, presumably, the big St. Louis *As You Like It*):

> and then devote all her energies for the next five years to acting the best roles she can find. After five years Miss Anglin will retire from the stage. (*Toronto Star*, 13.5.16)

Had she adhered to that resolution, she would have retired at forty-five, after her bravura performance in *The Trial of Joan of Arc* (which she would *not* have been producing and directing). As it happened, her acting career went on for another twenty-seven years, and she appeared as co-producer as late as 1937. In the *Star* interview M.A. observes that she had been "playing and producing continuously for 86 weeks," and she concedes that the strain of the dual role of actress-manager had "threatened her health." All the multifarious problems, frets and worries at the production level of the play represent "a drain on the nerve and concentration" of the actor-manager. "Such things," she says, "have hurt me as an artist. Unhampered by them, I think I could have done better acting":

> I dare say [she continues] if I had a theatre of my own things would be different—I would have my path made clear. But the trouble with the stage in America is its lack of organization. There is no economy of time. You spend a great deal of time on things that should be done easily. And you have to give too much time to others—there is no *esprit de corps*.

The whole interview has the slightly querulous tone of an outwearied woman. Nevertheless, the inner need to produce drama is still strong:

> If I had the two to choose from [she admits] I would rather be a producer than an actress. I like to create, I like to see things grow and happen. I would like to come into the theatre and see the work I have created; see how it goes; see it as others see it. An actress cannot do this. She can follow the production of the play and observe wherein it goes wrong—but only from her own point of view. In working as actress and producer at the same time, I find I have lost my point of view from the other side of the footlights.

Two months later thoughts of retirement had given place to a grandiose scheme for making movies—a scheme which was to end in costly liquidation a year later.   On 14 July 1916 the *Cleveland Plain Dealer* carried the announcement:

> The Margaret Anglin Picture Corporation has been formed to produce the famous star's pictures.   Miss Anglin is under contract with the company to appear in sixteen feature films within the next two years.   The scenarios are to be written by well-known authors.   The first picture, as yet unnamed, is in the process of production, the release date being set for September. The studio is in Detroit. . . .
>
> Miss Anglin's director will be Arthur Voegtlin, the man who conceived and produced many of the big spectacles of the New York Hippodrome.

Miss Anglin, whose democratic feelings were of a somewhat rarefied order, is quoted (in the same article) as saying: "It is the limitless democracy and the tremendous possibilities for artistic achievement that have made the screen irresistible to me." Unfortunately, the screen found her not only resistible but contraindicated—largely because M.A., that "natural" front-and-centre stage personality, was unaccountably "very camera shy" (W, 16.10.85), and apparently tended to petrify on film.   Besides, her deep doubts as to the histrionic value of the new medium were reinforced by Shelley Hull's empirical judgement: "Why, movie acting isn't acting at all.   It's just a species of pantomime" (DJ, 119).

In any case, her filmic venture was not only a theatrical non-event, it was a financial fiasco, and a sizable one.   The *N.Y. Dramatic Mirror* (2.8.16) gives us some inkling as to the extent of her monetary commitment to the scheme:

> The Margaret Anglin Picture Corporation has purchased a twenty-acre lot near Detroit, where a studio is in process of erection on plans drawn by Howard Crane.   The estimated cost is $100,000.   James D. Barton, president and general manager of the corporation, has entered into negotiations for a site for a winter studio at Dallas, Texas.
>
> Miss Anglin is said to have received an offer from William Randolph Hearst to appear in a picturization of *Medea*, the classic which she presented at the Greek Theatre in Berkeley.   She was obliged to decline, since she is already at work for her own company.   Her first picture will be released in September.

September of '16 in fact saw (as we have seen) a sound, substantial *Caroline* and not the ghost of a film.   Indeed M.A.'s whole film career, which kept almost happening for the next thirty years, is a spectral one.   Witness her "signing on," after her own company had passed into shadowland, as "one of the new screen stars of the Sanger Picture Corporation," to begin work immediately on a "melodramatic production" which, likewise, never happened (*N.Y. Telegraph*, 25.1.17).

But if the shimmery, airy soap-bubble of movie stardom (and moguldom) soon burst, the business of stage production soon re-quickened, for, in spite of her Toronto resolution, her *Caroline* production was a big touring success in late '16 and early '17, and by the end of 1917 M.A. had no fewer than three of her own productions—the revived *Lioness*, *The Open Fire*, and *Billeted*—more or less simultaneously on the boards. But we may consider that story to be part of the end-of-the-war years and our next chapter.

M.A. in 1920 as Vivian Hunt in *The Woman of Bronze*, a role she played a thousand times during the 'twenties in cities and towns all over the United States and Canada.

Chapter IX

Joan of Arc and *The Woman of Bronze*: 1917-1922

She says she is mystified by the character [of Joan]. In playing it she mystifies herself. She transcends herself. (Alan Dale, *N.Y. American*, 3.4.21)

Billeted, which was to be M.A.'s financial mainstay through 1918 and part of '19, began, not very auspiciously, under the title of *Lonely Soldiers*, on 24 September 1917 at the Empire in Syracuse. The evening began with the dismal discovery that the two cars carrying the scenery and costumes for the play had been "lost somewhere in the vicinity of Binghamton." But of course the show must go on, and so

> the house scenery was used in the emergency, while O'Malleys furnished the gowns, and the silver and glassware came from the Onanadaga Hotel. (*Syracuse Post Standard*, 15.9.17)

Miss Anglin played with perfect "naturalness and ease" and with unruffled charm "before a crowded house [featuring] many army and navy officers and people of social prominence," but her trouper spirits could not carry her through to the post-show party (given by the Syracuse Art and Music Club) at which she was to be guest of honor, and she begged off in favor of a hot tub and a long drink.

The show itself, "one of those typically English things, all dialog and practically no action," was well received, not because of any perceived intrinsic merit in the play (by the British team of Jesse and Harwood), but because of the uniformly professional poise and polish displayed by "the seven members of this remarkable cast."

Three weeks later the *Philadelphia Ledger* (19.10.17) spoke of a trimmed and tightened *Lonely Soldiers* as

> a fragile play, slender in thematic material, familiar in development of situation, yet informed with such a profusion of sparkling wit, and acted with such a rare sympathetic distinction and polish that it becomes a veritable gem coruscating artistic fires.

M.A.'s *Lonely Soldiers* may be thought of as a truly timely (even socially conscious) production, coming as it did less than three months after America's entry into the war (June

1917); but the fact is that although the male principals are British officers supposedly engaged in the Great Conflict, the play is in fact just another drawing-room comedy with uniforms instead of dinner-jackets. The trenches might as well be on the dark side of the moon. In the story, Betty Tarradine (Taradiddle?) a witty and flirtatious hedonist who has been a tartly merry grass-widow for some three years, offers to put up a couple of officers of the locally encamped regiment in her pleasant English village house. In order to finance her expansive entertainment of her guests, Mrs. T. kills off the absent Mr. T. (by telegram) and collects his life insurance. Needless to say, one of the new tenants turns out to be the unlamented lost husband, with a new name (Captain Rymill), a new moustache, and a new military bearing. After a suitable period of mutual non-recognition and recrimination (and partner changing), husband and wife are amorously re-united, while Colonel Preedy, the Captain's confidant, and Penelope Moon, Betty's confidante, are also happily spooning.

The piece was judiciously renamed *Billeted* for the New York season, and was accorded a sort of grudging acceptance by the *N.Y. Times* critic who found it, on the whole, "shallowly facetious." But "perhaps," he allows, "a light-hearted glance at the Great Struggle" comes not entirely amiss in "these depressing days":

> The play contains not a little clever dialogue [he concedes], but it also has stretches which are dull and even moments which border upon silliness. It is not a particularly deft play technically, and the authors have been decidedly lax in the drawing of character. It is only the art of Miss Anglin which served to make the principal character at all interesting, for as a character she had not one redeeming quality. In the hands of a less skilled actress the heroine would have been totally without sympathy. Miss Anglin, of course, found the simple requirements for the part easily within her grasp, and played with her customary poise and finish. (*N.Y. Times*, 26.12.17)

And, it would appear, gave the character a charm not explicit in her lines. Edward Emery was easily gentlemanly in the part of the hail-fellow Captain, Phyllis Birkett, a bright young English actress with a nice fluty voice, was agreeably sportive with the owlish Colonel, and "a good bit was contributed by Howard Lindsay as a Scotch bank manager with a burr."

Just before deciding on *Billeted* as *the* commercial vehicle for 1918, M.A. had been giving most of her time and energy to Hubert Footner's comedy *The Open Fire*, which (after seeing M.A.'s performance) the *Christian Science* Monitor (18.12.17) decided was "one of the more important American comedies of the first two decades of this century." *The Open Fire* tells the romantic comedy story of how a warm-hearted, absent-minded, "artistic" interior decorator, Laura Kevney (M.A.), wins out in spite of her butterfly improvidence, in life and love, over her cold calculating and conniving secretary Minnie Mockridge (Margaret Ferguson, later Blanche Bates) and the ruthless financier T.B. Avening (Howard Lindsay), and wins the love of the good-hearted young (blond) accountant and *honnête homme* Joe Pennock (George Howell). Miss Anglin, says the *Monitor*, produced a personal performance of "engaging warmth, wit and whimsicality" and a company performance of consistently high quality. Despite the *Monitor's* high praise, however, this amiable piece failed to do big box-office business, and M.A. wisely relegated it to second string.

Most of the New York reviews of *Billeted*, which opened at the Playhouse on Christmas night, were highly laudatory. The *N.Y. Herald*, for example, comments in passing

> It is in light social comedy of this kind that Miss Anglin shines with especial lustre. In it she has few if any rivals upon the English speaking stage, and when it is remembered how potent she can be both in passion and in pathos a true conception may be formed of the dominant position which she holds among the leaders in her profession.

As soon as she settled into the Playhouse with *Billeted*, M.A. immediately commenced rehearsal for her Carnegie Hall productions of *Electra* and *Medea*. Johnson tells us that

> She rehearsed *Electra* and *Medea* at the Fulton from the morning until the matinee or evening performance of *Billeted*. Usually after the evening performance of *Billeted*, the cast would assemble at Carnegie Hall. A rehearsal would last from twelve until three or four in the morning, or later. (J, 163)

Electra was originally scheduled for 6 and 15 February and *Medea* for 20 February, but the ticket demand was so heavy that M.A. agreed to a 7 March *Medea* and an 8 March *Electra*. The pace she set during these weeks was obviously a killing one:

> She was so exhausted by the activity [says Johnson] that she cancelled *Billeted* on March 6 and after the *Electra*

performance on March 8 left New York for some needed rest. Early in April of 1918, she resumed performances of *Billeted* in Chicago. (J, 163)

Johnson further observes that

to supervise every detail of a Greek production required enormous physical and emotional strength. Margaret Anglin was equal to the task. She had a fantastic capacity for work. By her own admission, she would spend eighteen to twenty hours a day handling the myriad details of play production. Before her 1918 production of *Electra* in New York, she said she worked steadily without rest for thirty-six hours before the performance: "I shouldn't have done it, because it wasn't fair to myself as an actress, but I had to do it as a producer." (J, 155-56)

And all that colossal effort resulted in a net loss to Anglin & Co., despite the fact that they sold out Carnegie Hall (capacity 3,000) for every performance—the take of $30,000 was not enough to cover expenses. M.A. herself put her own $500 per performance back into the financial melting-pot to prevent her backers and colleagues from losing money.

Still, the beauty and majesty had been achieved and did not lack praise. "Taken together," says J.R. Towse, "both representations are entitled to be recorded as among the most notable artistic achievements in the musical and dramatic history of New York"; while H.K. Moderwell asserts that "for sheer effectiveness and beauty, these stage pictures have rarely been matched in our theatre" (J, 152).

Much credit again goes to the visual genius of Livingston Platt for his grand and austere tableau effects ("vast and sombre" —J, 148) and his "fresco" costumes ("graceful in outline and delicate and harmonious in color" —J, 150), and *some* credit to Walter Damrosch, whose somewhat controversial Wagner-cum-Rossini music is probably fairly described as effective but slightly overdone mood music, "appropriate to melodrama" (J, 142). Once again, however, the music of the Anglin voice is at the centre of all, and Burns Mantle is moved to declare that

no other player of my time has ever extracted from spoken lines the very essence of soul-purging misery, or lived a heart-wrung grief, or launched the bitter, stinging curses of deep anger, or risen to the supreme heights of joyous gratitude for one beloved, with such affecting eloquence as Miss Anglin did yesterday. (*N.Y. Evening Mail,* 7.2.18)

Kenneth McGowan of the *Boston Evening Transcript* (8.2.18) gives M.A. all due credit for the versatility and resourcefulness displayed in playing *Billeted* in tandem with the Greek tragedies:—"That she could, while acting nightly with consummate skill in light farce, yet devise this production, marks her as a dramatic artist which this country cannot equal."

Arthur Hornblow returns to the Anglin voice for his central impression of the *Electra*:

> One of the best of our few real elocutionists, Miss Anglin, combining an expert knowledge of the technical and plastic phases of her art, gave an *Electra* beautiful in its grief and sisterly love and gorgeously moving in its outbursts of triumphant revenge. (*Theatre,* March 1918)

His impressions of the *Medea* are only slightly less admiring:

> Though the *Medea* is quite as sumptuous and gorgeous in production, I confess, in spite of the modernity of its appeal, I liked the *Electra* better. I would go so far as to suggest that the text be cut, for however great and able the exponent of the title role, there is something too much of Medea and her wrongs. Methinks the lady doth protest too much—still should the most lavish praise be paid to Miss Anglin for the vividly varied reading she gave of the Barbarian [sorceress-princess], the ill-fated consort of the [perfidious] Jason. As a declamatory *tour de force* it was remarkable. Aided by pantomimic intelligence and plastic grace that gave its varying words and eloquence added impetus, the performance was tremendous in its onrushing sweep of tragic significance. (*Theatre,* April 1918)

After the splendid Carnegie Hall run, a testimonial dinner was given M.A. by the Twilight Club on 24 February 1918 at the Hotel McAlpin. The *Brooklyn Eagle* (25.2.18) opens its account of the event with these lines:

> A score of leaders of the drama—playwrights, actors and actresses—and 400 friends of the arts joined last night in a tribute to Margaret Anglin in recognition of the distinguished career which has just been crowned by the presentation of Sophocles' *Electra* and Euripides' *Medea.*

The chairman of the dinner committee was Daniel Frohman, the toastmaster was the playwright Augustus Thomas, and the keynote speaker was the impresario Arnold Daly. The latter set the tone of the evening with these words of praise:

> Miss Anglin is one of the few people on the American stage who have suffered for its future, and unless it gathers recruits from her spirit it will have something to lament. She would have gained a perfectly comfortable living if she had been willing to cater to the popular appetite for mediocrity. But she has always fought for the best in the theatre. However, an American artist cannot do without backing. And if you think you can get backing for any high purpose from a commercial manager you are quite wrong, but it is not the manager's fault, it is the public's.

The other speakers were: Laurette Taylor and her husband J. Hartley Manners, Tyrone Power, Julia Arthur, Dorothy Dix, Thomas Wise, Nat C. Goodwin, George M. Whicher, Florence Reed, Ina Clair, Brandon Tynan, Edmund Breese, J.R. Grismer, R.C. Megrue, and Maclyn Arbuckle, "who once played Uncle Tom to M.A.'s Little Eva" and who "used Miss Anglin as a text for remarks addressed to the glorification of her sex." After being virtually deluged with expressions of praise, appreciation and affection from such a notable company, "Miss Anglin was so moved that when the toastmaster asked her to respond she could only say in a broken voice: "Good night, dear friends, and thank you."

M.A. successfully toured *Billeted* and *The Open Fire* for the rest of 1918 (barring midsummer) and part of 1919. However, on 3 February 1919 the *N.Y. Times* reported that her performance of *The Open Fire* at the Parsons Theatre in Hartford was cancelled due to illness, and on 19 February the *N.Y. Star* reported that her week-long Baltimore run had been cancelled due to what was "believed to be a nervous breakdown."

Perhaps a prime contributor (by way of delayed reaction) to that breakdown was the profoundly shocking death of her much loved brother-in-law, Shelley Hull, in January of 1919. The nearest thing the 1919 stage had to a matinee idol: "he was," said Otis Skinner, "one of the most glorious young men of our stage, and pretty nearly its 'white hope'" (*DJ*, 144).

After playing the lead in his long-running (war melodrama) success, *Under Orders*, on Wednesday, 8 January 1919, Shelley Hull went to bed feeling feverish. Six days later he was dead of pneumonia-influenza. Josephine's diary simply says, "He died at 6:55. My beloved, my life" (*DJ*, 144). Those who saw him in death—"so young, so beautiful"

—couldn't believe he was gone. He was just past his thirty-fourth birthday. The lights of Broadway that Tuesday night (14.1.19) were dimmed, and many a Broadway eye was misty—including Margaret's.

M.A., though she never played with Shelley and was not one of his intimates, had a high regard for him as a person and an actor and was "deeply saddened" by his passing. Howard, who had introduced Shelley to the stage (by way of *Florodora* [1901]), staunchly supported the shattered Josephine through the ordeal of the New York funeral and the bleak and bitter Boston interment (*DJ*, 145).

Whatever may have been the ingredients of the February breakdown, M.A. appears to have been fully recovered in March, and was getting good reviews and granting charming interviews in Columbus and Toledo; and on 3 April 1919 (her forty-third birthday) she was in St. Louis to do "the ceremonial planting of two trees at the main entrance of the Municipal Theatre"—the vast open-air theatre whose construction she had initiated in 1916. The two trees in question were a sycamore, called "The Site Discovery Tree" and a tulip tree, called "The Margaret Anglin Tree" (*St. Louis Globe Democrat*, 4.4.19).

High summer of 1919 found her (as usual in the late teens) at her Catskill country place near Katonah, N.Y., a domicile described by *Theatre Magazine* (5.21) in these somewhat extravagant terms:

> "Cedarwold," her extensive country estate in Westchester County, a picturesque hacienda of country manors, which has no duplicate, except perhaps in California, is situated on the highest point in the county overlooking six mountain ranges and the entire chain of Croton lakes. Farmland, pastures, forests and gardens are all included in its vast acreage.

And it seems the "nervous breakdown" symptoms had not altogether disappeared, for we find her remarking in a 7 August letter to Paul Kester, "Another bad mood, I wish these attacks would pass away from me." In February she had opened a letter to him with these lines:

> This morning, thank heaven, I woke up with something approaching a normal mind, by which I mean I could follow ideas through to their conclusion, and that has been hard and often impossible for me during recent weeks. . . . How good and kind and patient you were with me, and what a sorry thing I became. (K, 17.2.19)

Her edgy psychosomatic condition could scarcely have been improved by the actors' strike of 6 August to 6 September 1919. The Actors' Equity Association, which had been in rather ineffectual existence for six years, suddenly flexed its muscles and managed to persuade the overwhelming majority of New York actors to walk out when the theatrical managers refused to recognize its right to bargain for its members. George M. Cohan and David Belasco, the most vocal anti-unionists among the actor-managers, founded a rival union, called the Actor's Fidelity League, which was, in essence, just a sinking fund for actors' welfare, and was known to Equity as "Fido." "Among the actors who opposed Equity by joining Fidelity," recalls Brooks Atkinson, "were E.H. Sothern and Julia Marlowe, Mrs, Fiske, Margaret Anglin, Otis Skinner and David Warfield"—all of whom were also sometime producers (B, 186).

M.A.'s adamant opposition to the unionization of actors (which was maintained over the years and was to damage her career) is expressed early and urgently in a letter to Paul Kester, dated 26 August 1919, "Cedarcrest" [sic]:

> This appalling thing which has happened to the American theatre has for the past few weeks come between us and everything we have tried to do. Isn't it awful!
>
> Of course it is useless to make even the vaguest plan, and many of us face ruin, so far as we can see. If the labor unions get control of the theatres, think what they are going to become. Bad enough now, heaven knows, but individual effort was never interfered with or dictated to.
>
> Well, dear, enough of us and our perplexities. Howard and I are so glad you have found a nice house [in Port Hope, Ont.]. . . . It is lovely to feel that there will be a room there some day for us—but, in view of our imminent beggarhood, don't you think your offer fairly rash?
>
> Basil spent a few days here with us, and on Sunday we motored back to Albany with him in his new car. Oh, apropos of cars, the Studebaker finally blew up, much to our relief. Kemmet is now the proud possessor of a Maxwell, vintage of 1900, I should say.

From this last it appears that Ralph Kemmet (M.A.'s stage manager for fourteen years) was now a live-in member of the Hull family and its official driver.

She was also at this time in correspondence with Kester about the refurbishing of the French play *La Rivale* (by Henri Kistemaecker and Eugène Delard) which she had acquired, and acted as *The Rival* in 1910. The play was to be

As Joan of Arc: "I am a Roman Catholic and I have French blood in my veins, so Joan and her career have a special appeal to me." (1921)

thoroughly Americanized, and set in a Catskill estate, a lot like Cedarwold.   The subject of the bronze sculpture, the making of which stands at the centre of the drama, was to be changed from "The Dreamer" to "Courage," giving it a post-war significance, and its symbolic value was to be given clear recognition in the new title, *The Woman of Bronze*.   The re-edified piece tells the story of a famous and gifted sculptor's psychosomatic need of a young mistress and of his steadfast wife's eventual moral triumph over his philandering spirit and her musical sex-kitten (cousin) rival.   The central image of the play is the larger than life bronze statue representative of the heroic spirit of America which Leonard Hunt is sculpting. While his inspiration is the high-minded Vivian (his wife), the statute's expression is one of noble, altruistic resolve; when the inspiration becomes the nubile Sylvia (the cousin), the expression becomes one of amorous invitation, to say the least. But, as we have said, virtue is allowed to triumph and the inspirational statue finally goes forth duly dignified.

The new play opened at the Broad in Philadelphia on 25 October 1919 to a somewhat lukewarm response from the *Philadelphia Ledger* (26.10.19) critic who speaks, a little patronizingly, of M.A.'s resuscitation of the "older style of emotional acting."   It is, however, he concedes "admirably accomplished," and indeed "the excellence of the acting of the whole company, in almost every instance, suggests that painstaking rehearsal upon which Miss Anglin has always insisted."   Apropos of the Americanization of the piece, he remarks that

> although New York is the present locale, it all smacks much more of London, despite an occasional Americanism of phrase. . . . This British atmosphere is probably brought into the play by the presence in the company of several unmistakably English players, enacting British roles, while the beauty of Miss Anglin's speech and that of most of her coadjutors suggests the stage of London rather than that of America.   Nor is the speech alone responsible for this feeling of geographical dislocation; it is likewise traceable to the quietude of demeanor and bearing of nearly everyone concerned, a reflection of well-bred life, rather than the pace of cinematographic comedy.   For this speech and air of leisurely ease we are profoundly grateful in days when jazz has affected the tempo of even the dramatic stage.

This perceptive critic also picked up on the *Medea* echo in the big scene in which Vivian comes within an ace of stabbing her adulterous young cousin who is pregnant with her stepson.

One of the things that the new play did was to bring Howard (a prime favorite of Paul Kester's) out of the shadows. Probably at Kester's behest, the play was billed in these terms: "Howard Hull presents Margaret Anglin in Her Greatest Play *The Woman of Bronze* by Henry Kistemaecker and Eugene Delard." Another article in the *Ledger* (2.11.19), perhaps by the same hand, speaks of spending a number of "happy half hours during the last two weeks" with "the gifted Margaret Anglin and her clever and delightful husband, Howard Hull, devoted brother of Henry Hull, who has been Constance Binney's vis-à-vis in *39 East*."

"Mr. Hull," observes the reporter, "is a wit of fame." And he goes on to retail an exchange between Howard and Walter Hampden, "who was playing *Hamlet* matinees at the Broad last week." When Hampden told Howard that, whatever his doubts as to the quality of *The Woman of Bronze* as a play, he had to admit that M.A.'s performance was "marvellous," Howard replied: "Well, my dear Walter, let me say that whatever doubts I may have about your performance of Hamlet, I am bound to confess that you are in possession of a most excellent vehicle."

Glimmers of light on the "adorable" Howard also emanate at this time from certain phrases in letters from Margaret to Paul Kester. On 3 March 1919 she refers to Howard as "my mad dear one," and on 24 November 1919 she speaks of "mak[ing] Howard behave" at dinner, and reports that "Howard promises that he will not be 'individual' nor take off his shoes," and on 5 February 1920 she concludes a letter with the warning, "If you only had Howard's word for it, please remember his blissful state of irresponsibility."

M.A. was able to get a fortnight's booking in Chicago at the beginning of 1920, and Amy Leslie, in the *News* of 17 January 1920, gives voice to the general wish that her run had been longer, and she also appears to indicate that Henry Hull joined the cast of *The Woman* in Chicago:

Miss Anglin's brief season [she reports] has drawn huge numbers of happy people to Powers' theater and her brilliant demonstrations in *The Woman of Bronze* have marked a shining era in the drama of today. . . .
    It has been a festival of pleasant and profitable results, the flitting through of this remarkable artist. The adorable Hull boys, one of whom is Margaret's agreeable husband and the other that splash of lightning and ether Henry, of *39 East*, have enjoyed being here together under the worshiped pinions of their joint ideal, Margaret. Henry has jubilantly

thrust another Spanish tragedy at Margaret for next season and Howard says as near as he can translate the title [*La Maniatica Casera* (?)] it is *The Home Nut*, and the heroine is a rakish maniac with fits and starts of lucidity.

Later in January of 1920, in St. Louis, Howard shared an heroic moment with M.A. when she

> almost succeeded in capturing a burglar who entered her room at the Jefferson Hotel. The man escaped with $108.
>
> Miss Anglin was awakened and saw a man standing near her dresser. She screamed, and the man ran past her bed. Miss Anglin caught his coat, but, hampered by the bedclothes, was unable to retain her hold.
>
> Howard Hull, husband of the actress, chased the man down several flights of stairs, but lost track of him on the second floor.
>
> Miss Anglin told the police the burglar was about 40 years old, heavy set, and wore a dark suit and fedora hat. (*St. Louis Democrat*, 24.1.20)

The ever accessible and intrepid Howard did not believe in locking doors.

By the time M.A. brought *The Woman* to New York, on 7 September 1920, it had already begun to look like becoming her all-time standby, warhorse and money-maker, which indeed it did, in the course of over a thousand performances in scores of cities and towns all over the United States and Canada over the next decade. Alexander Woollcott subtitled his *N.Y. Times* (8.9.20) review "Miss Anglin Resplendent." Essentially, he says, the play is a rather threadbare version of the French *triangle sexuel avec temperament artistique* problem play, but Miss Anglin saves it, nay *makes* it, with her wonderful portrayal of the pent-up smouldering fury of a woman scorned. Vivian Hunt is a modern damped-down reprise of Medea (the Medean dagger appears in Act 2), and who other than Miss Anglin would one have to play her:

> It is an unforgettable experience [Woollcott avows] to watch her give expression to all the panic, fear, jealousy and murderous hatred for which the play is an excuse. The suggestion of inner tempest without any raging or even lifting of the voice above a despondent or frightened monotone; the suggestion of complete emotional abandon without the artist in her once releasing the tight sure grip on the reins—all these are memories of a dramatic adventure too vital, too moving, too glowing to be measured, except in memory.

While running *The Woman* in San Francisco, M.A. indulged herself in a long-cherished personal ambition; she mounted and produced on 12 April 1920 at the Columbia Theater Émile Moreau's historical tragedy *Le Procès de Jeanne d'Arc*, which she had had translated as *The Trial of Joan of Arc* by Miss Astrid Argyll.

It was yet another Herculean effort, an exhausting labor of love, for a money-losing (though sold-out) one-week stand; but that her efforts were fully appreciated by the cognoscenti is indicated by the *S.F. Chronicle*'s (18.3.20) laudatory judgement:

> In her production of *The Trial of Joan of Arc* Margaret Anglin has given San Francisco one of the most notable stage achievements in the history of this country.

She used several members of the cast of *The Woman* in *Joan*, including the two male stars, Fred Eric and Langdon Bruce, as Bedford and Warwick; but what with massive sets, lavish costumes, and "150 persons" involved in the production, expenses ran very high and a short-run loss was inevitable.

The staging of the tragic conclusion of Joan's meteoric career had indeed long been on the Anglin agenda, and the acquisition of the Moreau script finally gave her what she wanted:

> I have been contemplating producing a Joan of Arc play for eleven years [she told Colgate Baker]; in fact I have had it in mind ever since Mark Twain suggested it to me. . . . Mr. Twain thought of dramatising his *Life of Joan* and we talked the matter over many times.
>
> I am a Roman Catholic and I have French blood in my veins, so Joan and her career have a special appeal to me. . . . I began to dream of getting a play which would be in some measure worthy of the subject and practical for stage purposes. . . . I read innumerable plays about Joan before discovering *Le Procès* which Émile Moreau had written for Mme. Bernhardt. I loved it at first sight and immediately took steps to secure the American producing rights. (*N.Y. Review*, 16.4.21)

To Tom Nunan of the *S.F. Examiner* (18.3.20) she enlarged on her first discussion of the subject with Mark Twain on the occasion of his backstage visit after a performance of *Helena Richie*:

> It was when he came to see me in Daly's Theatre in New York about ten or twelve years ago. Tears poured down his cheeks and he shook his leonine head and that great shock

of white hair as he spoke about Joan. He told me that his book about her was the one thing he was glad to have written, his one book that he really loved.

M.A. then, at Nunan's instigation,

> declared herself an out and out believer in the divine guidance of the girl. It is *Saint* Joan of Arc with her and no possible doubt about it. Her acting of the role carries sufficient evidence of that, to be sure.

Her Joan's voices told her of a land called Holy France, one nation with her own king, dwelling in mutual loving-kindness under Christ, and so her Joan would dedicate herself to this ideal, and so she would live in love in the midst of hate.

M.A.'s friend and collaborator, the novelist Gertrude Atherton (*Black Oxen*), also a friend of Mark Twain's, was present at Nunan's interview, and was the other party to the rather surprising agreement that the reporter records:

> We all agreed that Moreau's *Trial of Joan* was the greatest play in Miss Anglin's repertoire, and, for acting purposes, one of the best in literature. It may stand like *Hamlet* as a test of ability. Thus far only Sarah Bernhardt and Miss Anglin have enjoyed the triumph.
>
> While we talked Miss Anglin repeated some of the lines in French as Bernhardt would speak them. It was Bernhardt's voice, the Bernhardt reading, in marvellous imitation. Ah, but Margaret Anglin can act!
>
> "And why not a Greek play this year," I asked.
>
> "Because," said the Actress, "there is no Greek play equal to this one. No Greek play that I have ever produced, or ever might produce, can compare with it."

The *Trial of Joan* was mounted again nearly a year later at New York's Century Theatre on Easter Sunday afternoon 27 March 1921, under the auspices of the Knights of Columbus, in aid of the Herbert Hoover Relief Fund. John Brockway of the *Brooklyn Standard* (28.3.21) reports on the benefit performance in this wise:

> Miss Anglin's staging of the Joan story was one of the biggest things New Yorkers have seen in a decade. The audience rose *en masse*, cheering and roaring their appreciation of the most remarkable and magnificent portrayal yet given by this great actress. For fully ten minutes this demonstration lasted.

In view of this reception it is not surprising that a limited run (12 April through 8 May) was immediately arranged.

Brockway goes on to declare that in this performance "Miss Anglin proved herself not only a great artist but a great spirit," and the critic for the *N.Y. World* (28.3.21), while duly noting the fact that a forty-five-year-old was playing a nineteen-year-old, is equally enthusiastic.

> While too mature for an ideal embodiment of the maid, Miss Anglin yesterday emphasized the character's spiritual meaning, expressed its compelling pathos, and arose to its heights of religious exaltation with that finished artistry which she now, among all our stars, alone controls. She spoke Moreau's florid line with the utmost beauty of diction. It was a performance in which intelligence, feeling and technical proficiency were perfectly combined.

Alan Dale of the *N.Y. American* (3.4.21) was also able to forget the corpulent, middle-aged woman in the consummate actress, for he declares that "The Joan of Arc that I saw in the person of Margaret Anglin was the visionary girl, the dreamer, the hearer of voices, the unforgettably pathetic figure." And the *Telegraph* (17.4.21) reviewer was even more carried away—"By some inner power she possesses [he says], an actual transmutation takes place. She changes in appearance before your very eyes. She becomes the wide-eyed mystical girl of the play. There is magic in it."

The entire company of "devoted and loyal players" comes in for considerable praise in most reviews, while, in particular

> Henry Hull, Miss Anglin's brother-in-law, impressed at a few hours' notice to act the important role of the Earl of Warwick, plays the part with such distinction and grace, one might have thought he had been doing it for a season. (*N.Y. Review*, 16.4.21)

Although Moreau makes abundant use of the actual transcript of the trial of Joan, J.R. Towse (*N.Y. Post*, 28.3.21) remarks that he "makes no pretense of being realistic," and that he renders the tragic episode "as an ideal in sentimental romance." The fact that the score of Tchaikovsky's opera *The Maid of Orleans* soared and fluttered and fell in the background serves to corroborate this statement. Thus released from the demands of realism, M.A. was able to make the most of her "splendid diction" and to create an eloquent Joan but one with, in the words of one surprised critic, "not a particle of rusticity and not much of religious exaltation." "Indeed," says Towse, "between them Moreau and Miss Anglin have very nearly made her clever."

But enough of such niggardly hedging. Colgate Baker who, to say the very least, found it "difficult to speak of the production and the acting of the star in measured terms," o'erflowed the measure in such terms as these:

> Behind the polished technic of her art glows such spiritual faith, such absolute conviction, the whole thing becomes almost supernatural. It is easy to understand after seeing this performance what a wonderful help to religion the mystery plays of the fifteenth century must have been and why they were so fostered by the church in olden times. Truly religion and the stage are closely connected, albeit they have drifted apart.
>
> In a word, what Miss Anglin does is to reincarnate Joan, inspired of God, martyred by the scheming politicians of France and England. Her Joan is the spiritual reality of the Maid of Orleans for the time being. . . . The dead heroic maid lives again for the nonce. Yet how is it possible for a living woman to bring this about? I think the explanation is that the actress is not in the ordinary sense of the word a living woman at the time of [her dramatic impersonation]. I think that her inspiration is so great—the rising of spirit is so obvious in it all, that for the time she is all spiritual force; but this is mystic speculation. (*N.Y. Review*, 16.4.21)

But, mystic speculation aside, Baker is ready to swear that "Margaret Anglin's *Joan* is the greatest spiritual inspiration our stage has ever known, bar none." He might have been even more impressed (if possible) had he known that ‑ M.A., weakened by fasting and lack of sleep, was invariably scarcely able to stand at the conclusion of the play "and more than once fainted at the end of the evening" (*GN*, 78).

Following the Herbert Hoover benefit performance Margaret was presented with a gold medal by the Consul-General of France on behalf of the Joan of Arc Committee of New York; and after a benefit performance of Act 3 for Actors' Fidelity on 5 June 1921, she was presented with a lavish floral tribute and a silken tricolor by fifty members of the Société de Femmes de France. Immediately following that she set sail for France. Her first stop (after Le Havre) was Domrémy—it must have felt like coming home (*Telegraph*, 5.5.21; *Telegram*, 7.5.21).

The other big event of 1921 was the Manhattan Opera House performance of *Iphigenia in Aulis* in which M.A. decided to give the title role to Mary Fowler (the pretty Sylvia of *The Woman of Bronze*) and to arrogate the more sombre role of Clytemnestra to herself. Almost as soon as *The Woman* opened in New York in September of 1920, M.A. began to plan another lavish Greek production and was soon rehearsing it while maintaining an uninterrupted run of her "commercial vehicle." Many and many an all-night rehearsal would find her at daybreak "with her head done up in wet towels to relieve the neuralgia from which she suffers, but still energetic, still full of zest and enthusiasm for the grand thing to be done. . . . 'As long as one is doing something worth while, something of one's own, one does not feel tired. It is not hard to do a thing when one's spirit is in it. After all, the spirit animates the clay'" (*Shadowland*, June 1921). Further complicating matters, of course, was the massive revival of *Joan* ten days before the staging of the Greek extravaganza. And to the foreseeable stresses and strains of such a situation were added the imponderable pangs of a germinating feud between M.A. and Walter Damrosch.

The two performances of *Iphigenia* at the Opera House were to be Damrosch's ceremonial farewell to the New York Oratorio Society of which he had been director for several years. He was to go out in a blaze of glory; *Iphigenia* was to be *his* show. But as rehearsals went forward, M.A., as usual, emerged as the dominant personality, and the exasperated, self-important Damrosch was moved to accuse her in full rehearsal of personal arrogance, managerial high-handedness and deliberate publicity-hogging. At this point we may let Maurice Browne, M.A.'s stage director of the 1921 *Joan* and *Iphigenia*, take up the story:

> She turned on him at last, justifiably, with all Clytemnestra's power of invective. He responded in kind. She swept out. I ran after her, a raindrop beating against Gibraltar. "I shall appear in the two performances, but I shall not act; I shall merely walk through the part and say the lines. Reproduce the play and give it to Iphigenia; keep Clytemnestra in the background. I shall not set foot in the theatre again until just before the curtain goes up, unless Dr. Damrosch apologizes." He would not; she did not. The play's last ten minutes had not one rehearsal.
> The players were unanimously on Miss Anglin's side, but were appalled by the thought of no further rehearsal with her, above all of no dress rehearsal. They were determined, however not to let the show down. She had no understudy; [assistant director] Nelly Van offered to read her

lines. Mary Fowler was Iphigenia; the two girls and Moroni Olsen, who was acting opposite Mary, rehearsed with me for nearly twenty-four hours, to give Iphigenia the play; then we took Mary through it with the Company; all of them met every demand. But there were still the last terrifying ten minutes. (*TLTL*, 254)

During that last ten minutes, after the noble voluntary departure of Iphigenia to the sacrificial blade and flame of Artemis, Clytemnestra remains on stage to call down passionate denunciations upon the messenger who claims to have seen a white hind miraculously substituted for Iphigenia, while the maiden herself was spirited off in a moony cloud, and upon Agamemnon who bids her rejoice at this indubitable sign of the gods' favour. Meanwhile the women of the chorus look on and it is through their eyes that the audience sees the indignant queen.

We were using a chorus of fifteen [says Browne]. All had been chosen for their acting ability, particularly for their skill in mime. Now while Nellie Van read Clytemnestra's closing speeches in as many different ways as she could devise, and moved in and to unexpected places, they improvised simultaneous reactions. And finally, when they seemed able to meet any emergency, she read the lines like a schoolgirl, gabbling them tonelessly and without movement; the girls made Clytemnestra appear a woman stunned by grief. (*TLTL*, 255)

And so Browne & Co. had done what they could to avert total disaster, but as the curtain rose on the afternoon of 7 April 1921 for the grand entrance of Clytemnestra they envisioned the "more than three thousand in front" with more than a little trepidation:

Miss Anglin [Browne continues] had just reaffirmed her decision; she would merely "walk through." Now, twelve feet away, she was standing in her two-horsed chariot with her charioteer, waiting for her entrance cue. The entrance was upstage left at full gallop, then across the back of the stage with exit upstage right and re-entrance downstage right, still at full gallop to centre, where the horses were pulled back on their haunches to a swift standstill. We had rehearsed with a piano. From the one hundred and twenty pieces of the New York Symphony Orchestra came a terrific chord. The startled horses reared, throwing Miss Anglin, a big woman, heavily to the stage. Before Bell or I could reach her she was back in the chariot, and the chariot was racing hell for leather past a wildly cheering audience. Nor throughout the play did one of those spectators suspect that, three seconds before, she had been bruised black and blue from heel to shoulder; the fall had given her such a shock that she chucked her decision down the drain and acted Mary Fowler, Walter Damrosch, her own Company and the entire New York Symphony Orchestra clean off the stage. (*TLTL,* 256)

Browne himself, watching the last ten minutes "from in front" was "dumbfounded" by the poised perfection of M.A.'s powerful control of a scene that had never been rehearsed.

Then the curtain fell—and the audience went mad. And I had played a small but integral part in this triumphant—and absurd—vindication of the theatre which I have loved. But at the moment that did not occur to me; for there was I cheering and stamping and beating my hands together as violently as the rest, and the curtain kept rising and falling, and Miss Anglin beckoned Damrosch on to the stage, and he kissed her hand, and she kissed him on both cheeks. And now she was beckoning to me; and now friendly hands were suddenly and surprisingly pushing me down the aisle to the pass door. And now it was I who was kissing Miss Anglin's hand, and she was kissing me, and Damrosch and I were shaking hands, and she was kissing Damrosch again. The eighteenth curtain fell; it was the last. She smacked his face. (*TLTL,* 256)

And that slap in the face, combined with the financial one, effectively concluded the ten-year Anglin-Damrosch connection. Henceforward her musical maestros got financial guarantees and kid-glove treatment.

Reflecting more reservedly upon the great fall from the chariot, Arnold Johnson remarks:

Although physically injured, she finished the *Iphigenia* performance as well as the evening performance of *The Woman of Bronze.* Such was the endurance of Miss Anglin. (J, 165)

The *N.Y. Telegram* (8.4.21) reviewer (quite in the dark about the injury) reacts to M.A.'s performance thus admiringly:

As Clytemnestra she dominated the scene intensely. Fiery in denunciation, melting in appeal, stalwart in defence of her daughter and poignantly tender in farewell, she stamped herself indelibly on the mind again as America's greatest tragic actress.

Her lines were beautifully read, so clearly they could be heard even in the last rows, and yet none of their finer shadings were lost in the huge auditorium. . . .

She touched, too, with understanding on those fleeting probings of Euripides into the mystery of grim human fate. In her final passages with the daughter she was to surrender to the

sacrifice Miss Anglin seemed to be speaking for all the
mothers of all ages. Here, too, Miss Mary Fowler showed a
flash of genuine power, speaking her farewell to her friends
and to Greece with the exquisite spirit of a swan song.

"This splendid production," says the same reviewer in
conclusion, "is by far the supreme dramatic achievement of
the season."

The *Brooklyn Eagle* (8.4.21) reviewer, who considered the
staging of Maurice Browne ("that apostle of affectation") to be
inept, gives the triumph entirely to M.A. (with honorable
mention to Mary Fowler, Moroni Olsen and Ralph Roeder):

> If she has ever done anything better than this performance
> [simple, forceful and lucid] of Clytemnestra, we have not
> seen it. . . . Ten minutes of Margaret Anglin in *Iphigenia in
> Aulis* is worth a year in the trashy melodrama, *The Woman of
> Bronze*, in which she has been appearing so successfully this
> season.

Trashy or not, it was *The Woman* which began making money
again for M.A. upon her return from a six-week holiday in
Europe. It was given some help by a refurbished version of
The Open Fire "for which [Hubert Footner] has written the
most lovely and fascinating third act you can imagine, though
the second act is still a bit shaky." This last to Paul Kester
from Howard (17.8.21) who adds, presumably with a note of
self-gratulation, "Footner has developed an amazing amiability
and has become transmuted from an incorruptible author into
a cocktail-drinking competent."

And speaking of making money, M.A. appears to have
been fairly flush these days, in spite of her quixotic devotion
to the classics and such non-lucrative religious fare as the Joan
and Magdalen pieces, in spite also of her liberal, if not
feckless, way with money, in terms of splurges, gifts and
charities (especially the ASPCA). While Cedarwold was, as
we have seen, a notable Catskill showplace, her beautifully
appointed 93rd Street house was accumulating an impressive
array of choice *objets d'art*, such as "a seventeenth century
Italian daybed covered with an early sixteenth century spread
of a deep mulberry shade, a lovely pair of seventeenth
century Flemish verdure tapestry chairs, an eighteenth century
mantel set given to her grandmother by Napoleon III," and,
covering an entire wall of the drawing-room, purchased from
a bankrupt Italian count, "one of the most valuable tapestry
cartoons in the country, a genuine Raphael of which there is
no duplicate—its rich browns and greens mellowed by the

centuries to exquisitely delicate shades, it represents the feast of Diana" (*Theatre*, 2.21).

M.A.'s car was no longer a 1900 Maxwell but "a 1920 Cadillac sedan," which, incidentally, was stolen one night while standing outside the Frazee Theater in New York during a performance of *The Woman*. It was recovered three weeks later in Utica and three crooks were apprehended (*N.Y. Telegram*, 12.1.21).

In August of '21 Margaret was saddened by the death in his twenty-first year, as the result of an automobile accident, of her "favorite nephew," the very personable and bright (B.A. aet. 20) Frank Anglin Jr., who was studying law at Antigonish N.S. but had "always wanted to be an actor." Ironically, M.A. had herself, as a young woman, "really wanted to be a lawyer instead of an actress" (*Boston Transcript*, 8.8.21).

In December of '21 she was the keynote performer at the ninth annual Sarah Greenbaum Guest Day at the Sinai Temple in New York. Her "Recitations" received top billing, above the renditions of the Philharmonic String Quartet. Earlier in the year (*N.Y. Telegraph*, 28.4.21) she had presented a program of "famous speeches of Shakespeare's women" to the Spring Session of the Women's Club of Orange N.J. In these two outings she seems to have set aside her mild prejudices against Jews and Orangewomen. As well, her early commitment to being an elocutionist, or dramatic reader, was being honored rather late in the day, and would continue to be, increasingly, as her histrionic star faded.

New Year's Day of 1922 saw her again riding the durable old bronze warhorse while continuing to cast about for a bright comedy suitable to an actress approaching a forty-inch waistline and a fiftieth birthday. It was at this becalmed moment that her dedication to Greek tragedy was re-fired by a letter she received from Don Louis de Bourbon. Bourbon, as PR director for King Constantine of Greece, invited M.A. to produce a Greek tragedy or two in Athens under royal patronage. "The Greek people," he told her, "are aware that you are the first great tragedienne to present a Greek drama in the United States," and he assured her that King Constantine was "most interested" in the possibility of hosting Miss Anglin's production of *Electra* and/or either *Iphigenia* or *Medea* (J, 263-64).

Miss Anglin responded to Don Louis most forthcomingly. She had "always dreamed of such an opportunity." She decided to present *Electra* with an English or American cast, and decided against having any Greek spoken in the production, as the melange of languages would be simply "incongruous."

> When she arrived in Greece in the summer of 1922 [says Johnson] she was invited by King Constantine to the Royal Palace. The King explained his plan to create a spiritual and cultural rebirth by presenting revivals of the ancient Greek plays. Miss Anglin promised to present her production in Athens the following year. Unfortunately, within a month after she arrived back in the United States, King Constantine was dragged from his throne and pushed into exile. His dethronement prevented Miss Anglin's realization of a dream. (J, 265)

Perhaps by way of consoling herself, she began almost immediately planning a truly grandiose production of the *Hippolytus* of Euripides for the Greek Theater at Berkeley in the spring of 1923.

Meanwhile *The Woman* continued to bring home the bacon, even when she could no longer walk, as we discover from this item in the *Bronx Home News* (27.4.22):

> As a result of falling down a flight of stairs in her 93rd Street home, Miss Anglin broke [i.e., severely sprained] both ankles; but, rather than break her contract, she played her role in *The Woman of Bronze* in a rolling chair [i.e., a wheelchair]. Last night she had to wheel herself out on stage twice to receive the plaudits of the audience. Her manager [Ralph Kemmet] said that, although she had not slept since receiving her injuries, she insisted on finishing her week at the theatre.

In the spring of '22 with the welcome of *The Woman of Bronze* wearing a mite thin, along with M.A.'s gusto (especially after seeing her meal-ticket variously misprinted as *The Woman of Brass*, *The Woman of the Bronx* and even *The Woman of Booze* [N.Y. *Globe,* 16.10.21]), and with things theatrical generally in low estate—all the fault of unionism, says M.A. ("Howard Lindsay has left me, . . . Miss Marlowe has retired" [K, 24.10.21])—the Hulls decided to abscond to Europe. The vacation of '22 begins on an idyllic note "motoring lazily from Genoa to Florence" (K, 5.5.22) in May, continues allegro with popping in on the King in June and cruising the isles of Greece in July, but ends on a distinctly minor dissonance: "We have been involved in a most fantastic and unexpected expense by Kemmet (at Cedarwold) to the tune of several thousands of dollars. This will throw the production of the new play back" (K, 23.8.22).

The new play in question was the stage version of Dickens's *Bleak House*, which she and Kester had been collaborating on for some time—of which more later. In the autumn of '22, M.A. was again touring *The Woman* in the provinces under the management of Kemmet, and in October Paul Kester visited the lonely Howard at Cedarwold and later wrote in this *penseroso* vein to Margaret:

> We do enjoy each other's company, and the place is not lacking in melancholy charm, but we missed you most lamentably. We spoke of you constantly, until it seemed we should hear your voice or see you come into the room at any moment, and when you didn't, it all seemed strange and vacant. Your personality is not to be subtracted from anything without a saddening sense of loss. We are all thankful for the better news of your dear mother. I was in New York yesterday and dined with Basil and Howard. Howard does me, a dull dog, a lot of good. Mrs. Marbury wants me to dramatize *The Age of Innocence* (1920) and *The Glimpses of the Moon* (1922), Mrs. Wharton's novels, but if I can survive without I'd rather not. (K, 29.10.22)

M.A. with Holbrook Blinn in *A Woman of No Importance,* 1926:
performances of Wilde's play subsidized the losses on the classics.

Chapter X

Hippolytus and *Lady Dedlock*: 1923-1926

Phaedra: Many a time in night's long empty spaces
I've pondered on the causes of life's shipwrecks.
I think our lives are worse
than our wills warrant.
(Euripides, *Hippolytus*, ll. 375-8)

With the big *Hippolytus* assuming ever more extravagant proportions in M.A.'s seething brain, it behoved her to get another commercial vehicle on the road which would be capable of subsidizing another sure-fire classical loser. To this end she took an option on the rights to *The Sea Woman* by Willard Robertson, a journeyman actor of her nodding acquaintance, who, in terms of later contractual bargaining "treated [her] abominably" (K, 1.2.23), causing her to lose her taste for the piece ("My heart went out of it"), whose film rights were later sold to the Hollywood scenarist June Mathis (*N.Y. Telegraph*, 30.4.25).

The Sea Woman, though flawed with "numerous dramaturgic shortcomings" (*Variety*, 17.1.23), had a large-hearted heroine and a strong streak of emotionalism, and that, for M.A. in full sail, was enough. The "unwieldy story-line" tells us that Molla Hansen, a lineal descendant of Leif Ericson, is rescued (as sole survivor) from the burning wreck of her father's ship by an heroic lighthouse-keeper who dies in the attempt but not before exacting a promise from Molla that she would take on his daughter (Pearl) as her ward. Pearl turns out to be a nasty (but plausible) piece of work from the beginning and ultimately (and not a moment too soon) commits suicide with her small-time-hood fancy man, but not before involving the tigress Molla in a series of harrowing rescues (including the shooting of an innocent man). At the end, however, Molla's seafaring lover (who was sure she had perished in the wreck) returns from the Antipodes; the shooting victim recovers, forgives and blesses; and Molly and Roddy sail off on amorous red sails into the sunset.

Howard liked the piece well enough to give the name "Molla" to a spirited red heifer out at Cedarwold.

M.A. opened fairly successfully in Stamford Conn. on 11 January 1923 in what the *Boston American* (17.1.23), with a hint of allusion to the Anglin voice, calls "a sere and mellow drama from the old hokum bucket." And indeed at the literary level *The Sea Woman* is, says the *Washington Times* (16.1.23), "undistinguished bombast fustian," but still:

> In the stalwart and noble Norsewoman Miss Anglin has a character that drips with primitive emotions. None of the contemporary stage can surpass her in portraying deep emotions, and the climax of the first act which finds her bathed in real tears is but another tribute to the spirit with which she endows the characterization.

The bad Pearl was played almost too convincingly by the "youthful" and almost too attractive "newcomer," Rea Martin (*Variety*, 17.1.23).

The Sea Woman, for which "Miss Anglin wore . . . bobbed hair, men's clothes, and brown skin," and for which she devised a "particularly appealing" Norwegian accent (*Variety*, 17.1.23), had a moderately successful run in Washington and the eastern seaboard states, and provided a welcome holiday from the "trashy" French triangle. But her bad relations with the author made it lose favor with her sooner than it might have done, and it was once again "old bronze" that took her west in the spring of '23. She began rehearsing *Hippolytus* during a May 7-21 Los Angles run of *The Woman of Bronze*. From 22 May to 1 June the company moved to Berkeley for intensive on-site rehearsals.

This most extravagant of all M.A.'s Greek puddings was only a qualified success in the proof, and this may well have been largely due to the fact that the fiery Phaedra hangs herself at the end of the third scene and leaves the somewhat unthrilling Theseus and Hippolytus (Henry Mowbray and Boyd Irwin) dangling despondently for the remaining three scenes. As both fiery and amorous, M.A.'s Phaedra was appropriately costumed by Livingston Platt:

> As the passion-racked queen of Troezen, Miss Anglin wore a red wig which streamed down over her shoulders. Her costume was a delicate pink garment with gold embroidery and a scarf of purple. The chaste disciples of Artemis were clad in dull grey; the priestesses of Aphrodite in yellow and orange. (J, 246)

The play held up, says Tom Nunan of the *S.F. Examiner* (3.6.23) as long as Miss Anglin was on stage—the presence majestic as ever, the voice rich and vibrant as ever, "fully competent to convey most movingly the pride, the passion and the grief of Aphrodite's queenly victim." But the rest of the cast simply didn't have the stature or the presence such major drama requires—besides, most of the actors involved "had no previous classical experience and no outdoor theatre experience."

Given this basic criticism, with which he agrees, it is a little surprising to find Clay Greene of the *S.F. Journal* (3.6.23) speaking of the production as "a high art success" and as "a noble production of beauty." Besides the acting of Miss Anglin, it was, as always, the splendid staging of Livingston Platt that did it for him. But in an article entitled "Vast Throng Held Spellbound by *Hippolytus*," Dudley Barrows of the *S.F. Call* (3.6.23) remarks that the play really was "over-produced"—after all, he says, "the important thing should be the text, not the large orchestra, immense stage crowds, spectacular staging, graceful posturing, beautiful costuming, leashed dogs, white doves." It was all rather kaleidoscopic —wonderful brilliant bits in a crazy quilt effect, while lines like "The apple tree, the singing and the gold" danced like sugar plums in the auditors' heads. And there was "too much singing," in the opinion of George Warren of the *S.F. Chronicle* (3.6.23)—composer Arthur Fisher had been given too free a hand in his quest for moving choric and orchestral effects, and the music, though sometimes "imaginably Greek," rather obscured than underscored the lines of the play. Part of the over-production was a forty-piece orchestra and a singing chorus of sixty.

According to her stage manager, Jerome Collamore:

> M.A. practically wrote the music of *Hippolytus*. Arthur Fisher, the pianist in the *Bronze* production, was selected to write the music. He and Mary would meet at the studio. Mary would read a passage and Fisher would improvise. When he got it right, Mary would say, "Good, write it down."
>
> The next day she asked him to play it, and he couldn't; he hadn't got it on paper. In a fury she grabbed a book and threw it at him. Mary told me she could never hit a person, but she could throw things at them. (C, 22.11.85)

"Rehearsals were always hectic with M.A.," says Collamore:

> she was always so far ahead of the players they had to run to keep up with her. She always had two different versions of all the big scenes. We'd rehearse the play with the first attack. Then at dress rehearsal she would suddenly spring

the second attack. I found this a trick of hers which kept the
company on their toes for the opener. (C, 22.11.85)

Not to say tenterhooks. Collamore also tells us that, in the course
of her 2-P.M.-to-midnight rehearsals, M.A. knocked back a two-
ounce highball, every hour on the hour—the genial cup-bearer
being the otherwise expendable Howard. She also had prompters
concealed at several strategic points in the set to give her her lines
when she dried up. But her inability to retain lines (says
Collamore) had nothing to do with drinking—she had already (he
believes) begun to feel the effects of cerebral arteriosclerosis. And
if her mnemonic faculty was failing, her aspiring spirit and
"enormous personality" were unimpaired. Her managerial style
remained comprehensively imperious and incisive, and she was
still able to explain to Henry Mowbray, that good-looking, good-
sounding dunce, "the difference between a syllogism and a
soliloquy" (C, 13.8.85).

When all the returns were in from this biggest and least
artistically successful of the Greek productions, M.A., for all her
toil and trouble, had sustained a net loss of something in excess
of two thousand dollars. The paid attendance was 5,837 (usually
reported as 10,000) and the gross receipts amounted to $11,295.
Immediately after the presentation of *Hippolytus* the company
began rehearsals of *A Woman of No Importance*, as Wilde was yet
again called upon to subsidize the classics.

This immediate resumption of commercial theatrical activities
constitutes a fairly clear contradiction of what she told "two
young women" of the press during the *Hippolytus* rehearsals. The
interview was reported in the *N.Y. Times* (22.5.23) as follows:

> Margaret Anglin will never act on a public stage again "here or
> elsewhere" if an actors' union is formed, she said today. . . . "I
> am violently opposed to a closed shop for the professional
> stage," Miss Anglin declared. "Artists are not bricklayers. They
> cannot be controlled by a union or by union rules. Neither can
> their emotions be controlled. Art is something spontaneous,
> which flows freely and uncurbed. Personally, my ability as an
> actress would be impaired if I was held down by iron-clad rules.
> I want to be free to express my emotions. Therefore it is very
> likely that this appearance of mine which I am planning here
> may be the last one I may give here or on any other stage."

The clear implication that neither she nor any of her actor-
manager colleagues could work as (or even with) union members
was a little more than M.A. was ready to go to the block with,
and the disdainful phrase "Artists are not bricklayers" had
evidently been generating more heat than light for a fractious

fortnight; so she issued this revised version of her anti-union creed to the *Times* (5.6.23), after *Hippolytus*:

> I said that I was in no way opposed to labor organizations or to those people who saw fit to join them, but for myself, naturally I was opposed to the proposed closed shop in the theatre which I had been given to understand would, if put through, force me to leave the stage, as I would no longer be permitted to act with my own company. I added that it was my earnest hope that all present difficulties could be adjusted.
>
> The exquisite and idiotic vanity which I understand is attributed to me by Frank Gillmore [head of Actors' Equity], in his implication that I would feel myself so hampered emotionally as to be incapable of acting under altered conditions, would be merely something to laugh at, if it did not seem to me the intention behind it was deliberately malicious. . . .
>
> So far as trade unionism in the theatre is concerned, and in this I allude to the stage hands' union, I have rarely had anything but fair play, and when a difference has arisen it has been the fault of the individuals, not the organization. I employ as well, and seem to make comfortable and happy, many members of Actors' Equity, but I did say that it was my personal belief that the rules which applied to other unions, such as plasterers, carpenters or bricklayers, could not be made to work successfully with the art of acting; that if a whistle were blown in the middle of a rehearsal it would be difficult to return on the next whistle and pick up emotions like a hod of bricks. Unfortunately, this is a phrase-snatching day, and in the statement alleged to have come from me the bricklayers seem to have won out over the plasterers and the carpenters, that's all.
>
> . . . As I am permitted, under present regulations, to appear on the stage for one more year, I would deem it a great favor if you would publish this merely to acquaint the members of unions who have worked for me with the fact that I am in no sense their foe, and to absolve me, in the eyes of such theatre-goers as are interested in me, from any ridiculous sense of my own importance.

She did have enough sense of her own importance, however, to want to decide for herself what her actors were worth. She remarked, during the *Hippolytus* rehearsals, to her stage manager, Jerome Collamore, on the markedly unequal talent of her company:

> And I have to pay them all the same. Equity has taken all bargaining power from me. I won't live to regret this, Jerry, but you will. Now the minimum is the maximum. The

actor playing beside you is not nearly as good an actor as
you, but he gets exactly the same salary. No one is paid his
worth. (C, 13.8.85)

Back at the Curran in San Francisco, as a companion piece
to *A Woman of No Importance*, M.A. introduced Orrick Johns's
"Joyous fantasy in three acts" called *A Charming Conscience*. It
tells the story of how the New York socialite Jacqueline
Fellows (M.A.) saves Penelope Sterling (Janet Cameron) from
throwing herself into the East River; how a revitalized
Penelope woos and wins Jackie's former husband, Freddie
(Henry Mowbray); how Penelope's own supposedly dead
husband, Forbes (Wheeler Dryden), turns up after she has
married Freddie; and how Jackie gets Penny back to Forbes
and herself back to Freddie; and how all troubled consciences
are charmed by the outcome especially Jackie's, which is, of
course, the conscience of the title.

What M.A. describes to Paul Kester as "a most amusing bit
of nonsense in which I think you would delight," *Variety* (9.8.23)
characterizes as "a futuristic, scenically crazy drawing room
farce . . . which keeps the audience, for the most part,
bubbling with merriment."

> The role of Jacqueline [it continues] is handled by Miss
> Anglin in her delightful comedy style, but with all her
> cleverness in this sort of vehicle she looks a bit too matronly
> to ideally suit it.

Very witty and urbane, nonetheless, and always hospitable San
Francisco was willing to embrace her *embonpoint* for the sake
of her charm; but other cities were less indulgent, and *A
Charming Conscience* was not destined to become a
breadwinner.

"Incidentally," says Jerome Collamore, "Wheeler Dryden,
who applied to me for a job in S.F., was a half bother to
Charlie Chaplin. Illegitimate. Chaplin would do nothing for
him and he didn't have enough to eat. I got him into the
company and he played well [the absent-minded, poetical,
'lost' husband]. Then he went behind my back and tried to
get my job from Howard" (C, 13.8.85). And Howard promptly
offered to send Wheeler back to short rations.

Before staging *A Charming Conscience* in August, M.A. had
introduced what she fondly hoped would be the *magnum opus*
of her middle years: this was the long-pondered and labored-
upon dramatization of Dickens' great mystery novel *Bleak
House*. She had more or less commissioned Paul Kester to

devise such a play for her, and as the script arrived in various stages of completion, usually at Katonah, M.A. would overscore it with the desired revisions and send it back—she described the process as "manufacturing Chesney Wold at Cedar Wold."

On Monday 16 July 1923 the play, entitled *The Great Lady Dedlock*, was unveiled at the Curran Theatre in San Francisco and was both indulgently and cordially received. Indulgently, because of the excessive length of the piece:—"The opening performance with its attendant delays dragged out to the midnight hour" (*S.F. Bulletin*, 17.7.23). Cordially, mainly because of its considerable success in capturing a genuine Dickensian atmosphere:—"The characters of this beloved writer literally step from the pages of his book and strut upon the stage, manifesting all of the quaint peculiarities with which their creator endowed them." *Variety* (26.7.23) praises the set designs of Dickson Morgan (Chesney Wold) and Dean Arnold (London slums) as "cunningly capturing the Dickens flavor. . . . The costumes, also true to the Dickens period, are by Lucien Lebaudt":

Margaret Anglin [says Walter Rivers of the *Bulletin*] deserves acclaim on two counts, first as a producer and secondly for her truly extraordinary portrayal of a dual role, that of the Great Lady Dedlock and the fiery, tempestuous Frenchwoman Hortense. The transitions of the star from the quiet sweet dignity of the name character to the cunning, scheming, temperamental and nefarious Hortense reveal the scope of her art beyond cavil. The role of Hortense gives Miss Anglin the greater opportunities, for as the unscrupulous serving woman she dominates every scene in which she appears.

M.A. (who played some of the Hortense scenes barefoot) went the length of having all of Kester's Hortense speeches translated into French (by R.E. Francillon) and then literally re-Englished (by herself), the better to show off her French accent, of which she said "I am a little vain."

It would appear that this characteristic over-extension of her physical and mental energies was her way of fighting off "the blue devils" which, as she began to "friser la cinquantaine" (approach fifty), were becoming ever more leech-like, visiting her especially with chronic insomnia (K, 14.11.23).

"Next to the star," continues Rivers, "the acting honors fall upon the shoulders of John J. Ivancovich as Mr. Tulkinghorn, the spider-like, pitiless solicitor." His performance "would have warmed the heart of Dickens" while it "chilled the spectators." "Inspector Bucket, as played by [the recycled] Wheeler Dryden, is the very essence of Dickens," while "Esther Summerson by Janet Cameron is a charming and sweet characterization." These sentiments are almost echoed in an unusually self-effacing letter from M.A. to P.K. after a week's run at the Mason Opera House in Los Angeles (K, 10.8.23):

> Ivancovich as Tulkinghorn was amazingly good. I hope we can hold him in reserve for future productions. . . . Dryden as Bucket was very well and workmanlike, but I covet a man of much more authority, more able to dominate me in my scenes. . . . Janet Cameron as Esther was lovely and a picture to look at. . . . I have a portfolio full of notes and impressions to be gone over and suggestions from people of taste and intelligence that I think worth considering, but I shall await consultation with you before acting on any of them.

In Chicago in March of '24, despite a number of trimmings and tightenings, the play still ran from 8:30 to 11:35, and that half hour of unpaid overtime tended to put the reviewers out of humor. Ashton Stevens of the *Herald* (12.3.24) supposes that the sheer physical strain of all the entrances and exits and costume changes hurt M.A.'s acting, which he describes as "falsely keyed" in both roles—Hortense too manic, Lady Dedlock too "heart-on-sleeve." Whereas Rivers gives the palm to her Hortense, "a vicious, fiery, vindictive, cunning creature . . . —a fine bit of artistry," William McDermott of the *Cleveland Plain Dealer* (25.3.24) prefers her sadly stately Lady Dedlock: "Miss Anglin can be regal with more grace and plausibility than any of her contemporaries with the possible exception of Ethel Barrymore, and it is as the imperious Lady Dedlock rather than as the wicked Hortense that she reaches her true stature in this piece."

> . . . When she is put on the rack, her past revealed, her daughter threatened with tragedy, herself thrown upon the mercies of a cruel and unscrupulous man, the drama assumes a life and a power to stir and enkindle that makes it first rate and memorable theatrical entertainment.
>
> I don't remember anything finer in the year than Miss Anglin's perfect evocation of a tortured mind and a torn heart.

Still, the play was clearly one that just missed, as did the accent that Miss Anglin devised for Hortense—both were just a little confused and confusing.

> Perhaps the basic problem [says the *Chicago Journal*, 11.3.24] is Mr. Kester's apparent assumption that his audience will have read the book, or at least a plot summary. That, in these days of the flying films and the raging radio, is an overestimation of the public's reading habit.

As for the dual-role performance (first conceived by Fanny Janauschek in a turn-of-the-century *Bleak House*), Charles Collins of the *Chicago Record* (12.3.24) allows that "technicians could ask for no more in such a cause, and Miss Anglin again gives an exhibition of 'acting as a fine art,'" but his implication has the same force as the flat statement of the *Christian Science Monitor* (19.3.24): "The feat has more the nature of a stunt than of characterization."

And speaking of feats, it was in the spring of '24 in Chicago that M.A. upstaged the great Marshal Ferdinand Foch at the opening of the Edward Hines Hospital. On that occasion she read, in French, Jules Bois' poem "L'Imitation du héros" to such telling effect that the largely unilingual audience was moved to tears, and the silver-haired marshal was moved to kiss the hand of the golden-tongued actress (GN, 72).

The Great Lady Dedlock, which was given some sixty performances in the summer of '23 and the spring of '24, was an expensive failure in terms of money and of physical and psychic energy for M.A., who was not only leading woman, manager and producer, but virtually co-author as well. And this ill-fated *Bleak House* play was to hang over her head (and Kester's), like a Chancery suit, until the conclusive New York, New Year's failure of '29.

After putting *Lady Dedlock* into dry dock at the end of August of '23, M.A. toured western Canada with *The Woman of Bronze* as her main vehicle, and Winnipeg at least was more than ready for her high-tension emotionalism. "Never," says the *Winnipeg Free Press* (18.9.23), "has the Walker [Theatre] season opened with such an abundance of creative worth. . . . Rarely is acting so impressive, imaginative and sincere seen on the stage today. The audience last night was profoundly appreciative of its unusual opportunity and following the frenzied outburst of the final scene recalled Miss Anglin after the second act again and again." This is a far cry from the chilly reception S. Morgan-Powell accuses Canada of according her greatest thespian, and it may well have been from just such a sense of warm Canadian welcome that Margaret was called to the deathbed of her mother in October of 1923. The sensitive and spirited Ellen McTavish Anglin (1843-1923) had been laid low by a stroke in the spring of '23 and had lingered through the summer and early fall in a condition of partial paralysis and almost total blindness, so that her passing on 25 October could not but have been seen as a blessed deliverance. And that is perhaps the sense we may gather from a reference to it in a letter from M.A. to Paul Kester (14.11.23):

> It must seem infamous to you that I have not contrived to get a line off to you since my desperate journey two weeks ago, but while there was much of beauty and consolation in everything that attended Mother's passing away and being laid at rest, I still took it rather hard in spite of my efforts to be sensible about it and it did not leave me in very good shape to renew my work.

The *Ottawa Citizen* (26.10.23) contains this retrospective paragraph:

> During her husband's Speakership Mrs. Anglin was regarded as one of the most cultured and accomplished hostesses in the brilliant social life of the Ottawa of the day. She possessed a cultured soprano voice of rare beauty, and her singing at the frequent evening entertainments in the Speaker's Chambers was a notable feature of the programme provided. She also took leading parts in operettas given at Rideau Hall during the brilliant Dufferin regime. During her life in St. John, N.B., also, she was widely known for her charming social functions.

"Mrs. Anglin," continues the *Citizen*, "is survived by four sons, all of whom have distinguished themselves in their various fields of endeavor." (In the cases of Frank and Arthur, big legal successes, and Basil, a success in oil, this was certainly true; but in the case of T.W. Jr. [Wanny], the charming black sheep of the family, a not very successful New York confidence man, it was perhaps stretching a point.) "Her elder daughter, Miss Margaret Anglin (Mrs. Howard Hull), the celebrated actress, was also present. Her younger daughter (Eileen), Mrs. Thomas Hutchins, the wife of Captain Thomas Hutchins, U.S.N., is at present residing in Peking, China."

The *Ottawa Journal* (26.10.23) tells us that "others present" at the funeral included:

> The Rt. Hon. Rodolphe Lemieux, Speaker of the Commons, the Rt. Hon. W.S. Fielding, Acting Prime Minister, the Hon.

L.P. Brodeur, Lieut.-Governor of Quebec, the Rt. Hon. L.P. Duff, M.P., Sir Louis Davies, Sir George Perley, Sir Henry Drayton, . . . [and] Thomas D'Arcy McGee, [B.A., LL.B., nephew of the assassinated "silver-tongued orator"].

Mary-Margaret had, of course, been very close to her mother in the early days of her career (after T.W.'s death), often travelling with her on her tours, later living with her in New York, and later still providing her with her own substantial apartment. After her marriage she even set mother up in a little villa near Verona where she could be near her voice instructor—Ellen at this time was pushing seventy, but Margaret had no hesitation in indulging her whim. In 1922 and '23 Margaret was paying her fairly substantial medical bills.

After finally having to concede a costly defeat in the *Lady Dedlock* venture in the spring of '24 (She told Kester in October that she had lost $27,000 on the production), M.A. found herself "prevented from playing through the summer by Actors' Equity" (K, 6.10.64)—earnings from which she had "counted on to finance a season in New York." But then, she couldn't get a New York Theatre anyway—she had already gone through "eight weeks of hell, 'unshirted hell,' as Howard likes to call it," at the beginning of the year in the effort (K, 9.2.24).

An article in the *N.Y. Telegram* of 19 April 1924 tells the story of the plight of the rising young actress Margalo Gillmore, daughter of the head of Equity. Equity, she feared, was about to call a strike, and her role of the heroine in *Outward Bound* might, in that case, fall to Ruth Chatterton "of the Fidelity ranks, . . . so that at least one good play and one leading theatre could remain open in case of the strike." The other leading roles were assigned by the theatrical speculators to Otis Skinner, Louis Mann, May Irwin, Margaret Anglin and Henry Miller. These staunch anti-unionists, incidentally, found a new or rediscovered amity arising from their common cause, especially the last two mentioned. As it happened, of course, the '24 strike was averted, and Equity had its way in all or at least most things, to the confusion of Miss Anglin and her colleagues of the actor-manager class.

Finally, on 2 September 1924, by way of the good offices of the Shubert brothers (Lee and Jacob), she managed to get permission to produce Pinero's *Iris* at Stamford, Conn., under the management of Fred Erlanger and Mary Kirkpatrick. The production began auspiciously enough, and was accorded laudatory reviews by *Variety* and by both the Stamford papers,

In the title role of *Caroline*, by W. Somerset Maugham, which played intermittently from 1916 to 1929: "America's Best Loved and Most Notable Star."

the *Sentinel* and the *Advocate*. The titular heroine, played, of course, by M.A., is a merry widow who, in course of keeping a rich ugly man and a poor handsome man dancing to her tune in tandem, finally gets caught out and thrown out. "It is a remorseful study of downfall," says *Variety* (17.9.24), "yet Miss Anglin makes a sympathetic role of the woman."

If *Variety*'s praise ("well staged," "especially capable company") is restrained, that of the Stamford papers is not:

> Miss Anglin dominates the play throughout [says the *Advocate*, 3.9.24]. In changing moods, and especially in passionate scenes, she is at her best. . . . Frequent applause indicated appreciation of superb acting.

And the *Sentinel* (3.9.24) appears to be reacting to the first night of a sure-fire hit:

> *Iris* is an exquisite jewel, flashing in its lines, with a brilliance which is a facet of the plot cut crystal clear. And from the depths of this jewel, Margaret Anglin, breathing emotion, lives upon the stage—not as the famous actress that she is—but as Iris Bellamy, a woman whose life is caught in the meshes of love and of luxury.

But (perhaps not surprisingly) this exquisite jewel failed to catch the frippery eye of the average theatre-goer and after a little over a month on the eastern seaboard it died and was quietly laid to rest. M.A. wrote to Paul Kester in October in this despondent vein:

> We tried out *Iris* hoping it might be something to go on with. It wasn't. And now I have had to sell myself to a further tour of one-night stands, playing an old play for Mr. [George C.] Tyler with William Faversham.
>
> Bills are facing me which must be met, and I need not tell you how thoroughly discouraged I am.
>
> I can get no one in New York to take the slightest interest in *Lady Dedlock*. I have tried in every way I know. I would have to have my own money with which to back it. I am out now on it over $27,000, and of course I don't have to tell you that I can't go any further. It is all a very, very bitter disappointment to me, and I have worried myself ill more than once over it.
>
> I am trying to arrange to go to Australia in the Spring, and perhaps I can produce the play there where I feel they would like it. (K, 6.11.24)

She was also, at this time, dickering with London re. *Lady Dedlock* ("it would be a splendid vehicle for me to have in London" [K, 10.12.24]), also some Wilde and Pinero stuff; but her resolutely high asking price spoke more of her pride than her pragmatism, and London backed off.

So she did sell herself to the gruelling business of seven months of one-night standing in an old play for Mr. Tyler. The play in question was the old English play *Forget-Me-Not* by Merivale and Grove cunningly revamped by Zoe Atkins ("author of *Déclassée*") under the title of *Foot-Loose*. The story concerns the skulduggery of the Marquise (Stephanie) de Mohrivart, a middle-aged courtesan whose son has committed suicide after involving a young upper-class Englishwoman, Alice Verney, in a compromising correspondence. The marquise (who now holds the letters) threatens to ruin Alice's marriage prospects if the Verneys do not make her (Stephanie) a member of their household and re-launch her into fashionable society. However, Alice's friend, Sir Horace Welby, digs up a Corsican called Barrato whom the marquise had commissioned to kill her aged husband and then betrayed to the police. Merely allowing Barrato to appear in the grounds is enough to rid the Verney household (in Rome) of the succubus-like Stephanie.

The reviewers are almost disconcertingly unanimous in agreeing with the *N.Y. Times* critic in considering the part of the poisonous marquise as "just right" or "an ideal role" for M.A.:

> Margaret Anglin [says the *St. Paul Pioneer*, 21.4.25] is indeed a shrewd selection for this unscrupulous intriguer. Her Stephanie is consistently hard and frivolous, a cynic whose moments of sentiment are never to be credited. Miss Anglin's brittle and staccato utterance serves continuously to deepen the impression of embittered ruthlessness. Her successful resistance of the temptation to sentimentalize the role is to be praised. She has painted the portrait of a middle-aged woman of pleasure grasping with desperation at the things [security and respectability] which youth was content to see flung away. As such it contains a great deal of artistry, —artistry of a strangely uncompromising sort.

The *St. Paul News* (21.4.25) is only a little less admiring:

> . . . as the marquise she is persuasively heartless, Parisian, and very hard. Some of her mannerisms are strikingly effective, although, to me, her habit of continually breaking off sentences by unexpected pauses becomes a little annoying. But then the Marquise de Mohrivart is supposed to be a little annoying.

In *Foot-Loose*, Zoe Atkins is treading the treacherous ground of the past and present of a woman of thoroughly bad character, whose peccadilloes include adultery, perjury, blackmail and murder, but she treads it lightly and artfully,

> and all references [to the criminous] have been clothed in refined language, wholly inoffensive, yet sharp and impressive. There is just enough comedy, contributed principally by Miss Anglin, to supply relief from the heavier moments. (*Yorktown Vindicator*, 15.5.25)

As for the acting of William Faversham, still an imperially slim six-footer and darkly handsome, though a touch grizzled, at fifty-six, the *Pioneer* is absolute in its praise of his portrayal of the resourceful Sir Horace:

> In this rendition those suave arts which one has long admired in him are revealed in their fulness. No one can play the mature worldling as he can. . . . That this role could be better played is simply unimaginable.

The tour as an extended nostalgia trip recalling the heady days of their 1900 hit *Brother Officers*, when she was "a jewel of a girl" as Baroness Royden, and he was "a tower of strength" as the stalwart Lieutenant John Hinds, V.C., had much of the shine taken off it by Faversham's ongoing affair with the play's young heroine Edith Campbell Walker who, says the *Vindicator*, "is extremely pleasing in the role of a fashionable, well-bred Englishwoman, observant of all the niceties of manner."

> Faversham [M.A. told Kester] is inclined to be very friendly, but, without wishing to be in any way scandalous (as I have no occasion to be), he has a shadow in the person of our leading woman, and I have not seen them apart for any five minutes since the company was organized. . . . Still he is very amiable when one does succeed in diverting his attention, and of course plays with great charm. (K, 1.11.24)

Before the end of the run, the twice-divorced Faversham had in fact married the extremely pleasing Miss Walker (thirty years his junior), but after six months found her less pleasing and added her to his list of discards.

Foot-Loose, which opened in Richmond Va. on 1 November 1924, headed south from there, and the *N.Y. Tribune* of 30 November 1924 reports that

> Margaret Anglin and William Faversham in *Foot-Loose* are said to be scouring the Southern one-night stands like a

vacuum-cleaner, for the play has developed the power of absorbing $20,000 worth of gold dust weekly.

So there were consolations for the lack of Faversham's urbane company and the rigors of touring.   M.A. (though she had very extensive experience of it) never did quite come to easy terms with the nomadic life of one-night standing.   She confessed to Kester (K, 25.11.24), apropos of her lengthy separation from the affectionate if inept Howard, "already I miss him bitterly."   Four years earlier (5.2.20) she had queried the same correspondent, from Omaha, "Are there such things as homes and decencies and comforts?—I'm beginning to wonder.   I'm beginning to feel like Padraic Colum's "Old Woman of the Roads."   This rueful allusion might well prompt us to remark that the actress had in her possession a copy of *Wild Earth* with this inscription: "To Margaret Anglin/Homage/Padraic Colum/New Year 1921."

Loneliness (more than melancholy) was at this time a word of sad might in the Hull ménage, with Margaret almost continuously on the road and an apparently business-wise incompetent Howard relegated to desultory superintendency at Cedarwold.   "I am trying," wrote Howard, "to justify your love, if only as a superintendent.   God knows, if I am half one it is more than we will ever get, I do be thinking."   As part of his caretaker's job, he was once required to replaster a wall, on which occasion he quipped, "I find I am better at this than the expert wop, and the only thing I ever plastered is H. Hull."   On 10 May 1925 we find an allusion in the *N.Y. World* to

> a recent magazine article [which tells] of the loneliness of the lives of three of our great actresses, Mrs. Fiske, Mme. Duse, and Margaret Anglin.

It is a subject upon which Margaret was usually tight-lipped, but Howard was not.   One of his letters ends with this abrupt *cri de coeur*: "I am so bloody lonesome, but I love you, and that is why."   Some of the other lonely valedictions are considerably less laconic, as for instance: "It occurs to me to say some seeming something, not of remoteness, just a deep sense of my uselessness, and you bravely going away with no sleep, and, selfishly enough, my loneliness," and:

> The carpenter made a mistake today and said, "You know, even carpenters make mistakes."   "Ah," said I, "true, but you have no right to make all of them, it is in violation of the anti-trust law."   Clever? No. Well. I must run down

to the post with this. I don't want, and I know you know I
don't want any particular commendation, but do tell me
sometime that these long pages, badly written and worsely
spaced, are not altogether tiresome. As I look at the pile of
stuff on the floor beside me I honestly have an emotion
more than akin to trepidation. But it is all the medium I
have to escape a searing loneliness, and in the hope that
they please you I find solace, but you mustn't put up with
them on that account, how silly you would never say, and
how more than silly I should never ask. Good night, sweet,
good night. K.

Howard (pen name "K" for Kitty) was, like his friend Don
Marquis's cat Mehitabel, "toujours gai," always the life of the
party between his second drink and his sixth, and he carries
out the role in the letters, but can't help tipping his hand at
the end of one of them:

By the way, the last sentence of your telegram from Ann
Arbor was as follows: "SIGURK AS YOU REQUEST." I give
it up. I did not request anything so immoral as SIGURK.
All my love. It is best to be gay if I can, and I know it is
better to amuse if I can, but there is a gnawing love for you
which will never be satisfied though I live for ever. My
love, good night.

It does appear that Howard's emotionally erratic and
slightly dipsomaniac ways combined to make him an
impossible business manager, but they never seriously
impaired M.A.'s deep affection for her "mad dear one," and
the fey grace of the best of the letters suggests the reason
why. Howard was wont to refer to himself (as a letter-writer)
as a "garrulous old fool," and sometimes that is a fair
description, but just as one is beginning to agree with him he
will turn a phrase like "Garrulity is a quality in others which
prevents one from talking as much as one wishes. We all
suffer from it."

Towards the end of the *Foot-Loose* run, M.A. had a brief
and rather floppy fling with a melodrama entitled *Mariana*,
which, said the critic for the *S.F. Examiner* (6.5.25), "proved a
peculiarly inert vehicle even for so sprightly a post horse as
Miss Anglin. The theme of the play is patience, and for
patience the matinee throng was model, and without patience
Mariana would have died in the first or second act. The
obvious was rubbed in pretty hard."

On 17 May 1925 the seven months with *Foot-Loose* was
terminated with sighs of relief and full purses all round, and
on 30 May M.A. and the restively rusticating Howard set sail

for Europe aboard the *France* with such interesting co-voyagers as the writers Alexander Woollcott and Edna Ferber and the actors Carl Randall, Mary Eaton and Ruth Gordon. Miss Anglin told the gentlemen of the press at dockside that she was for the nonce just plain old Mrs. Howard Hull and that she really didn't care to be interviewed or photographed ("I'm scared speechless of those flashlights anyway"); but she could tell them that she was "going to England to see Rebecca West who is writing two plays for me"—i.e., dramatizing her novels *The Return of the Soldier* (1918) and *The Judge* (1922).

As it happened, Miss West was doing nothing of the kind; she was merely making some character and setting notes for the stage-writer Miss Anglin was to engage. M.A. ultimately did engage Gilbert Emery—"a gentleman as abrasive as his name" (K, 29.12.25)—author of *The Hero* (1921) and *Tarnished* (1923) and brother of Edward, male lead in her production of *Billeted*. Apparently Emery, who was also to play the title role, did contrive a stage version of *The Return of the Soldier* (the tale of a shell-shocked, amnesiac, war hero and his tearfully staunch village-belle fiancée), but it was never produced, as M.A. came to think of it as "rather sweet" but "dramatically inert." Nevertheless, the project allowed Margaret (and Howard) to spend a pleasant week with the always stimulating Rebecca (and her entourage of pigs and cats) at her country place in Buckinghamshire (N.Y. World, 6.12.25).

She returned to New York on 28 June and entrained immediately for St. Louis where Livingston Platt and her company were awaiting her arrival to stage a twelve-performance run of *Electra* to inaugurate the new alfresco Garden Theater. As she remarked to Paul Kester, it was yet another "exhausting" production feat for her, for besides having to run rehearsals for eight consecutive days (and nights) to get the show ready, she had to contend with the atmospherics of an unusually hot summer:

> The heat has been appalling. It was warm in London and Paris, but I was scarcely prepared for this. We had to rush from ship to train, only to arrive here with the thermometer high up in the nineties, where it has stayed for three weeks. (K, 15.7.25)

The *N.Y. Telegraph* (1.8.25) correspondent adds that a bumper crop of mosquitoes "received Miss Anglin's *Electra* with open jaws."

> Towards the end of rehearsals under the arc lights [he continues], when the great open-air theatre fairly reeked with

oil of citronella and the actresses were forced to bite their tongues in order to make their hands behave after the Grecian classical manner, one member of the company suggested that *Elektra* be rewritten to include the business of burning Chinese punk. When bats joined hands with the mosquitoes the actresses couldn't tell one from the other.

Miss Anglin was highly gratified with the St. Louis reception of *Elektra*. The Greek piece ran for two weeks to packed houses, the Garden Theatre holding 3,000 persons.

"Sweet are the uses of adversity" was apparently again M.A.'s watchword, for

> although [as the *St. Louis Star*, 7.7.25, observes] this is her fourth production of *Electra*, her performance is wonderfully fresh and spontaneous in its evocation of the primal emotional impulses, the elemental human passions of filial love and hate and revenge.

The *St. Louis Globe* (7.7.25) critic characterizes the entire production as "a fine and stirring example of art in high degree, . . . just what we need to forget the heated season." He particularly remarks that for the "unbroken hour and forty minutes" playing time "the 3,000 spectators sat stilled and hushed as if spell-bound," but at the conclusion "the entire audience rose and cheered, yea, veritably made our suburban welkin ring with loud huzzas."

The orchestral music, the Furst score (all vocal music was eliminated), was excellently performed under William Parsons (J, 224); the massive set (Agamemnon's palace), by Joseph Solari, was sombrely, rather Egyptianly, impressive (J,235); while the overall staging, lighting and costuming were, as usual, excellently contrived by Livingston Platt. It all added up to what Richard Stokes of the *St. Louis* Post-Dispatch (7.7.25), a little hyperbolically, calls "a master work of all time, . . . a monument of fair and stately beauty." With such words from the all-too-often heartless press, how could Miss Anglin fail to be "gratified"?—especially if one were to add, as does Mildred Adams (*Toronto Globe*, 13.7.27), that "when she gave St. Louis two weeks of Greek tragedy, even the local baseball team fell into the habit of enthusiastic attendance."

This impressive production, whose expenses were underwritten by a committee of prominent St. Louis merchants, ended up with a net loss of $5,000, but M.A. was guaranteed $7,500 clear to pay herself, her company, and travelling expenses, which probably left about $2,500 for herself, and that was gratifying too (J. 187).

Back in New York at the end of July she graciously accepted a certificate naming her "honorary adviser" to the John Murray Milton School of the Theatre (*New York American*, 31.7.25); this certificate she was able to add to the one given her on 1 April 1924 at Berkeley declaring her "illustrious adviser" to the English Club of the University of California.   Such prettily documented honors were all very well, she thought, but they did not put bread on the board or wine in the decanter of one against whom the unionized theatre was steadily closing ranks.

Apropos of decanters, it may be observed that while Howard had a drinking problem, M.A. never did.   She quite simply accepted social drinking as one of the amenities of life, and never stinted herself or her guests, this side of intoxication—even in the dry years of Prohibition (1919-33). Indeed, a passage from one of her letters of this period (15.3.23) to Paul Kester suggests that Prohibition was less a serious hindrance than an amusing challenge to affluent drinkers of the twenties:

> We wished you were with us yesterday at Antoine's [in New Orleans] where we dined on such delicacies as only Antoine can provide, and *wined* via a green tea-pot, strainer and all—it was the most amusing camouflage I have seen up to date.

Among other tell-tale phrases in the Kester papers is the following: (K, 15.1.22).

> I loved your letter—it is locked behind the decanter [Scotch], as the only worthy shrine I could think of, to await Howard's return.

The Mary-Howard household, as it came to be known, seems always to have had a well-stocked liquor cabinet in season and out, and throughout the twenties Howard at Cedarwold can be seen manfully attempting to ration himself to six ounces of gin or scotch per day, and often succeeding. In one of his letters to Margaret we hear this protestation of injured innocence:

> I am a little bewildered about the blast of excoriation about the Capri bill—it was as much *ours* as anything on earth ever was.   Miss Johnson did come up and had meals with you and me, and took dictation and requests for errands, and got back to the *Globe*; also there was Alice [Kauser], Ralph [Kemmet] and innumerable times [Livingston] Platt. As a matter of fact, we rarely had a meal alone together, so

I may not rest under the imputation of mounting a huge bill, mostly for liquor—though I don't believe you really meant it. But one thing, as the fire dies, it was never rendezvous.

The rest of 1925 was markedly anticlimactic. Most of August and September was spent (reasonably unfretfully) loafing, hiking, riding and naturalizing among the pleasant wooded hills and streams of Cedarwold; most of October and November trying to find a theatre and financial backing for *Lady Dedlock* and/or *The Return of the Soldier*.

On 16 November 1925, after much cajolery and blandishment on the part of the "Vaudeville Solons," who had been "flirting with Miss Anglin for ten years," she finally succumbed to the lucrative lure of the "two-a-days." "Howard Hull," says the *N.Y. Telegraph* (19.11.25), "will attend to the active management." Her first vaudeville vehicle was "a witty comedy drama playlet entitled *Radio*," which tells the story of a woman who chooses the obvious loser of her two suitors because he and she happen to be on the same mental wavelength. In the course of rehearsal M.A. came to have increasingly serious doubts about the playlet's alleged wittiness, and abandoned it in favor of another triangular one-acter called *The Terrible Woman* by W.B. Steele in which the woman of the title, who is in reality an amiable scatterbrain, is by a series of ridiculous misunderstandings implicated in various forms of moral turpitude. This inane playlet, too, proved a barren stock, and M.A. herself broke off the trial-basis contract.

Indeed, so obscure was this effort that in February of '26, when M.A. again contracted with the B.F. Keith Co. for a vaudeville run, her opening was again generally referred to as her debut in vaudeville. This time, with a thoroughly congenial role, that of a famous actress at odds with a dramatist, a stage director and an envious husband, in Nita Faydon's *Nature vs. Art*, she was amply successful:

> The star of melodrama and classic Greek plays [says the *Brooklyn Citizen*, 21.2.26] takes to vaudeville with the ease of the true artiste at home in every department of the theatre. She has an unerring sense of place [sic] and tempo and has easily adapted her comedy methods to the conditions of the music hall.

The *Brooklyn Standard* reviewer is especially struck by the unexpected and arresting note of high drama that M.A. succeeded in injecting into the essentially frivolous music-hall ambience:

In what has been billed as a "sparkling little comedy,"
Margaret Anglin gives a tense few moments of acting
wherein she shows the difference between acting and reality,
a paradoxical situation nicely handled. In the play being
rehearsed within the play, Miss Anglin has the part of a
married woman who learns that her husband has just died.
The scene is carried on with a highly emotional flow of
words. A laugh follows, accompanied by the applause of
her co-actor. Then the maid brings in a telegram
announcing that the actress's husband has been killed. There
is a breathless catch of the throat, and a silence more
eloquent than any words could be. But then the husband
(tactless villain) saunters in, laughing at the joke he has
played on his wife. The sobbing cry of relief is echoed
throughout the theatre.

Nature vs. Art was performed twice daily at the Palace (and
then the Albee) at 4:09 P.M. and 10:09 P.M. It lasted exactly
twenty minutes and was followed hard upon by a new series
of burlesque sketches by

Frank Fay, Broadway comedian of the razzle-dazzle, jazz
type, whose low comedy stood in pronounced contrast to
Miss Anglin's high comedy. (*New York Telegram,* 16.2.26)

An incidental piece of intelligence arising from the *Citizen*
review of *Nature vs. Art* is that M.A., who at this time was
beginning to accept all invitations to do dramatic readings,
had (with the assistance of Alice Kauser) learned to read
Greek:

She has mastered Greek and could address an Athenian mob
in the language of Démosthenes. Her reading of Homer in
the original Greek is a delight to the judicious, her deep
emotional voice rendering the vowelled undersong of the
rolling hexameters in billowy cadences.

She also learned the "big speeches" of *Medea* and *Electra* in the
original, and doubtless it was in this version that she regaled
her husband, probably in the summer of '22—for according to
the *Oakland Times* (6.5.26): "While travelling in Greece she did
the big Electra speeches for Howard Hull alone at Epidaurus."
    After making a tidy sum in her three weeks of "vode"
slumming, in which she was joined by the operatic soprano
Grace Moore, and which she describes to the *N.Y. Telegraph*
(16.2.26) as "great fun," she revived Maugham's *Caroline* (under
the management of William Streett) and opened on 12 April at
the Capitol in Albany, thence working gradually westward
with the object of joining Blanche Bates in San Francisco in

July for a collaborative summer season and of staging another *Electra* at Berkeley on 24 July. The adjective "sparkling" continues to appear regularly in the *Caroline* reviews, as the provinces remained dutifully appreciative of the breath of sophistication which the artificial comedy breathed. The Metropolitan in Minneapolis was appreciative enough to bill the leading woman as "Margaret Anglin, America's Best Loved and Most Notable Star."

At the age of 53, M.A. played the lead in the witty domestic comedy, *Candida*. (1926)

Chapter XI

Candida, Met. Electra, Macbeth: 1926-1928

Naught's had, all's spent,
Where our desire is got without content.
(Shakespeare, *Macbeth*, 3.2.5)

Before she happily joined forces with Blanche Bates in late June the tender-hearted Margaret was saddened by two middle-distance bereavements in mid-April. The first blow was the rather sudden and unexpected death (*aet.* 67) of Henry Miller (whom M.A. had always loved, in her fashion) from lobar pneumonia on 10 April 1926:

> I cannot tell you how shocked and saddened I am by the news of Mr. Miller's death. My association with him goes back to my early days in the theatre and there are many close ties between his family and mine. He was at all times a positive and powerful contributor to the life of the American theatre, and this nation has lost a fine actor and a true gentleman. (*Albany Times*, 11.4.26)

The other death (15 April 1926) was that of the cultivated and gracious Harriet Kester (*aet.* 81), the gently possessive mother of the rather lonely bachelor-playwright. News of Harriet's passing reached Margaret a week late, and she assures "dearest Paul" that

> had any word of it come to me earlier you should have had at least a poor message of love and sympathy —perhaps more love and sympathy than from anyone else . . .

It was the little-boy-lost, waif quality in the slim, attractive Kester that most appealed to M.A., and she wanted to mother him (at least by telepathy) in his time of sorrow:

> Howard is at Cedarwold and longs to have you spend the summer with him there. Can't you just shut up Wirtland for a while—I can't bear to think of you alone there.
> I feel you would have easy freedom on our little hilltop. Lena will see that you are well fed and decently cared for. You can be as much or as little alone as you choose—I won't be about to disturb you, except that my spirit will hover about you with loving tenderness. Ever your devoted Mary. (K, 21.4.26)

When she arrived in San Francisco on 23 June the *Chronicle* interviewer found "the great tragedienne" not the least elegiac in mood or manner:

> She is [on the contrary] filled with a distinctly modern pep and verve. She is keen and snappy and up to the minute in her ideas. Her blonde hair is bobbed in the latest shingle, her hat and frock have the Parisian touch, and she shows an almost prophetic understanding of the psychology of modern audiences and admits that she goes to the movies to find out just what are the going things.

And she finds that movie fans like melodrama, the vigorous play of strong emotions, "hate and fear and love and hunger," and they like to be scared by "the great crisis, the great and daunting question, death." And, therefore:

> This year I am planning as the big feature of our season to produce *Tosca*. It has not been given as a dramatic production except in opera form for years. It was written for Sarah Bernhardt and was played with great success by Fanny Davenport. It has the romance and the emotional quality that I feel sure people want.

But the big *Tosca* went the way of the big *Romeo and Juliet*, up, for want of backers, in a slightly acrid smoke of "regrets."

The Bates-Anglin opening was, however, everything the two divas could have wished. The *S.F. News* (7.7.26) headline runs: "Anglin-Bates Season in Brilliant Opening," while the *Chronicle*'s reads: "Anglin, Bates, Co-Stars, Win Deserved Ovation." Blanche Bates starred in the one-act opener, *Peg the Actress*, adapted by her husband George Creel from Charles Reade's novel *Peg Woffington*:

> As the fiery Peg, actress of parts and of which her heart is no small bit [says the *News*], Miss Bates has a role which, with its rapid transitions from comedy to heartbreak and back to comedy again, affords her, in the short space of time allotted, full opportunity to run the gamut of emotion and to carry her audience with her in rapt attention through both laughter and tears.

The same critic contents himself with simply asserting that "as Caroline Ashley, to whom the realization of widowhood falls far short of anticipation, Miss Anglin is at her brilliant best, than which higher praise cannot be written."

Edith Bristol of the *Chronicle* is a little more specific:

> Miss Anglin's ability in comedy of the subtle, satiric variety animates the play and gives the motif for a production that

is at once delicate, deft and delightful. The lines have a wealth of not unkind, but truly keen wit, quite the Maugham touch in the phrasing and quite the Anglin touch in the intonation.

Miss Bristol concludes her review with the observation that the collaboration of the Misses Bates and Anglin provides "not only a rare opportunity for San Francisco audiences":

> but it constitutes, both stars declare, the gratification of a long-cherished ambition ever since as two young girls in New York they played together in the company of James O'Neill in *The Three Musketeers*. Their friendship has continued since that first engagement together, but this co-star appearance is their first opportunity to play together.

Thirteen years earlier the *Theatre Magazine* (August 1913) interviewer confessed to Miss Bates that she and M.A. were his favorite actresses:

> When I told her how often I had wished to see her and Miss Anglin as co-stars, she said that she had dreamed of such a combination herself, and had even talked of it with Miss Anglin, but that when "Maggie" had suggested that they start with *East Lynne*, her courage failed her, as she felt herself unable to contend with Miss Anglin in such a part as Lady Isabel.

The genial Blanche, by the way, appears to be the only one who ever called Miss Anglin "Maggie." M.A.'s pet name at home was "[Queen] Mab," or, occasionally, perhaps cryptically, in Howard's letters, "Anemone."

Margaret and Blanche, coincidentally, both came out professionally in 1894 and both were big successes in the *Shrew*, and while Margaret was starring in *The Great Divide* the Oregon-born Blanche was scoring in *The Girl of the Golden West*. Blanche also shared with Margaret her love of horses and opera and her conversational aplomb. Despite being very similar positive charges (and physical look-alikes to boot), they combined well both histrionically and socially. Indeed, in the fall and winter of '27 Margaret took over Blanche's flat in Manhattan. At the time of their west-coast coalition Margaret was just past fifty and Blanche just shy of fifty-three.

The next Anglin-Bates collaboration was *Candida*, in which M.A. took the title role. Of this production the *Chronicle* (20.7.26) declares:

> It is to be doubted that this charming and mordant domestic comedy has ever been done so wittily this side of London.

Margaret Anglin as the keen, subtly understanding and quietly dominating wife and Blanche Bates as the self-sufficient and surprising typist Prossy, give finished portrayals.

The *Los Angeles Express* reviewer is particularly impressed with Miss Bate's adroit handling of the role of the pert Prossy "with a whimsical turn and quaint touch that are delightful." The article goes on to observe that

> Beauty and drama are nicely blended by Miss Anglin in the triangular situation in which Candida is made to choose between her husband, the parson, and the sensitive, love-hungry poet of eighteen.   Her expressive voice and simplicity of movement lend strength and nobility to the scene.

The Swinburne-like Marchbanks is played "with apt aestheticism" by Ralph Roeder (himself a youngish poet), while the muscular-Christian Morell is played with equally apt "hale-fellow-well-met-ism" by J.R. Tozer—two of M.A.'s regular male leads.

Candida was followed by, and later alternated with, a production of Zoe Atkins' comedy *The Texas Nightingale*, in which (according to the *S.F. Examiner*, 20.7.26) a suitably "mercurial," and even "mellifluous" Blanche Bates took the title role of Waco's slightly addle-pated answer to Jenny Lind, "while Miss Anglin appeared as the manageress, a shrewd and witty businesswoman—a role completely different from anything she has yet been seen in." And, indeed, the shrewd businesswoman is something completely different from anything Miss Anglin ever was.

In order to simplify the double life of the Anglin-Bates summer season in San Francisco and Los Angeles and the July rehearsals for the Berkeley Electra, M.A. took to living in the theatre.   The *S.F. Examiner* of 29 June tells us that "Miss Anglin has rented the entire fourth floor of the Columbia Theatre and has fitted it out as an apartment."   It was to this warehouse-cum-apartment that George Warren of the *Chronicle* tracked her down on 5 July 1926, and there she told him this story of her Greek travels:

> When I was in Greece three years ago I made a pilgrimage to the places associated with the tragedies. I was in Corinth where Medea lived, and in Mycenae, which Agamemnon ruled.   I saw Aulis from a distance.   It is a rocky and forbidding coast, a fit setting for desperate deeds and dire resolutions.

When I was in Athens I had a wonderful day with Andromeda, the daughter of Heinrich Schliemann, the excavator of Troy and Mycenae. She allowed me to cherish in hand a wonderful array of ancient Trojan ornaments: rings and bracelets and other adornments, exquisite bits of carving—no jewels; just the gold, chased and engraved, and all so beautiful.

She asked me if I believed the body her father had taken from a tomb was really that of Agamemnon. I answered that I certainly did. "I am so glad," she said. "You know, we had it in the house here for a long time."

Her mother gave me a portrait of herself showing a headdress of gold that is believed to have belonged to Helen of Troy.

Once again Dionysus smiled on *Electra*, according the production a fine, sultry, starry night, a full house of 7,500 (doubled by one enthusiastic reporter to 15,000), and a near flawless performance by the company. By now M.A. had given seventeen performances and four productions of *Electra*, so it is not surprising to find that her performance on Saturday 24 July 1926 is described by the *S.F. Examiner* (26.7.26) as "magisterially secure."

Miss Anglin in the title role [says John Piper of the *News* (26.7.26)] was superb. As the daughter of a murderess sworn to avenge her father's death she faced the necessity of creating sympathy, while all her actions and words breathed hatred. This she did with subtle art . . . Her big scenes provided drama so gripping that to compare it with anything on the stage today would be travesty.

The fully expected Greek Theatre success prompted M.A. to schedule *Electra* performances at UCLA and the Hollywood Bowl in September:

Irving Pichel [Arnold Johnson tells us] was hired to make the arrangements; and Lloyd Wright, the son of Frank Lloyd Wright, was also commissioned to design the palace facade for the performance in the Hollywood Bowl—but the whole program collapsed when Miss Anglin could not get the needed sponsorship. (J, 267)

Earlier that year she had proposed to do a Greek season at Lewisohn Stadium at New York City College, but that institution had balked at her "extravagant" logistical demands (J, 266). Johnson also tells us that in 1924 she had offered to open the 80,000-seat Chicago Stadium with a synthetic trilogy of Greek plays to be made up of the *Iphigenia in Aulis* of

Euripides, the *Agamemnon* of Aeschylus and the *Electra* of Sophocles, to be presented on successive nights.

> She told the authorities [says Johnson] that she had the costumes and props but thought perhaps the productions could use at least twenty chariots and from two to three hundred supernumeraries. Although she spent many hours working out the details, the planning was wasted. Officials informed her that the Chicago Stadium was so wide that "no human voice could satisfactorily be heard in the auditorium."
> (J, 265)

As things worked out, M.A. continued her collaboration with Blanche Bates through the first fortnight of September, during which they played in the Hawaia Theatre in Margaret's dream city of Honolulu. After that "lovely little run," M.A. toured the south (minus Miss Bates) with *Candida* and *Caroline*, mostly the latter, mostly to "large" or at least "fair-sized" houses.

Salt Lake City found her performance of Caroline Ashley "brilliant and exhilirating" and loved the look of her play:

> *Caroline* [says the *Tribune*, 3.10.26] is charmingly adapted to Miss Anglin's delightful personality. She wears gorgeous Paris gowns, is seen in a boudoir scene which is the last word in stage settings, and makes every woman envious of its occupant.

This tour continued into the early weeks of 1927, at which time M.A. broke off to begin preparations for the *Electra* to end all *Electras* in response to an invitation from the Board of Governors of the Metropolitan Opera House of New York City. At the same time she was carrying on a series of negotiations with Minnie Fiske toward the establishment of an Anglin-Fiske coalition which would (of course) inject new life and brilliance into the now sluggish and turbid stream of the American theatre. For if Blanche Bates was a ranking exponent of domestic comedy and melodrama, Mrs. Fiske was widely considered to be the finest American actress in the area of social and psychological drama (J, 32), and (*pace* Julia Marlowe) M.A.'s chief American rival in high-style acting.

The overture to this proposed alliance would seem to have been made by Mrs. Fiske on 23 October 1925, for M.A. telegrammed an acknowledgement of her "most interesting scheme" on 24 October 1925. The scheme seems to have been that they should join forces in producing *The Merry Wives of Windsor* and take the parts of Mistress Page and Mistress

Ford.   M.A. asks at the end of a follow-up letter (29.8.25): "Which of the women would you like me to play? It is some years since I read the play and my recall of the parts is vague."

The next significant item of correspondence, a night letter dated 21 August 1926, finds Mrs. Fiske inviting M.A. to take the part of the maid Regina (the "good" Captain's illegitimate daughter) in her production of Ibsen's murky melodrama *Ghosts*, in which Minnie, of course, would play the multifariously tormented Helen Alving.

> Your superb performance [says Mrs. Fiske] would illuminate Regina which is actually one of Ibsen's most skillful parts. Will gladly play second fiddle to you in a future play. Think dignified joint appearance fine prelude to next season's big departure. Please wire soon.

The requested wire reads thus:

> Would love to play any fiddle with you. Cannot at present see my way out of existing plans. Might possibly find some way of compromising if could know date and tour, but not very hopeful—also feel too mature for part.   Sailing Honolulu Saturday.   Hawaia Theatre.   Return Sept. 15th. Address: Columbia Theatre, San Francisco. Love, Margaret.

The original plan seems to have been to play *Ghosts* at the end of '26 and begin *Merry Wives* in the spring of '27, but, as we have seen, M.A. followed the line of least resistance and readiest cash by taking the two Cs through the south at the end of '26 and working on the Met *Electra* in the spring of '27. In the spring of '26 (21 May) she had told Minnie that she was already drumming up publicity for the Fiske-Anglin company and that the "$2500 or $2600 a week" Minnie had offered Otis Skinner (as Falstaff) was much too high—he would surely settle for about half that, for "I do not think anything in the world would induce him to relinquish the opportunity with us."

But still Miss Anglin waffled, would not give Mrs. Fiske the clear and unequivocal commitment she needed to get the show on the road, and on 21 February 1927 Minnie wrote from Chicago to her husband-manager Harrison Fiske in New York:

> It is too bad that Miss Anglin has desired this long delay in announcing next season's plans. However, announcements or no announcements, I know you will be firm in following Mr. Erlanger's advice to begin the booking for next season in

a week or two. . . . The crazy bookings of *The Rivals* cost us a fortune in railroad expenses. We cannot afford this risk in the much larger enterprise of the *Merry Wives*.

But apart from all this there must come a time before many weeks when we should make a very earnest request to Miss Anglin that the announcement may be made.

On 21 March, Harrison Fiske felt so sure of M.A.'s ultimate agreeability that he issued a press release concerning the formation of "the Fiske-Anglin Theatre, a national touring organization":

> *The Merry Wives of Windsor* will be the first production of the Fiske-Anglin Theatre, Mrs. Fiske and Miss Anglin playing the two merry wives, and Otis Skinner, as guest star, will play Falstaff. . . . This production will be made on Oct. 24, when a 30-week tour of brief engagements will be begun.
>
> Modern American and foreign plays may be produced from time to time, but for the most part the two allied stars, with occasional guest stars will keep to the classics. We are confident that these annual tours will elicit such critical acclaim that the Fiske-Anglin name will constitute an iron-clad guaranty of high quality entertainment to audiences in our smaller cities. (*Boston Traveller*, 21.3.27)

Shortly after this manifesto went forth, Miss Anglin (perhaps unconsulted?) simply said "Thanks, but no, thanks" and "withdrew from the venture" (*MF*, 354). "Mary told me," says Jerome Collamore, "that Mrs. Fiske was hogging all the good parts, so she dropped the whole thing" (C, 3.8.85). Mrs. Fiske, shaken but undaunted, went ahead and signed Otis Skinner to a fat contract and engaged M.A.'s erstwhile neighbor and occasional rival, Henrietta Crosman, to play Mistress Ford. She produced the *Merry Wives* with moderate success in the spring of '28.

An overlay of irony now attaches itself to the laudatory article written that May in the *N.Y. Herald* (21.4.27) by Burns Mantle in which he votes for Margaret Anglin as "America's greatest actress" and which concludes:

> Next season, if present plans carry, Miss Anglin is to tour with Mrs. Fiske and William Faversham [sic] in a revival of *The Merry Wives of Windsor*. And, unless this prophet is completely out of touch with the sentiment of his time, that will be the supreme attraction of the theatre season of 1927-28.

And an air of the apocryphal attaches itself to the well-known anecdote, presumably referring to this time but given wide currency some years later by *Reader's Digest* (24.5.42):

> Margaret Anglin left the following note on Mrs. Fiske's dressing table: "Margaret Anglin says Mrs. Fiske is the best actress in America." Mrs. Fiske read it, added two commas, and sent it back to Miss Anglin. It now read: "Margaret Anglin, says Mrs. Fiske, is the best actress in America."

If the collapse of the Fiske-Anglin alliance was a sour note for M.A. in the spring of '27, the winning of the Laetare [Rejoice] Medal was a distinctly sweet one. The medal was awarded annually by Notre Dame University to the most illustrious and meritorious American Catholic layman not previously so honored. M.A., though her practice was not always perfect, was always proud and grateful to be a Catholic and always maintained many cordial clerical friendships. Thus it was with a full heart that she heard His Eminence, Patrick Joseph Cardinal Hayes, M.A., D.D., Archbishop of New York, welcome her as Guest of Honor to his house upon Ascension Day (5 May) 1927, and heard the Rev. Dr. P.J. Carroll, C.S.C, Rector of the University of Notre Dame, address these words to her before a select gathering of church and theatre notables:

> In your art and profession you have played many parts conspicuously well; and always in your portrayal beauty and virtue have gone together. This, we think, is not faint praise. For it is no small accomplishment to have always followed the guiding of an ideal, waving aside the hour's popular favor for the permanent recognition of the wise and for the comfort that comes from an approving conscience. Indeed, it is hardly less than heroic in these days to fight a good fight against the allurements of a success that is measured in money, and to stand in the ranks of those who patiently carry on the traditions of a very venerable art. You, whose name is already secure in the roster of theatrical nobility, are to prove yet again that there is no greatness but that which is erected on truth, no worthiness but that which is established upon virtue.
>
> The medal, then, which the University of Notre Dame confers upon you is not a gesture of encouragement for the rich promise of a flowering, but an act of recognition for the fullness of a fruitage. . . .

And so a misty-eyed M.A. ceremonially (officially, 26 March) joined the ranks of rejoice-worthy Catholic celebrities—a list which included a dozen literary persons, six jurists, four medical doctors, two generals, one admiral and, up till then, no actors. Among the scores of congratulatory letters and telegrams that reached her, two were particularly gratifying. The first (1.3.27) was from the eminent critic and director George Pierce Baker of Yale University who wrote: "It was a genuine pleasure to state to the University authorities my assurance that you thoroughly deserved the medal. It is an even greater pleasure to know that it is awarded to you." The second was from M.A.'s favorite actress, Julia Marlowe (Sothern), who wrote (27.3.27): "Edward and myself read with great satisfaction this morning of your new honors from the Notre Dame University. How wise they were to do this! And we are both very glad for your sake."

The presentation plan advocated by Professor (and poet) Charles Phillips of the Notre Dame English faculty was that the ceremony might take place on the stage of the Metropolitan Opera House either just before or just after the performance of *Electra*, but the rector of the university, though he was "personally very happy" to be the announcer and bearer of the prize of "the golden rose," was not quite willing to tread the boards to present it—hence the in-camera ceremony at the cardinal's residence.

The Met. *Electra* (3 and 4 May '27) was perhaps the greatest single success of M.A.'s career, and, considering the journeyman nature of her career over the past six years during which she had been a weary wayworn exile from the Great White Way, it came not a moment too soon. Frank Vreeland reviewing the play for the *N.Y. Telegram* at last produced the inevitable headline: "An Electric *Electra*." The electrified crowd, he tells us, "hung enthralled on her every word"; and if "the star" was at times "a little hoarse," still

> she seemed to me to be greater than ever, more spacious than ever, more like a harrowing cry from the lost centuries and the dead divinities.

And if she was "more ample of figure" than of yore, still

> that detracted not a whit from the statuesque sublimity of her performance. It made her power more all-embracing, like a prima donna voicing the Valkyrie cry of vanished cultures. In spite of her soon-forgotten matronly appearance, she managed to convey magically, hypnotically, the sense of a young, passion-driven creature caught up in a storm of grief and hate and vengeance.

Most of the critics were almost adulatory in their reviews, John Anderson of the *N.Y. Post* (4.5.27) being a notable exception in

MARGARET ANGLIN
AS ELECTRA

JAMES MONTGOMERY FLAGG
1927

For Mary —
from her
affectionate Aunt
Mary.

Still youthful and very beautiful, M.A. was painted by Montgomery Flagg in 1927.

his slightly acidulously expressed opinion that Miss Anglin felt
the ambience of the Opera House so strongly that she felt
compelled to sing her part:

> Upon the ironclad beat of the verse she set sail as upon the
> metallic sea at Coney Island, to rock back and forth in
> sonorous rhythms of rich and unrestrained declamation.
> There is, though, a dynamic and unfaltering power behind
> the portrayal, wrought into a sustained portrait of
> commanding proportions. While it tends strenuously to the
> same pitch, it is a robust picture, oracular, but woebegone.

R.D. Skinner of *The Commonweal* (18.5.27) agrees that vocally
she overpowered her co-players, but,

> though her diction did have the quality of a chant, the fine
> rhythm of a sustained phrasing, it was without the suspicion of
> being sung. It had, so to speak, cadence without cadenzas. It
> had the surge of tides but no scurrying wavelets.

Her Electra did indeed especially overpower Ralph Roeder's
rather pallid Orestes—and the big recognition scene, because
of his dimness,

> became a scene, not of mutual joy, but of momentary
> exaltation for Electra alone, made strong only through the
> seemingly boundless reservoir of Miss Anglin's power. Hers,
> after all, was the only performance of true greatness. I am
> not sure, in retrospect, that it does not stand forth as the
> only momentous and truly great performance I have seen on
> the English-speaking stage.

The great Polish pianist-composer-statesman, Ignace Pad-
erewski, concurred: "Yours," he told her after her opening
night performance, "is the power of great art."

Perhaps the most balanced and judicious critique was
contributed by Alexander Woollcott of the *N.Y. World* (4.5.27),
but even that sober critic allowed himself a rhapsodic

> Miss Anglin was, I thought, magnificent. At first she
> seemed to me a trifle prim and conscious of herself, fussing
> with her robes and getting all prepared to wince when
> Orestes should come on and ask, a thought critically, "Is this
> Electra's form I see?" But by the miracle of her voice
> always she filled the vast spaces of the Metropolitan with an
> ancient and matchless music. And when, as in the
> incomparable tingle and excitement of the recognition scene,
> she forgot herself and how she looked, forgot the audience,
> forgot the modern world and the last 3,000 years, a mighty
> glow was on her, and I knew again what I had known

before, that here at least was an actress whom one could call great, one who, from Sarah Siddons and a long, thronged past, caught up and handed on the torch of a great tradition.

And who, in turn, would one say, caught up that fiery torch of "the great tradition" from *her* hand? or, might one say it proved too hot for the after-comers to handle?

On the second night 3,500 spectators again packed the Met., and 600 last-minute ticket-seekers were regretfully turned away *(Toronto Globe, 13.7.27)*, and 18 curtain calls were answered by M.A. and all and sundry officially involved in the production, while a bravely and slightly tipsily smiling, unemployed Howard stood in the wings with M.A.'s pro-tem secretary and niece Basile Anglin, and intoned for her ears alone: "They also serve who only stand and wait."

In June, by way of coming down to earth, M.A. revived *The Woman of Bronze* at the Lyric on Broadway "at popular prices ($2 and down)." At these prices she got full houses, and for her own performance she got respectful notices. But the gallantly "serviceable" Bronze Jade fared less well. As Brooks Atkinson sees it,

> Even Miss Anglin (splendid though she is) cannot spare *The Woman of Bronze* the false theatricalism of motivation, characterization and dialogue. Seven years ago this melodrama seemed mildly distressing, though serviceable. Now it is lurid and mawkish. *(N.Y. Times, 16.6.27)*

Alison Smith of the *N.Y. World* (16.6.27) begins her review with this commentary on the datedness of the piece:

> Last night the Lyric Theatre again echoed to the choked sobs and murderous laughter of a wife who learns that her husband loves another. A few blocks down the street, at the Maxine Elliott, another wife makes the same discovery, greets it with sympathetic and tolerant calm and straightaway buys a ticket (for two) to Capri. And between Margaret Anglin's revival of *The Woman of Bronze* (dated 1920) and Ethel Barrymore's *The Constant Wife* (of the present season) there stretches a chasm of changing sentiment which might well represent seventy years instead of seven.

And E.W. Osborn of the *N.Y. Evening World* (16.6.27) ends his review, which harps on the same datedness theme ("Seven short years ago, but ah! the difference to now"), with the note:

> Details intended to give *The Woman of Bronze* a touch of up-to-the-minute were, besides others, a cigarette for Mrs.

Courtney [Marion Barney], a reference to Beatrice Lillie and a mention of Gershwin's music. And for the women, the short skirts of 1927.

As for the star herself, Osborn concedes,

> she acted with much of the fine distinction that is always hers. To us it seemed, pathetically, that there dwelt back of her endeavor of the evening a sort of courage which was not merely that of the woman of the play, facing desperately the issues of desertion and a perished dream . . .

A nice piece of detection, that, of Miss Anglin's sense of the handwriting on the wall of her own craft or sullen art, and of her ability to derive from it an extra fillip of stage pathos. She was in this effort stagily supported by a "picturesque" Mary Fowler "in a series of stained glass attitudes," and by Pedro de Cordoba, "looking like a distracted Dante in a frock coat."

In response to a personal invitation from Prime Minister Mackenzie King (10.5.27), M.A. interrupted the heavy schedule of *The Woman* ("9 performances a week" [K, 22.6.27]) to make a flying trip to Ottawa to read Bliss Carman's ode on the diamond jubilee of Confederation. Actually she had been asked to read a longer piece by Sir Charles Roberts, but she decided that brevity would be the soul of wit on such an overloaded oratorical occasion, and she undertook to get Bliss Carman to do a made-to-measure piece for the ceremony. She received this response (15.6.27) from New Canaan, Conn.:

> Dear Miss Anglin:
>
> "We strive to please" is our motto, so here you have the best the New Canaan School of Verse can do for you on the present occasion and trust it will serve.
> I enclose an extra copy which you might send to Mr. Mackenzie King, so that he can have it in time to use in any way he cares to. No copyright required.
>
> Sincerely,
>
> Bliss Carman.

Since Carman wisely omitted this poem from his collected works, it perhaps behoves us to reproduce it here:

> Dominion Day, 1927
>
> From Grand Pré with its brimming tides
> And orchards on every hand,

To our western gate on Georgia's Strait
Where wondrous mountains stand,
Whether bred to the sea or the hills or the plains,
We are born to one sacred land.

Our freedom we brought from Runnymede,
Our blood from Senlac Hill,
The heritage of our fathers' faith,
Good heart, and a steadfast will
To receive and uphold the living word—
These are our watchwords still.

The din of nations on the march
Resounds. We wait the Voice
That shall to every living soul,
Proclaim the mightier choice—
The reign of brotherhood, wherein
The man-god may rejoice.

The actress, it may be said, wafted the ode with more élan than its rather pedestrian lines invited. This sixty-six-second performance (Canada's "premier actress" reads Canada's "unofficial laureate") was delivered to M.A.'s largest-ever audience:

> Upwards of 30,000 [reports the *Toronto Globe*, 2.7.27] gathered on the velvety lawns of Parliament Hill, and every coign of vantage on adjacent buildings was occupied.

and another *Globe* headline reads: "Millions Listen and Hear Clearly Message from Ottawa":

> The Signals from the key station CNRO, Ottawa [the article begins], were picked up and rebroadcast by a chain of 23 stations across Canada, and, via the Marconi beam wireless at Montreal were hurried across the ocean for rebroadcast by the British stations.

The pleasant ceremonial occasion, on "a smiling day of rippling breeze and azure sky," was one which allowed Miss Anglin to hob-nob again with vice-royalty. In this case she found herself seated on the dais next to and chatting amiably with Viscount and Viscountess Willingdon. It may have reminded her that eighteen years earlier (N.Y. *Star*, 12.6.09) she had met the then governor-general, Earl Grey, after he had invited her to act as a judge in a drama competition under his sponsorship. On that occasion, as on this, she was the guest of her elder brother Frank, now Chief Justice of Canada. She may also have fancied she could remember being chucked under the chin as a tiny tot by Lord Dufferin.

Towards the end of July, M.A. traded in *The Woman* on a new play called *Gypsy April* by Lois Compton (produced by Carl Reed, staged by Cecil Owen).   She opened at the Broadway, Long Branch, N.J., on 26 July 1927 to a respectful review, and three days later the *Ashbury Park Press* (29.7.27) began its coverage with these lines:

> Securing suitable plays for theatrical luminaries that are out of the flapper class is a task that tests the mettle of producer, manager and playwright, especially when raucous talents of the cabaret character hold the boards. In *Gypsy April*, which opened last evening at the Savoy, an attempt has been made to supply a proper vehicle for one of the greatest living actresses—Margaret Anglin.

It seems to have been decided that a suitable role for the fifty-one-year-old M.A. would be that of a liberated grandmother. The highly convoluted, obscured-identity story concerns the troubled pursuit of a sister-soul relationship by the artist-grandmother (Deborah) and the bohemian granddaughter (April) in the teeth of general philistine opposition. In the hard-won dénouement, art and love and liberalism gratifyingly win the day:

> The final revelations [says the *Long Branch Record*, 27.7.27] make wonderfully strong and fascinating scenes and give Miss Anglin opportunities to display her marvellous art. In fact, she brought tears to the eyes of many.

There was general agreement that the "exposition" of the story was "inadequate," that the piece lacked "plausibility" at the level of characterization and motivation, that Miss Anglin's tempo in act one was "too impetuous," that the grandmother (M.A.) looked no older than her daughter (Beatrice Terry). The *jeune première*, (Claudia Wright), however, was declared to be "charming," "a winsome *ingénue*"—fine words which would butter no parsnips for M.A.

Gypsy April carried M.A. through the fall of '27, and then it was time to seize the opportunity she had been waiting for for years—a run of *Electra* on Broadway. Lee Shubert staked her to two weeks at the Gallo Theatre, and that run, well-attended and generally praised, was virtually everything she could have wished it.   The *N.Y. Times* (2.12.27) reviewer speaks admiringly of M.A.'s characteristically powerful, characteristically "Greek," conveyance of "the stark and still abandon of a fine-drawn creature in the clutch of overmastering fate." The *Brooklyn Times* reporter simply says "Miss Anglin's personal triumph as the vengeance-obsessed princess is too well-known to require further elaboration."

"Beautifully staged, and played in an almost faultless manner," says the *Brooklyn Eagle* (2.12.27). But J.B.C. of the *N.Y. Evening World* demurs. To him "the performance as a whole seemed to be at too feverish a pitch." Everything was either "starkly tragic" or "abysmally sepulchral." "In plain English, it was overacted." Still, he concedes, the "thunderous ovation" at the close "demonstrated that a very large portion of the audience was not of my mind."

After thirteen performances at the Gallo the production was moved, lock, stock and barrel, to Philadelphia where it played to an audience of 3,000 (J, 190) at the Metropolitan Opera House under the sponsorship of the Philadelphia Art Alliance.

The Philadelphia critics seeing the production for the first time were understandably more thrilled than their New York confreres who were perhaps seeing the Anglin *Electra* for the third time in the Gallo performance. The *Ledger* (17.12.27) reviewer avers that

> Miss Anglin's interpretation of the play, both as to her personal performance and her staging of the tragedy, although deviating now and then from some of the accepted standards, was a glowing, vital, vibrant thing. She is just about the only actress of our times who can play such a role with the sweep and sublime passion which it requires.

while the *Inquirer* (17.12.27) reviewer was moved to

> fancy how this play must have stirred the emotions of enrapt audiences in Sophocles' day. . . . There is in its story of grief and revenge a primitive emotional appeal that is gripping in its ferocity and moody passion. In their revelation Miss Anglin rose to the heights of grandeur. . . . Her wonderful voice melodiously filled every nook and cranny of the big Metropolitan with her litany-like delivery of passages that contained majestic dignity and intensely appealing beauty of phrase and vowel.

For the Gallo and Philadelphia productions M.A. had replaced her usual Clytemnestra (Ruth Holt Boucicault) with the young Antoinette Perry whose admirable "restraint, poise and dignity" was praised by the *Evening World*. (Miss Perry's name has since become memorialized in the Tony awards.) For the New York Met. production M.A. had engaged Michael Strange (Mrs. John Barrymore) for the part of Electra's younger sister:

> Of the attendant company [writes Alexander Woollcott] I was most interested in the performance of that exceedingly intermittent actress, Michael Strange, as Chrysothemis. She came on with startled hair and a pink costume, vaguely suggesting a Gibson Bathing Girl of the now derided nineties. Then she moved with the paralyzed awkwardness of a frightened, gawky

girl in a high school cantata. Yet her really enchanting voice came rushing to her aid, and the moment she had recovered from the anguish of a prancing entrance which compelled her to cry out:

> In pure delight, dear sister, thus I rush,
> My maiden grace abandoning, to come
> With swiftest foot,

she, too, caught and shone with the glow of an undying scene and played it, I thought, extraordinarily well. (*N.Y. World*, 4.5.27)

The very substantial popular and critical success of the '27 *Electra* prompted M.A. to excogitate some rather grandiose plans for the Greek Theater at Berkeley. On 30 December 1927 she wrote to William Popper, chairman of the Music and Drama Committee at Berkeley apropos of discussions they had had about the possibility of committing the Greek Theater to an annual summer festival (with M.A. as director):

> If anything permanent is to be accomplished at Berkeley [she contended] some definite organization will have to be undertaken. The dreams I once had for the Greek Theatre were perhaps over brilliant; but Walter Damrosch and many other knowledgeable people encouraged me to feel it should and could be made to the drama and its allied arts what Bayreuth was to opera, and since then Salzburg has become to the theatre. But one performance given every two or three years cannot accomplish this. A definite program to be carried out through a period of time each year would have to be selected and adhered to—say a Biblical drama, such as Racine's *Athalie* with its great choruses, a Shakespeare play, and a Greek play, to be enacted two nights of each week; perhaps then to go to the University of California for two performances on the Monday and Tuesday of each week . . . This is just a scheme, somewhat in the large, offered merely as a suggestion.

She was later to become quite specific about the necessity of an up-front guarantee of $100,000 to secure a three-year plan for the Greek Theater Festival, and she was able to enlist the active support of W.W. Campbell, president of the University of California, in an effort to secure such a guarantee by way of pledges of support from "wealthy Californians." Campbell was able to get her a guarantee of $25,000 for one year, but that was all, and a slightly miffed M.A. said that if they didn't want to bank on her for three years they couldn't have her for one, and thus she bade a regretful (almost) farewell to the Greek Theater of happy memory—for she was never to produce there again, though she did play there, as "guest star," twice more.

A note in the *N.Y. Review* of 22 January 1928 gives us the incidental intelligence that "Margaret Anglin and Juliet Gaultier de la Verendrye will entertain tonight at the Catholic Actors' Guild quarterly meeting at the Roosevelt." Also in January of '28 the genial impresario George C. Tyler conceived the idea of an all-star revival of Victorien Sardou's Victorian (1877) spy-melodrama *Diplomacy*. The cast list (always headed by the name of Margaret Anglin) "reads like a who's-who of American thespians" (*N.Y. Telegraph*, 30.1.28)—it includes: Cissie Loftus, Helen Gahagan, Frances Starr, Jacob Ben-Ami, Rollo Peters, Charles Coburn, Tyrone Power, Sr., and William Faversham. M.A. who had impressed twenty-seven years earlier in the sometime title role of Dora was cast in the briefly brilliant part of Lady Henry Fairfax.

The new *Diplomacy* opened on 30 January 1928 at the Garrick in Philadelphia and Arthur Waters of the *Ledger* (31.1.28) thought the effort to bring it "strictly up to date" a misguided one, since much of the dialogue and many of the basic social assumptions simply didn't work in modern dress. This *Diplomacy* often "creaks audibly," but still, he allows "in exciting action and in the presence of many stars it emerges as pretty good fun." "Margaret Anglin," says Waters, "appearing in only one act was brilliant if a trifle over-articulate in her staccato comedy." But if Waters thought the new *Diplomacy* creaked, Martha Wheatley of the *Binghamton Press* (8.5.28) was readier to be dazzled by the stars:

> With a less capable cast, the situations, which once seemed so aptly planned and so convincing, might now appear to be hopelessly old-fashioned misfits. But under the magic of the multitudinous histrionic gifts of a cast of stellar achievement, there is no doubt as to the delight of the entertainment.
> ... Miss Anglin's all too brief appearance in the second act [for a delightful example] provides a choice bit of work, rich in humour and brilliantly acted by this notable woman.

On 11 May T.M. Cushing of the *Washington Post* led off his remarks on the Tyler revival, which had "come to town on the wings of a successful tour of leading American and Canadian cities," with these deferential words:

> Heading the cast is Margaret Anglin, one of the grandest of our grand actresses, now in the full bloom of her career.

Just four days after that glowing notice, Miss Anglin had yet another of her periodic encounters with madfolk ("I seem to be a magnet to them"). On the night of 15 May 1928 the performance of *Diplomacy* at the Capitol in Albany was brought to a screeching halt by the galvanizing appearance of a ranting madman with a

particular grudge against M.A. (again, one supposes, based upon
unrequited love).   A fairly succinct account of the incident is
given in the *Portland Evening Express* (17.5.28):

> In the middle of the first act a religious maniac dashed down
> the main aisle to the orchestra pit, crying out that the show must
> stop and that he would shoot Miss Anglin. . . .
> Old timers at the theater thought Sardou's drama had been
> rewritten to get in a vaudeville touch, when Vincent Frost, 47, of
> Pittsburgh Pa. stalked down the aisle and demanded that the
> show be stopped.   The illusion was heightened when Charles
> Coburn, playing Baron Stein, asked in his best stage voice: "Who
> are you?"
> It was soon evident, however, that Frost, a powerful man,
> was not an added attraction. He burst into a stream of profanity
> and the curtain was rung down while he and a theater attache
> swapped punches down by the footlights. A panic was averted
> by four male spectators who seized Frost and subdued him.
> During this tirade at the footlights Frost demanded that Miss
> Anglin be produced [presumably as a moving target].

"'Bring out that Anglin woman!   This play can't go on!' he
kept shouting" is the *N.Y. Sun*'s (16.5.28) version of that demand.
     The *Express* piece goes on to say that the six-gun psychopath
was discovered to be a religious loony, "a college graduate," and
the author of several "crank letters" (of an obscure amorous drift)
to Miss Anglin and Frances Starr, the Dora of this production.
The *Boston Traveller* (16.5.28) adds the important fact that "Miss
Anglin, who was not scheduled to appear until the second act"
could not (not surprisingly) bring herself to go on.   But she was
all right the next night in Portland knowing that the fiery Mr.
Frost was cooling off in a padded cell back in Albany.   "I have
nothing but sympathy for the man," said Miss Anglin.   "Insanity
is a terrible thing and he is not responsible."   Still, the burly
figure of Mr. Frost could now be added to the angular one of Mr.
Freund to form a composite nightmare figure.
     When the *Diplomacy* tour was in Providence, just a week after the
Frost affair, M.A. took a leisurely late morning stroll in Roger Williams
Park. Suddenly she stood transfixed in front of the massive Benedict
Monument. This, she told herself, is a heaven-ordained setting for my
Electra—two great fake marble wings and a door in the centre, and it
is Agamemnon's palace (J, 168, 235).   She forthwith proposed to the
Providence Music League that they sponsor two performances of
Electra in the park.   They agreed with gratifying alacrity, and as soon
as *Diplomacy* reached New York on 28 May for a forty-performance
run, M.A. started *Electra* rehearsals which, of course, had to be worked
around the *Diplomacy* performances.

On 5 June 1928 [Arnold Johnson tells us] work began in Providence to change the Benedict Monument into the façade of a Greek palace. Miss Anglin and her company arrived in Providence two days before the performance. In the typical Anglin style, rehearsals were conducted "around the clock." This production was to be Miss Anglin's last venture as a producer of Greek tragedy.

And by all accounts she went out in a blaze of glory. Under a headline reading "8,000 Sit in Awe/Anglin Scales Heights" the *Providence Journal* (27.6.28) says,

A spell-bound audience massed upon the hills around the Benedict Monument to Music in Roger Williams Park last night sat awed and silent before the march and majesty of Sophocles' *Electra*.

Startled to admiration by the incredibly beautiful setting and the lofty production led by Margaret Anglin, the throng in the night-shrouded amphitheatre passed under a spell that is older than written history. It left us all lost and shuffled together in the black night, so everlastingly real, that applause did not break loose until the lights were given back to us.

There is no space, and not much object, in appraising the large and distinguished cast, one by one; but I must write it down, in black and white, that Miss Anglin's interpretation of Electra deeply impressed me as one of the finest and most moving performances in its order I have ever seen. I can only write of it, and of her, and of her vision brought to fact, the one preciously preserved word, "Superb."

"Anglin," says the *Boston Evening Transcript* (27.6.28), "was a primitive passion unleashed. . . . It was wonderful. It was the playwright, surely: but it was the actress too." The *Boston Herald* rejoices in the return of the mellifluous Fuller Mellish as the Guardian and then revels in the lovely looks of the show (as devised by Livingston Platt):

Always, whatever the action, the stage presented a beautiful picture. The Argive women, the palace attendants with their bare bodies, their glistening fillets, their spears or flaming torches, the attendants of Clytemnestra in brilliant greens and purples and blues, the jades and cerises of the flowers and fruit on the altar—the grouping and coloring during the whole performance was like a brilliant canvas.

Such magnanimity of effort and effect—and, again, after all, done almost gratis. The gross receipts were in fact gratifyingly large and the Music League was comfortably in the black, but M.A. told Randolph Churchill that she "personally received only $5,000 to pay the company; needless to say, [she] did not clear much for [her]self" (J, 191). It was still the old story of love's labour's struggles to break even.

Incidentally, for both the Providence and the Met. *Electra*, M.A. assigned the position of "director" to her sister-in-law, the clever comedy character actress, Josephine Hull. However, as Josephine's biographer William Carson says:

> When it came to Mary's *Electra* productions, Josephine might well have joined her voice with Figaro's in "Largo al factotum." The star was her own director, and Josephine a short-of-glorified stage manager. . . . At the Met, there were two performances before "enormous brilliant" houses, but whether Josephine got anything more out of the adventure than aesthetic satisfaction she does not say. (DJ, 188-89)

Carson also tells us that despite the great admiration the journeyman Josephine felt for M.A.—"one of the great *and* grand ladies of the stage (as difficult to handle as she was fine)"—she felt the patronage and the easy assumption of superiority of the elder (by two years) actress; and, as Carson remarks, "Mary's calm acceptance of the gap between their positions did occasionally get under her skin." Nevertheless, "*out* of the theatre, the relations between the two were warm, even affectionate," and

> When in later years her own fortunes rose and Mary's declined, her heart was touched and her loyalty was unabated. Mary, beset by many trials, would run in for comforting talks, "sweet and sisterly." And in her last months, though she was too ill to know it, no small part of the care she enjoyed she owed to a legacy from her "little sister-in-law." (DJ, 187-88)

In September of '28 she accepted, against her better judgement, the urgent invitation of the Drama Department of the University of California, and once again (after a lapse of eighteen years) played the title role of *Antigone* under the not entirely acceptable direction of Charles von Neumayer, professor of speech and drama at UCLA. In fact, the company rehearsed, until the eleventh hour, without Miss Anglin "who arrived at Berkeley on the day of the performance" (J, 6) and had only one rehearsal run-through. Still the *Oakland Tribune* (17.9.28) begins "Miss Anglin Triumphs . . ." and the review speaks of her "unimpaired vocal richness" and "pathetic appeal" and of her amazing ability to make us forget her fifty-two years in her "capturing of the spirit of a loving-hearted and fiercely loyal Grecian damsel."

Just as M.A. had fallen from the zenith of her St. Louis *Electra* in '25 to the vaudeville nadir of *Radio* and *The Terrible Woman*, so after "Scaling the Heights" in her Providence *Electra* in '28, she fell (with a passing clutch at *Antigone*) to the two-a-day lows of George Kelly's tragi-comic one-acter *Smarty's Party* about an arrogant and selfish rich-boy who marries a vulgar and mindless flapper and is told by his aristocratic mother (M.A.) that he is (literally) not her son and that he will have to find his niche in the riff-raff house into which he has so thoughtlessly married. The *N.Y. Times* (25.9.28) gives this production a fairly cool reception:

> Another prepossessing entertainment is at the Palace, where a capacity house turned out to see it yesterday afternoon. The technical headliner is Margaret Anglin, appearing in the George Kelly playlet *Smarty's Party*, before starting rehearsals as Lady Macbeth. The first audience, which gave the sketch respectful attention, found Mr. Kelly and Miss Anglin at something less than their best—a circumstance for which the author seemed as much to blame as anybody. Of the supporting cast, Betty Barlow, playing the Brooklyn girl who indulges in matrimony, contributed the outstanding performance.
>
> [In another turn] there is a young dancer from the Hollywood picture lots who was not without her adherents yesterday. Her name is Sally Rand and her act was one of the bill's brighter, if earlier, moments.

The mention of Miss Rand perhaps provides a clue to the coolness of Miss Anglin's reception at the Palace, while the mention of Lady Macbeth brings us to the serious business of yet another slippery milestone in the Anglin career.

Throughout the summer of '28 M.A. had been in correspondence re *Macbeth*: first with the impresario George C. Tyler, who was positive; then with the famous British designer Gordon Craig, who was polite but cool; then with her co-star Lyn Harding, who was bland and courtly; and finally with the Anglo-Scottish director Douglas Ross, who was self-impressed, and ultimately struck a frustrated M.A., who was putting it mildly, as "pompous and demanding."

M.A. was actually the linch-pin of Tyler's *Macbeth*. He signed her first and then got the "heroic" Lyn Harding (a big man with a big voice) to complement her. Harding, in turn, got in touch with Gordon Craig who agreed to design *Macbeth*, but he would not direct it, nor would he come to America to supervise the construction of his sets. Tyler then hired Douglas Ross (who had done an all-male collegiate

Macbeth at Yale) as director. And it is to Ross, as director and producer, that we owe the debasement, in the direction of stockish realism, of Craig's "highly poetic" scenic conception.

Ross was a foppish, unimaginative egotist who was confronted in M.A. with a stylish, imaginative egotist. They were "à couteaux tirés" from the outset, for, as Paul Sheren says: "Margaret Anglin clearly saw *Macbeth* as *her* production" (GC, 175). In any case, Ross was predisposed to discover an enemy in her, as this dire entry in Craig's "Daybook" makes clear:

> Ross had received a message warning him to "beware of Miss Anglin" who was, said the message, "a bitch." A nice world, this theatre. Ross went over thoroughly scared (or cross), on the lookout for Miss A. (GC, 176)

Jerome Collamore adds a footnote to the story of the animosity which existed between Ross and M.A. from before the beginning:

> As to the *Macbeth* production, M.A. told me that Ross (who was a blatant fairy) had his followers lying about the stage and Mary had to climb over them to rehearse her scenes. She wanted out almost as soon as she met Ross, and she told Tyler to ask Florence Reed to take over. (C. 15.8.85)

Florence Reed was a good actress with "a lovely husky voice," but virtually no Shakespeare experience, and she gave, as might be expected, an "insecure" performance.

Paul Sheren makes this comment on M.A.'s well-publicized defection:

> On November 6, Tyler announced the change of stars. Press releases told that Margaret Anglin had injured herself in a motor car accident just before opening and had been playing the role in Philadelphia bravely under incredible stress and pain. This was, of course, completely fabricated. Miss Anglin was coldly severing her relations with *Macbeth* with no mention of a sore foot. (GC, 179)

But there was real pain and stress and soreness, for she would surely have loved to share a triumph with Ellen Terry's son (Craig); and there can equally be no doubt that if the production had been given to her (and Platt), and given half the money Tyler expended on "the Craig *Macbeth*," it would have been successful. She never failed with a good play—even though, in this case, she admitted that that role in "that play" (which should remain nameless) held "obscure terrors" (GC, 173) for her. In any case, weeks of intensive study went up in smoke for her when she gave it up in "cold" anger. And, after all, it appears she was well out of it, for when it was laid to rest after twenty-five rather dismal weeks, it had realized a net loss of $76,462.97 (GC, 191), and the amiable George Tyler had been thus financially savaged for what Sheren calls "a terrible artistic failure" (GC, 191).

Having said all that, it perhaps behoves us to glance briefly at the critical reception the production was accorded while M.A. was still with it.

One of the most striking things about the direction of the energetic but acerbic Ross (who also played a rather dour King Duncan) was its stringent Scots aversion to the vivid emotionalism that both Anglin and Harding could have brought to the production, and most of the reviews do in fact remark on the "coldness" of the performance:

> Miss Anglin's reading [says the *Inquirer*, 30.10.28] was a meticulously correct elocutionary effort that was, unfortunately, without any real warmth of feeling. To this reviewer, hers was a curiously disappointing rendering in the earlier scenes, although she did reach more eloquent heights in her later essays when fear and remorse and their allied reactions were crowding close upon her.

The *Ledger* (30.10.28) is also "disappointed" in the M.A. performance:

> One would have expected to find in Margaret Anglin a Lady Macbeth that would take its place among the greatest interpretations of the famous role. Miss Anglin, however, scarcely achieves the distinction here that was hers in the revivals of the Greek classics. Vocally she is sonorous and compelling; histrionically she contributes little to the role. Her Lady Macbeth is scholarly and sincere, without once lifting the onlooker out of his respectful calm.

Arthur Waters commenting a week later (4.11.28) in the *Ledger* expresses a similar disappointment in these words:

> Margaret Anglin, save in her sleep-walking scene, which she portrayed with a shivery potency, was, frankly, not what we had hoped. Her Lady Macbeth lacked range and dominance. The original tremendous power of the woman was almost obliterated; hence her final weakening lost much of its point. . . .
> Miss Anglin's performance, however, was considerably more arresting than that of Lyn Harding [whose "coldly classical spouting" was without "force or feeling"]. It was

hard to believe that here was the same man who performed so magnificently the part of Henry VIII against Beerbohm-Tree's Wolsey.

If M.A.'s Lady Macbeth lacked color and contrast, so did the botched Craig staging, which was expected to be the real star of the piece. This *Macbeth,* according to the *Ledger* (4.11.28), "was played in semi-darkness throughout with few, if any, relieving moments," so that all the excitement and feeling to be gained from a shift from light and color to dark and gloom was forfeit. "Somberness," said the earlier *Ledger* reviewer, "is carried to an extreme, and the result was that every scene was played in shadow, obscurely and indistinctly." Still Craig's generally deplored "super-poetic treatment," says Waters, deserves some credit.

> The famous cauldron scene, which has been a favorite of artists for many, many years, has been created with a fine imagination and a grim and eerie quality. . . . The banquet scene has been invested with a somber gorgeousness . . . Lady Macbeth's night-walking scene is also assisted by a long, spectral staircase that seems to emerge from some secret chamber of the Thane's turreted home and to descend into purgatory itself. On the other hand . . . .

But (after toughing out the Philadelphia fortnight) M.A. was done with Craig and Ross and Harding, and her innate leeriness of the British, which kept her on a number of occasions from achieving a London season, at length seemed fully justified.

After three weeks at home (E. 39th St.) licking her wounds, she decided to try *Lady Dedlock,* in one last revision, one last time, and December '28 was devoted to putting together an unexceptionable production with which to usher in the new year with resolution and independence.

CHAPTER XII

Security, Lady Windermere, Ann Arbor Antigone: 1929-1933

Yet if it does not seem a moment's thought,
Our stitching and unstitching has been naught.
(W.B. Yeats, "Adam's Curse")

All that stitching and unstitching left the play, as it seemed to Robert Garland of the *N.Y. Herald* (2.1.29), "sprawling, overstuffed, not particularly worth while. . . . A couple or three years ago [he adds] I saw this same dramatization of *Bleak House* in Washington. It seemed dull then, just as it seems dull today." And it seemed very long. "For a time [says William Trapp of the *Evening World*] it looked as if the play would be the longest of the century, beginning in 1928 and ending in 1929."

M.A. was not deceived by the polite applause of the nearly full house at the Ambassador. She knew the feel of failure and its bitter taste, and as the taxi bearing her and Howard and Basil and Basile and Gaylord Tucker inched its way through the crush of New Year's merry-makers in Times Square she sat in stony silence, alone with her defeat. There would be no champagne party tonight, but there might be some stiff whiskeys.

Jerome Collamore writes:

> I was playing *Potiphar's Wife* at the Craig when M.A. was doing *Dedlock*, but I caught one of her performances. Much as I hate to say it, M.A. was not good. Her French (?) Hortense went off into Spanish, Italian and every other accent. Also, she was too heavy to do the quick changes with ease, *or*, to give the illusion of being a different person when the change was made. When I came out I heard two young girls saying "What is this? Hasn't she enough money for a maid and she makes out she has one?" I remember when we played it at the Curran (S.F.) I overheard a man say to a group in the lobby "Now Anglin is travelling with the graveyard." It hurt me and shocked me to hear such a crass remark, but that sums up the history of *Dedlock*. (Of course a "graveyard" play is just one in which the heroine dies—but perhaps you ought to leave that line out of your book.) (C, 13.8.85)

Wilella Waldorf of the *N.Y. Post* managed the more-in-sorrow-than-in-anger tone (which was that of most of the reviews) best:

> The attention and care which Miss Anglin and Mr. Kester have lavished upon *Lady Dedlock* deserve serious consideration, and it

M.A. played the dual roles of an excitable French maid and, shown here, the title role, in *Lady Dedlock*. (1929)

is therefore doubly disheartening to have to state that whatever "irresistible comedy and vivid romance in dramatic terms lie hidden in the crowded and brimming pages of *Bleak House*" [the words of M.A.'s blurb] lie there still quite undisturbed. Mr. Kester has indeed brought some of the familiar characters and a section of the plot upon the stage, and Miss Anglin acts no less than two major roles with all her might, but the result is curiously lacking in drama. Miss Anglin has yet to convince us that Dickens dealt "in dramatic terms."

While the scene-changes were found to be unconscionably long, the *mise-en-scène* (by Livingston Platt and Carol Sax) and the costumes (by Lucien Lebaudt) were generally liked. Alison Smith in her dissenting essay, cunningly entitled "Jarndyce vs. Broadway," remarks:

> The cast in general appeared in admirably designed make-up and with that air of conscientious quaintness which is fondly supposed to create a Dickens atmosphere. This was an error. For it really does take more than a picturesque assortment of Cruikshank figures to do justice to the interminable intricacies in the case of Jarndyce and Jarndyce. (*N.Y. World*, 2.1.29)

Some critics liked the abrasive performance of "the red-headed, excitable, [murderous] French maid, Hortense," while some liked the stately sadness of Lady Dedlock—few liked both, and all disliked the "trickiness" of the dual-role performance, and all felt the "uneasiness" it engendered in the audiences:

> As her Ladyship [says Alison Smith] with her "insolent resolve" and her "exhausted composure," Miss Anglin gives a neatly designed picture, only to shatter it with her next entrance where the shrewish Hortense rips out her Gallic insults with the uneasy consciousness that she must soon dash into her other make-up and become a lady again.

"It *is* a trick part," agrees Trapp, and therefore distracting:

> But Miss Anglin shows herself mistress of all the tricks, playing the dissimilar roles splendidly, with fine voice and feeling.
> But there were two other characterizations that seemed to this reviewer to catch the Dickens spirit even better than Miss Anglin did. They were the Tulkinghorn of John Ivancowich and the Bucket of Hubert Druce.

Ivancovich perfectly captures the "sinister rustiness" of the spider-like solicitor, while Druce is engagingly knowing and humorous as the double-dyed cockney Inspector Bucket of the Yard—though his all-too-authentic accent was a bafflement to some.

Clearly the critics in general were letting her down lightly—damning with at least faint praise, but the failing show was drummed out of the Ambassador after a fortnight of steady decline, and staggered through another three sickly weeks at the Waldorf. Management, consisting of Murray Phillips and J.J. Levanthal, insisted on covering their own expenses first, so that by the fifth week with total receipts of only $700 a night "some of the actors received as low as $2 or $3 apiece" (K, 4.2.29) and M.A. as director and dual leading woman was receiving nothing per night. Still she "had hoped that we could push the play to six weeks" so that it could look like a winner to the London producers and the Hollywood "talkies"—the two wealthy customers to whom she proposed to sell the *Lady Dedlock* rights—but the Dedlock name remained one of grim appropriateness, and no happy issue whatever eventuated.

And so, having absorbed another financial drubbing as a producer, M.A. was glad enough to accept the managerial patronage of her old sparring partner Lee Shubert and the "all right" direction of the youngish Stanley Logan, ten years her junior, in a new play entitled *Security* by Esmé Wynne-Tyson. This is the story of Jane Mapleson whose wealthy businessman-husband, James, is a heartless cheating philanderer with a front of perfect respectability. Jane is the conscientious protector of the front, mainly for the "security" of her two lovely, about-to-be-well-married daughters (but with a nod towards her own security as well). But when one of James's cast-offs (most awkwardly in the family way) shoots herself, and he confesses all to Jane, who already knew but didn't want to be told, she says *Now* I must disown you, and *he* promptly goes out and shoots *him*self. An anticlimactic and discordant third act shows Jane making a new life for herself in almost merry widow fashion.

The play opened on 3 March 1929 in Washington (the scene of the *Great Divide* fiasco of twenty-three years earlier) to mixed reviews:

> For two full acts [says John Daly of the Washington *Post*, 4.3.29] it drags bottom, as the divers have it, and then emerges into an incongruously lightsome third act. . . . The play has depth, of that there is no doubt. Too much depth, in fact. It is, to boot, a perceptive study of a wife's

compulsion to save a family's honor, even when that honor has been systematically undermined by a sinful paterfamilias. . . . But it is a talky play—good talk, some of it, but almost always more than enough.

The tribute to Miss Anglin is that she kept the vehicle moving all the time, even through one of the longest speeches of the season.

Most of the critics found the dialogue not only lacking in terseness and pointedness but often stilted and contrived. Robert Littell of the *N.Y. Post* (29.3.29) is, therefore, the more enthusiastic about M.A.'s deft handling of the often refractory lines:

> Quite likely [he supposes] she too had her quota of stiff, oratorical lines, but they were not noticeable, for whatever words she says are spoken with an extraordinarily skillful naturalness and variety, and an expertness in change of pace that takes your breath away.

The *Brooklyn Eagle* (29.3.29) likes the look of *Security* with its single elegant Regent's Park drawing-room setting (by Rollo Wayne). "It provides, also, one of the nicest looking casts to be seen along Broadway, and it is too bad that the things its members have to do grow a little mawkish as the evening proceeds." This critic also has words of commendation for the "engaging" supporting performances of the two daughters by Anita Kerry and the delectably (desperately?) named Hope Drown—"the latter charming as well as comely."

Robert Littell raises again the increasingly sticky spectre of datedness in the slightly tongue-in-cheek conclusion of his review:

> Coming after so many plays in which husband and wife are perfectly frank about each other's affairs, this jump back into a past when the adulterer's chief mistake was to get caught is refreshing. Or it would be, if the motives were made half plausible, if the dialogue were not so unashamedly 1898.

The *Eagle* reviewer is more precise in his charge of theatrical datedness:

> Miss Anglin has in *Security* a role that ten years ago no doubt would have been the material for a hit, since it is the kind of role she acts with great effect. Unluckily, today a number of those effects she knows so well how to gain seem scarcely worth winning. They seem empty and tricky. This [incredibly loyal] wife is what used to be considered a first rate "acting part." Consequently, almost inevitably in this kind of old fashioned vehicle, . . . Miss Anglin is more often the actress than the woman.

The "gentlemanly" Brooks Atkinson begins by wondering "how an actress of Margaret Anglin's dignity and insight comes to be associated with so trifling, so sterile a play as *Security*." After having his say about dialogue stilted with "stencil phrases," plotting denatured by "serial-story factitiousness," motivation "beclouded by sentimentalism," and structure skewered by the "fortuitous and gratuitous" scherzo ending, he allows himself to revel in M.A.'s performance *qua* performance:

> As the dissimulating Mrs. Mapleson, Miss Anglin plays with her familiar authority, speaking with a clarity rare in the theatre, molding the phrases of her dialogue into an intelligible form and relating gestures to the scene. All these technical accomplishments Miss Anglin has made so much a part of her act that they give a satisfaction of themselves. Hers is a bow with more than one string. From the emotionalism of the first two acts she can pass to the glinting comedy of the last act without violent transitions. (*N.Y. Times*, 29.3.29)

The less deferential E.W. Osborn of the *Evening World* (29.3.29) echoes Atkinson by misquoting Molière;—"What in the name of all that is theatrical, Margaret, are you doing in that gulley?"

Security had a respectable twenty-four performance run at the Maxine Elliott in New York and was allowed to die thus modestly dignified.

Towards the end of June M.A. revived *Caroline*, yet again, and revived, as well, one of her old romantic leads, Pedro de Cordoba, who played ("with Latin charm") her sentimental lover. She ran this production through July in the red-barn Berkshire Playhouse in the pleasant hill-country village of Stockbridge, Mass., and the summer people found her still "sparkling" as the wittily but discreetly amorous grass widow. That easy audience may well have taken their evening at the Playhouse for a nostalgia trip.

In August she took up briefly with a new play called *My Son*, in which she played an attractive Portuguese matron of fifty (Dona Ana) whose handsome profligate son contracts many debts of a courting and gaming nature, and takes to jewel thieving to cover them. Dona Ana has the two-fold dilemma of deciding whether to turn her son in, or cover up for him; and of choosing between a rich-practical-grave and a poor-poetical-gay suitor.

The play, which ran only a couple of weeks for her in the southwest, seemed to have the stuff of engaging drama,

> but somehow [says the *Kansas City Independent*, 13.8.29] its climacteric cliffs left the onlooker somewhat unresponsive except to the earnestness of Margaret Anglin's acting. Indeed, it may be suspected that this finished actress put more into her interpretation of a devoted mother than was provided by the script. The Portuguese woman was gentle and good and not without refinements that her social betters might well have coveted, yet withal, not very thrilling . . .

Miss Anglin's vaunted "urbanity" was not called for by this role, and therefore one thought the role was not quite her. Besides Miss Anglin's adroit strokes [continues the *Independent*] which unquestionably lifted the play out of mediocrity, Allen Moore's tenacious grasp of an unsympathetic character, the son, went far towards sustaining the pivot of the piece. Gladys George jumped into the scantiest swimming suit ever seen on conservative Cape Cod, disclosing a symmetrical figure suitable for a bathing beauty derby at Atlantic City. . . .

No wonder the raffish boy became a poor man's Raffles in order to ogle the glamorous Gladys. Miss George, of course, went on to be a star in her own right in *Personal Appearance* (1934) and *Lady in Waiting* (1940).

At the end of August, upon the demise of *My Son*, M.A. turned yet again to *The Woman of Bronze* and contracted to do a limited run in the title role with a Milwaukee stock company. However, when she arrived in Milwaukee on 1 September she was in effect locked out by Actors' Equity. The *N.Y. Tribune* (2.9.29) reports that

> When Miss Anglin went to the theater last night, Sherman Brown, theater manager, told her that an understudy was to play her role because Miss Anglin had not attended rehearsals. Miss Anglin replied that, having played the role more than a thousand times she did not feel that she was needed prior to the performance. Brown, however, said that her failure to appear had broken their contract, and that Miss Anglin had been cited formally to Equity.

The Equity sanctions (unspecified here) would appear to have scuttled this last fling with *The Woman*, for we hear no more about it. And maybe M.A. was not all that sorry

to be prevented from playing Vivian Hunt for the thou-
sand-and-first time, for we find her a week later writing in
good spirits to Paul Kester:

> Dearest Paul,
>
> It's been an age since I've written you. I've been
> junketting about ever since May—Kansas City, Rochester,
> Pittsburgh, the Berkshires, Long Island, Bar Harbor
> —summer engagements, keeping the pot simmering if not
> boiling. . . .
> We have made a new and good contract in the
> talking picture field, and I think I can resell *Beverly* and
> perhaps one of your other mss. I think we ought to
> change *Beverly* a little to make it more [cinematic]. I
> don't want to take your time from an important novel,
> but I think this would be worth the effort. (K, 11.9.29)

Again the bright elusive butterfly of the pictures, and
again nothing materializes—mainly, perhaps, because
wayward Howard was in charge.

The next view we have of M.A. in the theatre—the last
for some time—is at the onset of winter in windy
Montreal. And here she had the pleasure of seeing (and
perhaps helping to compose) the magniloquent ad
published by His Majesty's ("Montreal's Leading Theatre"):

> The Orpheum Players [it proclaims] take pleasure in
> announcing that they have engaged this theatre for the
> week commencing Monday Evening, November 25th,
> during which they will present as their Guest Star
> Canada's Most Celebrated Lady of the Stage, Miss
> Margaret Anglin, in Oscar Wilde's famous masterpiece,
> *Lady Windermere's Fan*, in which she will be supported by
> the entire Company of the Orpheum Players and an
> augmented cast.

No sign here of a spirit in any way cowed or even
humbled, and indeed the *Montreal Gazette* (26.10.29) assures
us that, whereas the fire had gone out of the furnace at
His Majesty's, it had certainly not gone out of M.A.'s
acting:

> A large and unusually smart audience for a Monday
> opening gathered at His Majesty's last night to see
> Margaret Anglin play with the Orpheum Company in
> *Lady Windermere's Fan*. And it was richly rewarded for
> its discrimination. Miss Anglin's suave, beautifully

polished work, Oscar Wilde's scintillating wit and the very competent support of the local players combined to provide an evening's most excellent entertainment, which warmed even the shivering audience in the bitterly cold theatre to enthusiasm. . . .

As for the outcast adventuress who rises to the heights of sacrificial nobility for the sake of the daughter who reviles her, Margaret Anglin plays with consummate artistry. She savors hugely every ounce of the rich humor of her lines, and in their savoring shares them fully with her audience. Her audacity is delicious while the melodrama, toned down by her splendid naturalness, becomes fine drama—poignant, human and convincing.

The next theatrical venture for M.A. (nearly six months later) was a ten-performance run of *Antigone*, beginning with an opening night in Kalamazoo and going on to a nine-performance run at the Lydia Mendelssohn Theatre in Ann Arbor. If the play was *not* produced in a manner of which she could approve, it was advertised in a manner of which she could:

Robert Henderson [the ad declared] has the distinction to present MARGARET ANGLIN, AMERICA'S GREATEST STAR, in Sophocles' thrilling masterpiece *Antigone*, with a brilliant New York cast. . . . (*Ann Arbor Daily News*, 25.5.30)

Once again, as in the Berkeley *Antigone* of '28, M.A. was, to say the least, not in perfect accord with the academic producer-director—in this case, Robert Henderson. Once again she was restive under the direction of a rather bumptious "young man" (several years her junior) who had, she thought, not much feeling for the "religious" quality of Greek tragedy and none whatever for its "daunting" potential. She did, however, respect the sterling vocal resources of the British actor, Ainsworth Arnold, who scored solidly as Creon.

When she arrived [says Jerome Collamore] Henderson showed her the set: a spiral staircase running up to nowhere. "Isn't it wonderful?" he said, "You make your entrance and run up the stairs to the top." "No, I don't," she said, "You can send one of your girls up there." He had college girls with long beards playing the Theban elders. (C, 14.11.85)

Notwithstanding Miss Anglin's brooding air of disapproval and occasional tetchiness, Henderson's *Antigone* seems to have come off reasonably well:

He gave us [says Ralph Holmes of the *Detroit Times*, 25.5.30] a drama so filled with fundamental truth it seemed miraculously modern. Margaret Anglin with her cello-like voice touches our hearts instantly. It is a superb production. Ainsworth Arnold as Creon proves to be one of the finest actors who ever reached this part of the country.

That for the Kalamazoo opening. Alison Ind of the *Ann Arbor Daily News* (27.5.30), while deferential in her treatment of the Ann Arbor opening, allows a clear note of ambivalence to be heard in her praise of the star:

> Some will have left the theatre convinced that Miss Anglin over-emotionalized. There is authentic ground for such criticism. But hers was a role of consistent tragedy, unrelieved by lighter moments, either in lines or action, except when she achieved heights of emotional projection—and these moments only intensify the tragic power that is Anglin's. Paradoxically, perhaps, these moments were not achieved with a crescendo of declamation and gesture but came when voice and gesture were at a minimum. It is in the vibrating alto tones that Miss Anglin thrills.

A large "formally attired" audience turned out for this opening, in order to "pass judgement on the heralded bearer of the title role"—some were thrilled; some were not. In any case, they were treated to an evening (introduced by an orchestral rendition of Beethoven's *Egmont* overture) conceived of as a symphony—"a symphony of rhythm, poetry, movement, tone, color and emotion." Again, for some this conception was largely realized; for others the various elements "didn't quite come together." Still, says Miss Ind, "Mr. Henderson has made a worthy attempt" to produce high theatrical art.

The following week the same company changed masks and presented M.A.'s own well-travelled production of *Lady Windermere's Fan*, in which Robert Henderson "endowed the romantic Lord Darlington with appropriately soulful looks and dulcet tones," Ainsworth Arnold "played that demned fine feller, the philandering Lord Augustus Lorton, as to the manner born," and Amy Loomis was appropriately "sweet and pretty and colorless" as Lady Windermere. As for Miss Anglin's Mrs. Erlynne, it was characterized by her usual "regal presence" and "crystal diction"—"a performance of splendid assurance, but withal, a little weary" (*Daily News*, 3.6.30).

Indeed, the old trouper was finding it just a little harder each time to get "up" for a performance, let alone a run. After over eighty starring roles, the marvellous machine was beginning to run down, as arteriosclerosis began its insidious and inevitable destructive course.

As Mrs. Erlynne in *Lady Windermere's Fan*: "a performance of splendid assurance, but withal, a little weary." (1930)

Through the latter part of 1930 and all of 1931, M.A. was still promoting herself as a going theatrical concern, but Broadway producers who, in any case, shied away from her maverick intractability, saw only the marked diminution of energy and incisiveness. Even the backers of the Greek Theater, who still believed in her, shied away from her extravagance. Thus the invitation she received "to inaugurate the Greek Theater at Griffith Park in Los Angeles" (J, 272) in the summer of '31 was ultimately withdrawn, after much planning by M.A., when it was discovered that her initial request for $13,000, up front, did not include her own salary as actress and director or the salaries of her designer (Livingston Platt) and her stage manager (Jerome Collamore). Nor indeed did it include the salaries of the orchestra conductor and twenty-three musicians, which she considered minimal. For a two-night stand with *Electra* and *Medea* the projected cost, in a depression year, was obviously prohibitive.

By August M.A. seems to be settling down to easy terms with neglect, and writes comfortably, ramblingly to Paul Kester from picturesque, breezy Cedarwold:

> Sally [Williams Riegal] is up here spending a day or two with me. Howard seems better than of yore. We all send you love—I more than the others. I often get lonesome for a glimpse of you. I am doing "Poetry" on the radio now and getting a most interesting return from it. There is some prospect of my returning to the stage again in the autumn—I wish now there weren't—the theatre has somehow gone by me. (K, 24.8.31)

If one remembers that the most notorious of the Broadway hits of 1931 was *The Constant Sinner* with Mae West, this last remark is placed in a justifying context. But still in the same year, M.A. might have seen her erstwhile protégée Alla Nazimova starring in *Mourning Becomes Electra*, whose author she had known as an engaging eight-year-old. Years later (1917, 1922, 1926?), according to Jerome Collamore, "Eugene O'Neill visited her backstage in Portland Oregon, and said that his greatest desire was to write a play for Miss Anglin" (C, 28.10.85). Whether or not he had her in mind for his Electra does not appear. In any case, M.A., living largely at Cedarwold ("I have a small apartment at 400 E. 49th St.") did not go to the theatre.

In the late summer of '31 M.A. became a regular contributor to radio station WOR, New York (dial 710)—every Wednesday evening at 8:30 the radio log listed "Margaret Anglin reading."

The radio readings at their best had all the majesty of the theatrical "readings" of her prime; at their worst they were off-puttingly slack and wobbly—but the average apparently remained quite high. Her greatest radio fan was the doggedly loyal Howard, and his letters to M.A. in the early thirties (unhappily undated) are replete with laudations of her readings, of which the following are fairly typical:

> Your voice was flawless, and you played with certitude and, wherever possible, fervor the verses Miss [Elinor] Wylie gave you.

> The reading of Keats did not seem like reading at all. I have never received such an indelible impress of no one writing words but of someone telling me them.

> It is evening. I have rarely, though of course often, heard your voice more lovely. "The Dauphin" was superbly done. I will not go into details about any ones we know, but there are those who would say "Very able, Mary," and I would have to serve drinks. I don't *mind* carrying water to God's pansies—if you see what I mean.

> The programme was lovely, *précieuse* of course, but what would you? one can't always do [Goethe's?] the Erl-Koenig.

> I have been moved, I have been touched, and once or twice stirred, but your "Hervé Riel" made me wish I was fifteen. I can understand your greatness and Browning's better now that fifteen is a dead milestone, but at fifteen—well, I wished I was fifteen . . .

This and much more in praise of M.A.'s reading; much in dispraise of the competition ("who called that S.O.B. Charles Daly a poet? . . . his voice a succession of queasy *aufgangs*")—"and I know *something* about poetry":

> I have heard some God-awful poetry readings over the air, but the depth, the height of incomprehensible awfulness and self-satisfaction was Edna St. Vincent Millay. I have heard Alfred Granger do Matthew Arnold, I have heard preachers in First Methodist Churches, but that terrible woman, I suppose she can write (I don't think so), but I am dogmatic about her reading, it is as poisonous as a clogged sewer with a dead dog in it.

Howard never did produce his promised volume of poetry, but he indulges in "spreading [him]self" fairly frequently in his letters to M.A.—as for example, in this musing opening:

> The shadows are lengthening, in fact they are so long they cover the ankles of the dusk. The brook has ceased murmuring, it

says it has been murmuring now for so many verses and cantos that it is going to quit. The crocuses have sung their eventide song, and put their little ones to sleep under the frightened, moon-illumined snow. A black tree is still as black as it was this morning, but no gilded rays touch its top; they can't of course since it has no top, but in case it had. And the day is done.

Everything he wrote in a fanciful or poetical or sentimental vein was written to, for, and about her ("White Lady," "Moon of my desire"). He tended to think of himself as Queen Mary's (or "Queen Mab's") demented troubadour, her *Pierrot lunaire.* One of his many pages of scribbled notes for poems that never got written runs thus:

> I find nothing in the moon
> to make me say it is you—
> I find great loneliness
> that makes me yearn more
> for you.
> It may then be I can
> never reach the moon
> and so
> I am lonely
> as I can never touch you—
> All I may do
> is to yearn for you
> and look
> at the moon.

When in disgrace with fortune and M.A., he begins another fragment with the despondent lines, "I never saw a moon so black / As things she said," or in prose protests, "I feel like Manfred, but I aint done Astarte nor nobody no harm." But his loyalty was unshakable, his vassalage complete—"I loved you when you were rich, now that you do not *appear* to be so rich, it's just the same I love you."

"Mr. Hull," says housekeeper Emmy Wittich,

could have been a fine actor. He was brilliant and a gentleman. He had a good sense of humor. He spent much time writing and lots of poetry, but M.A. didn't want him to send anything for publication. They were very happy together, and Howard was hers. (W, 16.10.85)

Jerome Collamore agrees with Emmy about Howard's histrionic potential—"I saw him play the desperate young Parmelee in [P.E. Browne's] *A Fool There Was* (1909) and he gave a most telling performance." But his flicker of theatrical genius seemed to be snuffed out "by M.A.'s dominating personality." He had real literary talent, too:

> He would write reams and never edit. And when he and Mary were at Booth Tarkington's home she spoke about it and Tarkington said, "Come with me," and took him up to the study and showed him his current work [*The Magnificent Ambersons*?] where he had changed a word 6 or 7 times. But I don't think it impressed Howard. (C, 3.8.85)

Collamore also tells us how M.A. got started in radio drama. The NBC radio show *Cuddles and Monty*, which he wrote and in which he starred (with his wife, Helena, an occasional M.A. supporter), had "gone off," and he had "hit a low in activity." Also Helena had a slight stroke. They were "just about flat broke":

> We had to leave our hotel, leaving our trunks there. When next I saw M.A. she slipped a fifty dollar bill into my hand and said, "This may help." Later, since she was spending so much time in Katonah [Cedarwold], she suggested we move into her apartment, which we did, till we got on our feet again. Then she got me to help her adapt Father [Robert Hugh] Benson's *Upper Room* for radio. She sent it to NBC, and it was turned down flat. I then took it to Alfred McCosker at WOR. He accepted it, and gave M.A. all the rehearsals she wanted. We rehearsed it for a week—unheard of for radio. When it went on the air the actors knew their parts and it was acclaimed the best of the year's radio. The head of NBC called her and asked why she hadn't brought it to him. She told him that his program director, Wm. Rainey, had refused it, and Rainey got a calling down. But that opened the way to do *Iphigenia, Joan* and others on NBC, which, in turn, led to doing more things on WOR and into her poetry hour.

Emmy tells us that the poetry half-hour was "a regular production for three years (1931-33), and that M.A.'s readings were backed by "the WOR Symphony Orchestra with Philip James conducting. The music was a beautiful background for poetry. It was very successful and well-liked. I know I picked up bundles of fan-mail from WOR once a week" (W, 16.10.85). Jerome Collamore remembers one particularly tearful evening upon which

> M.A. did a poem called "The Dancer" by an English author. It was a simple poem of a dancer who refuses to dance, for she's going to her dead lover. M.A. brought deep imag-

ination to this, and when she ended you were moved tragically with tears in your eyes. Then she read "Danny Boy" and had you weeping tears copiously. (C, 17.10.85)

As well as for the heart-pieces that "would bring your tears," Basile recalls M.A.'s penchant for "aspirational" soul-pieces. Especially she liked Dr. Holmes's "Build thee more stately mansions, O my soul" ["The Chambered Nautilus"], both for its fine sonorous rhetorical flourishes and for its lofty philosophy of life which was, she said, "essentially [her] own."

Howard and Margaret were both excellent readers of verse, and liked to read to each other by the fire at Cedarwold. Also, they cultivated the acquaintance of a number of prominent American poets. In December 1932 we find Howard writing to M.A.: "Did you think of a card for Charlie Phillips [the Notre Dame poet] and Eddie [Edwin Arlington] Robinson? I doubt if Kipling would understand, so you might as well leave him off the list."

One piece of poetry which Howard and Margaret were able to make entirely their own was occasioned by the plane-crash death in 1931 of the great Notre Dame football player and coach, Knute Rockne, whom they both knew. According to Emmy, NBC produced "a special radio tribute for him. Mr. Hull wrote a very beautiful poem, which M.A. read over the radio" (W, 16.10.85).

But "the nicest thing" she ever did in the way of reading was Oscar Wilde's fairy tale, "The Happy Prince." She probably first did it in '33; then in '36, as Emmy recalls:

> M.A. did a production of it at the Music Hall. It was one of their Easter shows. It was done like a pantomime. It was gorgeous. Most beautiful scenery and beautifully costumed. M.A. was the narrator, beautifully costumed also. Alexander Woollcott spoke of her "golden voice." (W, 16.10.85)

But before that there was *Martha Washington*. On 7 February 1932 at 5 P.M. there was a "trumpet flourish" on WOR followed by the stentorian tones of Mr. Floyd Neil resonating "Margaret Anglin presents Martha Washington." This was the first of a four-part series to be aired on successive Sundays from 5 to 5:30, in which Martha Washington was to be rescued from her relegation as "a simple, kindly gentlewoman" and given her due recognition as "a wise companion, a discerning diplomatist, and as an eager participant in the full activities of a great man." "I have given the dialogue what I deem to be an appropriate eighteenth century flavor," wrote the author, Montrose Moses, to Howard Hull (14.2.32), "and Miss Anglin is wonderfully at ease with it, and makes Martha just as warm and vivacious and keen as I had hoped she would be."

She also played Martha Washington in Percy MacKaye's grandiose pageant-drama, *Washington, the Man Who Made Us*, for the Washington bicentennial on 22 February 1932 in Constitution Hall in Washington, D.C., "with 1,000 amateurs" and "before a most distinguished audience" (W, 16.10,85).

It is rather difficult to trace M.A. through 1931-33, for she apparently did not get, and seems not to have been in quest of, any plays during that period—she had become essentially the elocutionist or "dramatic reader" that she had told her father forty years earlier she intended to be, and, as such, she was not accorded much press coverage. Still, the new line kept her fairly busy and, at times, quite mobile. Thus we find her writing to Paul Kester on 13 January 1933:

> January has me on the run—three more engagements: Newark, Providence, and the Actors' Fund. These will none of them be theatrical, but "platform," a new form of entertainment for me, which I approach with no great ease.

A week earlier (4.1.33) she had sounded Kester on the possibility of his co-authoring a play with her:

> What I have in mind is a humorous play with one underlying serious motive laid in the brilliant Saratoga days of the '80s. That was the peak of Saratoga's brilliance, when the President [Grant] and the fashionable world and the Blue Drawing Room and the rest of it, all flourished. Anyhow, let's talk about it. . . . Bronson Howard's *Saratoga* is naive to the point of absurdity.

Six weeks later (3.3.33) she was again sadly rubbing elbows with senior ministers of state (including the prime) and vice-regal persons on the occasion of the death of her eldest brother, Francis Alexander Anglin, P.C., LL.D. (1865-1933), Chief Justice of Canada (1924-1933). The scrupulous author of *Trustees' Limitations* was a man of high probity and solid intellect, but one apparently deficient in humor, warmth and charm, and hence not much allied in spirit to the vivacious Margaret. Still, one was cognizant of his "unfailing liberality" as a host, and one could not but be moved by the death of so Trojan a worker falling just twenty-four hours after the effective date of his retirement.

Mackenzie King, who had conferred the Chief Justiceship upon Frank, wrote Margaret a long letter (5.3.33) of condolence, which concludes in this highly characteristic vein:

> You know, I think, how deeply I have felt for you all along the *via dolorosa* which you have been called upon to walk anew. Death continues to be the greatest of all mysteries, next to Life. I have come to view it simply as life, momentarily shrouded with a veil, so far as we here are concerned, and life unveiled for those who pass through its portal. But be our beliefs what they may, we cannot part, even for a brief space, from those we most dearly loved, without experiencing pain at parting, especially where the passing is surrounded by mystery. And so I have felt deeply for you, and shared your grief in greater measure than perhaps it would be possible for you to know. It was splendid of you to give up everything to come, and I am so glad you were here at the end. The glimpse of you was like a burst of sunlight through the clouds. I hope you were able to carry away in your heart some of the sympathy that I felt for you. With much affection. Believe me, dear Margaret, yours with truest sympathy and understanding. Billy.

In March of '33 an ailing Howard, heroically rationing himself to "six drinks a day," was almost certainly already in possession of the throat cancer that eventually killed him. On 9 March M.A. wrote to Kester to tell him of "Frank's funeral," and added the P.S.:

> Howard has been rather wretched for the past ten days, and the doctor has been coming every day since my return. I hope sunshine and treatment will put him on his feet again.

Howard was indeed perky enough later in the year to comment wryly on one Mrs. Vogel's observations on the rise of the Third Reich:

> A collection of people assembled last night and said vitriolic and terrible things about Hitler. Mrs. Vogel, who is chronically social, sat and looked like von Moltke at the battle of Dettingen. Mindful of my instructions, I said nothing, but when James W. Gerard opened up I left the house and sang a soft little song to the moon, and came back when I heard a waltz.

It is perhaps in 1934 or 1935 that Mrs. Vogel is mentioned in dispatches again:

> I am here alone. I have been catechized by a woman who is largely deaf and completely puzzled. She doesn't know why

the Kaiser can't come back, since he didn't start it, and no, no argument at all. Poultney Bigelow does not help out our peace of mind by declaring that the stories of Jewish atrocities are as false as those told of Germans at the beginning of the [First World] War. And Mrs. Vogel knows Poultney.

On 20 June 1933, M.A. lost her faithful friend and correspondent of half a lifetime, when the gentle and gentlemanly Paul Kester died suddenly in his sixty-third year of heart failure at his home at Lake Mohegan, just ten miles across the hills from Cedarwold. Her sadness on that occasion must have been deep, but we have no words of hers to report. She did, however, ask Emmy and Christine Ruhl (her secretary) to make her old friend, the honorary Gypsy, "a spray of flowers from the garden" at Cedarwold. "I remember," says Emmy, "making a spray, with Christine, with 3 shades of delphinium, pale pink roses and baby's breath" (W, 16.10.85). "Sweets to the sweet," as M.A. doubtless would have said. Henceforth her premier correspondent was to be Randolph Somerville, a big, sometimes bearded, "theatrical" man, professor of drama at NYU and minor Shakespearean actor. For years he and M.A. were always on the verge of doing something splendid, but, so far as one can gather, they never quite did.

The fall of '33 and the Cass Theatre in Detroit saw Margaret Anglin, actress, briefly back in harness, again under the direction of Robert Henderson. Her part in Ivor Novello's *farce à clef* entitled *A Party* was that of Mrs. MacDonald ("a great actress of yesterday"), a thinly disguised caricature of Mrs. Patrick Campbell. Other persons represented in the piece are Novello himself, Sir Gerald DuMaurier, Talullah Bankhead, Lady Diana Manners, and the critics James Agate and Hannan Swaffer (played with venomous panache by Ainsworth Arnold). Miss Anglin made her show-stopping entrance with the little white Pekinese and the big black cigar of Mrs. Pat, and according to the *Detroit Free Press* (24.10.33) "went on to impersonate that erratic grande dame of the stage with effortless fidelity." If she lost or garbled a few lines, only her stage interlocutors would know or care. The assignment of the role of the dotty old diva represented fairly blatant type casting.

The other star turn of this production, the tiny, spritely, Corsican-born musical-comedy star, Irene Bordoni (*aet.* 38), played herself "doing her famous impersonations" and singing her (and Cole Porter's) hit song (from *Paris*), "Let's Do It."

"When you speak of Bordoni [says the Cass program], you think of Paris—of France—of charm and sophistication and irrepressible sparkling brilliance." Miss Anglin, who was "sometimes sad" in those days, liked to think of such things and liked Miss Bordoni who "made her laugh" (W, 16.10.85).

A Party, which ran for the week of 23-29 October to nearly full (half-price) houses was followed immediately by a one-week run of the "elegant" Edgar Wallace whodunit *Criminal at Large* (1931). M.A. was cast as the prime suspect, Lady Lebanon, the enigmatic and daunting chatelaine of the ancient and atmospheric Mark's Priory (Sussex), who appears to be positively riddled with guilty secrets about the mysterious death of her husband and the subsequent murders of the chauffeur and family doctor. As it happens, it is her nincompoop son, the nineteenth viscount, the "harmless nit," who is the triple murderer, and the "blood-proud" matriarch is simply trying to keep him out of the clutches of the hangman until he can beget an heir to the thousand-year-old house. The *Free Press* (31.10.33) reports that "Miss Anglin makes a most impressive *volte-face* from the mad-cap Mrs. Pat to the suavely menacing Lady Lebanon. The measured stateliness of her pacing is nicely offset by the businesslike briskness of Lester Vail as Inspector Tanner and the diddly ditherings of Director Robert Henderson as her schizophrenic son, Willie (Lord Lebanon)." The stately pace sounds just a little like something M.A. was getting away with—making a virtue of necessity, but it clearly served her well enough for the nonce.

And so Henderson's "rather bedizened" productions allowed the fading star to glitter fitfully for a fortnight, but the late fall and winter saw M.A. back in New York doing poetry and whatever radio work came to hand, and "working on her scripts." In all the time (1930-46) that she was with her, says Emmy Wittich, M.A. was always tinkering with scripts—to the early thirties Emmy assigns "*L'Arlésienne* [Alphonse Daudet], *Athalie* [Racine], *The Trojan Women* [Euripides] and *Boadicea* [Wm. C. de Mille]" (W, 16.10.85).

Jerome Collamore remarks of the fallow thirties that, even though she was no longer up to her ears in stage production, "she was a truck-horse for work. Up early every morning with a hundred new ideas. She wanted to start early in the day, and I'd be at her apartment by 9 A.M. I spent hours at the library reading poetry, and leaving with a string of books to take to M.A. . . . She was always gracious, but you never got over the sense that this was a powerful personality" (C,

22.11.85).   The high-wattage Anglin charm had a way of wilting sensitive plants of the Collamore kind.

Nineteen thirty-three was the year in which the infrequent, flitting, but always "sweet" visits of the shy Paul Kester ceased to grace the hills and dales of Cedarwold, but it was, by way of compensation, the year in which the Hulls saw the most of the genial and debonair Livingston Platt:

> He was indeed [says Emmy Wittich] a very dear friend of Mr. and Mrs. Hull.   He was always at Cedarwold.   M.A. and Mr. Platt went always for long walks.   Always making plans.   If not talking theater, they would rearrange gardens or something else on the place.   At the dinner table they loved to talk about cooking and food.   There was no end to it, and always about the most fattening food.   M.A. didn't need that, as she always had a weight problem.   She always asked me to make those heavy English dishes, like kidney and beefsteak pudding and other suet dishes, like steamed apple and blueberry pudding served with hard sauce. Cedarwold had lots of fruit trees, blueberries in the woods, and wild strawberries, bayberries and blackberries in the meadow.   Mr. Platt painted the outdoors a lot.   He was a great artist.

It is pleasant to imagine Livy (*aet.* 59) and Mab (*aet.* 57) at sunset, in the twilight of illustrious careers, climbing apple-tree knoll, and talking idly in the mellow air of Shakespeare and larkspurs—old friends, fitting like old gloves on old hands, yet not feeling old.

Noted New York portraitist Montgomery Flagg's 1927 drawing of Howard Hull.

Chapter XIII

Fresh Fields, Retreat,
Howard's End: 1934-1937

Poor Kit, farewell!
I could have better spared a better man. . . .
(Shakespeare, *1 Henry IV*, 5.4.103)

Towards the end of 1933, M.A. seems to have replaced her one-time supporter Laura Hope Crews in Clare Kummer's frothy comedy *Her Master's Voice*. The only evidence at hand is a passage (December '33?) from one of Howard's letters:

> McCosker said he and his wife were thinking of the people they loved, and she said, "Start with an A for Anglin" . . . and I said you were in Cinti [Cincinnati] with a play called *Her Master's Voice*, and I personally think she's gorgeous. "You're telling me," he said, "she's the greatest comedian in the world. But she wouldn't be there if the board [of WOR] hadn't outvoted me, but she'll be back as soon as I can make a break.

On 11 April 1934, M.A. paid a flowery visit to her most esteemed brother, Arthur, "the King's Counsel," in Toronto, and the next day graciously accepted an invitation to appear as the "guest artist" at the "Founder's Dinner" of the Pleiades Club of Toronto. She was eruditely introduced by the Hon. Charles McCrae, minister of mines, as "a bright star of the constellation [Pleiades]; indeed, the Electra of the group." She gave the distinguished company the proem to *Evangeline*, a humorous piece by H.H. Munro ("Saki"), and "O Canada." In the rendition of this last she experienced some embarrassment because of a mislaid script and had to confess she could not go beyond four lines from memory. When the script was found she read the lines as though they were inscribed on her heart. It was on this already somewhat heart-fluttering occasion that the unexpected appearance of the tiny, frail figure (bearing "an armful of roses") of Miss Jessie Alexander, her elocution teacher of half a century ago, brought tears of tragic joy to Miss Anglin's eyes (*Mail and Empire*, 13.4.34).

On Monday 9 July 1934, M.A. made a more or less triumphal return to the legitimate stage after a virtual four-year absence—*pace* Detroit and Cinti. On the evening of that day Messrs. Leslie Casey and James Littell took pride in presenting (in conjunction with the World's Fair), at the Blackstone in Chicago, "Margaret Anglin in the American premiere of Ivor Novello's *Fresh Fields.*"

The story is that of two daughters of a peer of the realm, the younger, the aesthetic, ultra-refined spinster, Lady Lillian (Alexandra Carlisle), the elder, the satirical, pragmatic widow, Lady Mary (M.A.). The middle-aging noblewomen (as a result of the market crash) find themselves penniless and facing the loss of their elegant Mayfair house and their faithful (and impeccable) retainers. While Lady Lillian sits down and weeps, Lady Mary goes out and rents the second floor to an Australian family with the wealth of Croesus and the manners of kangaroos, and thus, while their sanity is threatened, their property is secured. Eventually the *précieuse* Lillian marries the bull in the china-shop, big Tom Larcomb, while the dashing vulgarian Una Pidgeon marries the languid dandy Tim Crabbe (M.A.'s son):

> Miss Anglin [says Charles Collins of the *Chicago Tribune*, 10.7.34] is carrying the weight for dowager comedy roles now, and is acting the character of Lady Mary Crabbe, a needy patrician who rented the second floor of her London mansion to a trio of crude colonials, with consummate skill. Her touch is crisp; her character drawing is shrewd; her humor ripples with polite irony. . . . Miss Carlisle is equally adroit in a more fluttering vein.

Mrs. [Lottie] Pidgeon, a down-under version of Mrs. Malaprop, was played "satisfactorily" (if a little over-pointedly) by sister-in-law Josephine Hull. Collins was apparently enough of a snob to like the play (few American critics did) and concludes his review with these words of commendation:

> Altogether this production is a vast improvement upon the general trend of recent Chicago theatrical adventures. It has that admirable quality which is vaguely called "style."

Two weeks into the run of *Fresh Fields* M.A. accepted an offer to do a radio production of scenes from Schiller's *Mary Stuart* (1800), in the scripting of which Howard may or may not have had a hand ("Am looking at Schiller's *Mary*"). The Australian-born-and-educated tragedienne, Judith Anderson (*aet.* 36), took the part of Elizabeth, while M.A. (*aet.* 58) played Mary. (Schiller makes Mary 25 and Elizabeth 28). In this case, all the laurels went to Miss Anderson, and in hindsight M.A. might well have conceded that she was ill-advised to accept the challenge in the midst of a rather "difficult" run. The *N.Y. Dramatic Mirror* (27.7.34) has this to say about *Mary Stuart*:

> On the basis of this performance at least, one would have to say that Margaret Anglin's voice is not attractive on the air, while her style seems ponderous and old generationish. She was distinctly outshone as a microphone personality by Judith Anderson. . . . It is perhaps unkind to make contrasts, yet they are inevitable when two legitimate theatre actresses play together, and hence it must be recorded that the Anderson tones were crisp and sure while the Anglin interpretation was less vivid. . . . It sums up as one of the less memorable excerpts offered on the Fleischmann programs.

"Nonsense," says Jerome Collamore (C, 9.9.85), "Mary carried Judith in this one. Judith had played Elizabeth old; she played this young Elizabeth exactly the same." Emmy Wittich believes (W, 16.10.85) that Miss Anderson played the title role in the radio *Iphigenia* to M.A.'s Clytemnestra, probably in '33.

From William Carson's account of Josephine Hull's involvement with *Fresh Fields*, we learn that it ran a rather turbulent course, marked by frequent "ructions" between M.A. and management, by Alexandra Carlisle's snitching on a script-revising M.A. to "Novello's agent" ("Disgusting!" says the loyal Josephine), and by other forms of dissension, until 1 September, at which point M.A. handed in her resignation. She stayed on long enough, however, to help coach her replacement, Gladys Hanson, who remarks that (in spite of her generally imperious ways) "Miss Anglin was most charming to me—upon the several times I saw her in my rehearsals" (DJ. 217-218).

M.A. then set about bargaining for performing rights to *Fresh Fields* so that she might take it to Broadway for the fall/winter season of 1934-35. While she was engaged in these ineffectual machinations she apparently turned down an offer from Messrs. Arnaud and Connors of the starring role in *The Widow's Walk* (N.Y. *Herald Tribune* 10.3.35); Howard's steadily worsening health may well have been a factor in her refusal of a play of such a title. Meanwhile dear Josephine was giving up good offers to keep herself available, and by the time M.A. had *Fresh Fields* ready for Cape Cod in the summer of '35, Josephine, who was stony broke, had had to accept a poor part in a George Kelly farce at Bar Harbor. Relations between the "sisters" (mediated by "Mother [Elinor] Hull") were strained to the breaking point: "Am I simply to wait her beck and call, and starve in the process?" asked the long-suffering Josephine.

With the Australian outbackers turned into Wyoming badlanders (because of accent problems?), and with Eda Heinnemann playing Lottie less "satisfactorily" than Josephine, *Fresh Fields* opened ("with an eye turned hopefully toward Broadway") on 22 July 1935 at the Cape Playhouse, Dennis, Mass., under the management of Raymond Moore. The summer folk apparently "took some pleasure" in the Novello farce of manners, says the *N.Y. Times* (23.7.35) reporter, "more by virtue of the principal players than by that of the quality of the play":

> The performance [he continues], particularly in the case of Margaret Anglin, who plays the sweeping, bluntly humorous Lady Mary in entertaining manner, is better than the play deserves. The actress carries the action by sheer force of her personality. Mary Sargent is admirable as the willow-weeping Lady Lillian, attractive enough to warrant her belated romance and annoying enough to provoke boundless irritation. Eda Heinnemann clowns the parvenu mother a little too much.

Fresh Fields paid its way (and M.A.'s) that summer at Dennis, Newport (R.I.), and Bar Harbor, but it failed to attract a Broadway angel until the following February. In August of '35, M.A. was dickering with William Popper of the University of California over terms for doing either *Athaliah* (Racine) or *The Persians* (Aeschylus) at the Greek Theater. She was also trying to work out an arrangement to do some unspecified modern play (probably Kelly's stage-life farce, *The Torchbearers*) "for George Kelly and Homer Curran in San Francisco" (S. 4.9.35). But everything fell through, partly because "Neil [her black chauffeur] had to go to Carolina because of family trouble" (S. 4.9.35).

And, speaking of family trouble: in fairly close succession, in 1935, two members of M.A.'s "family" got into some very murky troubled waters. In the first instance, her brother, Timothy Warren Jr., was apparently arraigned for fraud. He was eventually acquitted, but he died either during or shortly after the painful and expensive process, in which M.A.'s resources were used unstintingly. Wanny, according to Emmy Wittich, was "a handsome, quiet and distinguished man," who was, at the end, a victim of slander and "blackmail" (W, 24.11.85).

The second case was the arraignment of Livingston Platt (a virtual member of the Hull family) on a charge of homosexual soliciting. Once again, an acquittal was won. In both cases, apparently, the aid of former Governor Alfred Smith (a longtime friend of M.A.'s) was obtained.

Platt however, disappeared under a cloud, spent a couple of years painting in Belgium, under the name of Paul Aumond, and then returned ("heavily bearded") to set up ("with Eddie Strawbridge") a cut-rate "scenic studio" in New York (C, 16.10.85). When he first returned ("flat broke"), M.A. allowed him to live rent-free at Cedarwold in the winter, but she forgot to leave him enough fuel, and, according to Basile Anglin, she used to get "rather pathetic" letters from him, saying "it's lovely out here, but it's perishing cold." Cold as he was, however, he did paint a couple of charming Cedarwold winter landscapes which, of course, he gave to his patroness.

It is perhaps not very surprising to find M.A. writing at this time (21.10.35) to Randolph Somerville:

> As for correspondence, I have been shabbily neglectful of many dear friends, but the truth is, I have been sailing in troubled waters for some time past, and I haven't wanted the wash from my boat to reach the shore of my friendships. An emergence is, I am sure, imminent. Anyhow I *want* to see you, if only for a handclasp, and *soon*.

The fall and winter of '35 also saw M.A. once again giving much of her time and energy to radio work, consisting mainly of a Sunday evening series on WOR. Howard recalls her all-but-valedictory words ("vibrant cello-like words") at the close of the penultimate program of that series:

> "I have been asked to read Tosti's 'Good-bye'; I find I can't do it; it seems so final—and yet my next Sunday is my last here. I have for two and a half years, or almost as long, been so surrounded with care and thought by everyone. Next Sunday, my last, I have a surprise for you. I have been fortunate enough to obtain the permission of Mrs. Dwight Morrow to read some poems of her internationally famous daughter, Anne Morrow Lindbergh, and so till then to all my audience, Good night." Such simplicity [says Howard], such stripping of the words of any possibility of a tear, merely saying them, you seemed to be smiling gratefully and thankfully to, oh, ever so many people. I saw old and young, maybe children, who paused and wondered what it was all about, and the elders paused, too, who knew what it was all about. They will pause always when the name of Anglin is mentioned.

On Monday 10 February 1936, as Edward VIII was acceding to the British throne and Hitler was remilitarizing the Saar, Margaret Anglin was returning to Broadway, after an absence of seven years, in a throwaway piece of outmoded class-conscious nonsense.   That, at least, is what the earnest critics called it, and most of the New York reviewers seemed immune to the humor of *Fresh Fields* though not, fortunately, to the tart charm of M.A.'s acting:

> Carrying a comic characterization to the breaking point of burlesque [observes Howard Barnes of the *N.Y. Tribune*, 11.2.36], Margaret Anglin dominated the stage of the Empire Theater last night in what might be described as a trouper's holiday.   As the star of Ivor Novello's *Fresh Fields*, she summoned a multitude of thespian wiles to make one remember the funny interludes in a shiftless comedy and forget the piece as a whole. . . . Her personal triumph was not matched, however, by an increase in her artistic stature.

Richard Lockridge of the *Sun* (11.2.36) suspects that some of M.A.'s thespian wiles were not entirely appropriate to the vehicle:

> Returning after some seven years in circumstances which seem to me rather inauspicious, Miss Anglin gets a bit of sharp bite into Mr. Novello's elfin lines.   Her career in Greek tragedy has, however, imparted measured stateliness to her acting and her timing is not, I rather fear, the timing of farce.   This contrast between method and material often gives one the impression that Miss Anglin is playing in a rather more serious, and probably good deal better, play than anyone else.

Lockridge finishes his article on a note of puzzlement about "the title" which "doesn't seem to mean much more than the play."   It would appear that the title is a corruption of the famous final line of Milton's *Lycidas*, "Tomorrow to fresh Woods and Pastures new," which carries the apposite suggestion of a transition from aristocratic *inertie* to demotic *élan*.

Brooks Atkinson of the *Times* (11.2.36) has this to say about M.A.'s Lady Mary (and her famous handkerchief):

> Although the part bristles with a brand of snobbery which many people, including this playgoer, find especially distasteful, Miss Anglin plays it with a dry wit that is happily caustic.   She has been absent from Broadway for a very long time now, but she has not lost either the gleam or the mischievous handkerchief that used to give her comedy

playing its mettle. If it is possible to make peace with the old drawing-room comedy Miss Anglin knows how to turn the trick. . . .

Through all this mincing blither Miss Anglin moves majestically, crushing her handkerchief to her sententious lips and looking maliciously into the scenery. Whatever Mr. Novello's style may be, hers is that of a thoroughbred.

The pragmatic Jerome Collamore puts the long teased-out make-believe triumph of *Fresh Fields* into realistic perspective:

> In the spring of '34 I was trying to persuade M.A. to do *Medea* at the Met.—she was inclined to listen, but she said she'd have to slenderize. She certainly thought hard about it, but the next time I came to 149th & East River she had got hold of *Fresh Fields*. She thought she could raise money on Novello's name, but later found he'd done something which put him in bad with the critics, and she had difficulty raising money. Then she got hold of Casey and Littell who produced it in Chicago, and they proved to be crooked and so she got out from under them and Mrs. [Anspacher ?] came to the rescue. Then she got Alfred de Liagre to do the New York production. Mary wanted me and Josephine. Liagre said I was too Greek and also vetoed Josephine. Mary was sure he bilked her over production costs. *Fresh Fields* was not the huge success she had hoped, and she played for the Equity minimum of $50 a week to keep the play going. And after a run of 80 performances it closed. But this was a good enough run to sell it to the summer circuit. (C, 11.9.85)

And so, after a respectable run at the Empire, *Fresh Fields* had a "decent" fortnight in Philadelphia in May, and was played through the latter part of June and July at White Plains and Mount Kisco, both within thirty miles of Cedarwold (Katonah), and later at Northwestern U. (Evanston) and Union College (Schenectady) and Ogunquit (Maine). Again the Novello farce, with its "New York cast," proved to be "highly acceptable" summer fare, and therefore reasonably profitable.

In the midst of her immersion in frivolous froth she was still seeking to reanimate her career as a Greek tragedienne. According to Jerome Collamore, "In 1936 she tried to organize a production of *The Trojan Women* [of Euripides] with Jane Cowl, Lenore Ulric, and herself in the role of Andromache" (J. 274). But once again she was unable to scare up the necessary (heavy) financial backing. M.A. was also "muchly put off" by overhearing Jane Cowl telling Collamore she would be glad to talk turkey with Margaret, "but I hope it isn't about Greek

Photo courtesy of Basile Anglin

M.A. as Lady Crabbe in *Fresh Fields*, 1936: a triumphal return to the legitimate stage after a four-year absence.

stuff." That just about "derailed the whole scheme" right then and there (C, 14.9.85).

In the winter of '36, M.A., well into her sixty-first year, fat and tired and low-spirited, and obviously over-the-hill career-wise, made a quite astonishing last grab at youth and glamor, and here we may let Emmy Wittich take over:

> She agreed to do a very strict diet and beauty treatment, combined with *Vogue* magazine and Richard Hudnut's Fifth Ave. beauty salon—all under doctor's care. This was to be a before-and-after article for *Vogue* with loads of pictures. This was the toughest thing M.A. ever did. It was a daily procedure for over six months. A terribly crash diet, daily exercise, paraffin baths and massages. . . . By May 1937 M.A. lost 65 [198-133] pounds. She looked gorgeous, about 25 years younger. Beautiful clothes were bought for her, lots of photographs were taken to be published in *Vogue*'s July issue. (W, 16.10.85)

It is nice to think that M.A. derived a good deal of satisfaction and pleasure from her rejuvenation, and much praise from the fast-fading but still-smiling Howard. But it was all just a little like whistling past the graveyard, for Howard's decline in the spring of '37 began to be quite rapid. M.A.'s letter of 2 August 1937 to Randolph Somerville contains this account:

> The doctors informed me at the end of April that Howard had no chance of living beyond a few months. I knew he was ill—he had not been strong for years—but the shock of the news affected me more deeply than I want to think of. It has been hospitals and doctors ever since. He had to be driven in from the country every day for many weeks. He suffered greatly, but with magnificent consideration for others, and with courage. I took these summer engagements that I should not have to leave him—but the effort and strain thro' disastrous rush and other matters connected with the performance of an insufficiently prepared play etc.—and a twenty-hour-a-day schedule during the heat wave—was too much for me (plus a bit of sunstroke), and I cashed out in Dennis, and there gave only half a performance when I did get going.
> On my return I found a fatal retrogression in H. I won't go into further details—of what this last or past week has been.

One of the things M.A. did at the end was to pull Howard out of the New York General (where he was simply ignored and left to fend for himself as best he could) "and take him to

St. Claire's where the nurses of the Catholic order gave him good care" (C, 14.11.85).

The 28 June opening of M.A.'s much-labored-over new play, *Retreat from Folly*, by Amy Kennedy-Gould, Eileen Russell, *and* Margaret Anglin was, at least in Wilella Waldorf's account, a full-blown fiasco.

In the story, Flora Lowell (M.A.) is the English widow of an American millionaire who, upon her return to London, is waylaid by her English ex-husband with a tale of woe about his and *her* wayward children, whom she has not seen since their infancy. She manages (incognito) to rescue her son from a course in car-thievery and her daughter from the lascivious clutches of an old flame of her own, and then remarries the for-the-first-time-duly-appreciative ex-husband. All this is confusing enough, says Miss Waldorf (*N.Y. Post*, 30.6.37),

> but by the middle of the second act it occurred to us that Miss Anglin had not only rewritten the play but appeared to be still revising as she went along. Such heartfelt lines as "I don't think I can stand this much longer" acquired a double meaning as the actors struggled through.
>
> There were times when this reporter, too, was on the verge of giving up the fight. But Miss Anglin, who isn't daunted by much of anything, even writing a script as she acts it, waded triumphantly through a maze of chatter, and when she couldn't think of anything more to say, laughed and laughed, or cried and cried. In moments of extreme anguish she laughed and cried at the same time. It was a highly emotional evening.
>
> Only Miss Anglin herself knows how she felt at the end of it, but this reviewer left the theatre a limp damp rag of a thing, and it was a cold, cold night.

The *Variety* (7.7.37) critic tells us that Miss Anglin not only substantially revised the script but also "assumed a heavy share of the director's duties," and he ventures to suppose that "the net result would have been more praiseworthy if Miss Anglin had been content to do less." This reviewer also speaks quite frankly of the "lapses of memory" on M.A.'s part that Miss Waldorf so broadly implies.

The part of Flora Lowell, says Douglas Gilbert of the *N.Y. Telegram* (30.6.37), ought to be a "supremely sympathetic" one:

> but Miss Anglin, long a distinguished figure in our theatre, lays waste her powers by the most exaggerated

Photo courtesy of Basile Anglin

A 1911 photograph of Howard Hull, who died August 7, 1937.

playing I have seen in years.   Here is the outmoded technique of the chuckle, the lifted eyebrows, the facial emoting, the false movement, the "beseeching" style of the old school of acting that, in its excesses, demands, instead of wins, attention.

That sounds like a list of don'ts that M.A. herself would give to an aspiring actress, but it is clear that she was running out of control.   For almost the first time in forty years she was considerably worse (rather than considerably better) than her material—and in this case it would appear that she herself also had a hand in botching the material.

One long-term plus for M.A. in *Retreat* was her introduction of a newcomer to the summer circuit in the person of Dan Duryea who "contributed capably" in the small part of a young con-man called Conway.   Duryea, of course, went on to become a well-known film actor, "specializing in whining villains," and scoring notable successes in *Black Angel* (1946) and *Chicago Calling* (1951).

The diabolically appropriately named *Retreat from Folly* ran a ragged and "woeful" week at Mount Kisco, another marginally smoother week in the Country Playhouse in Westport, Conn., and then quietly gave up the ghost, without even the faintest whisper of Broadway to be heard anywhere. M.A. next appeared on 14 July at the Cape Playhouse at Dennis, Mass. in Raymond Moore's production of *Marriage Royal* by Robert Wallsten, a somewhat derivative new play "with echoes from *The Queen's Husband* [a Gladys Hanson success of 1928] and *The Masque of Kings* [a Henry Hull success of 1937]."   The *N.Y. Times* (15.7.37) notice goes on to say that "The opening had been postponed from the previous night owing to the indisposition of Margaret Anglin, the star," but that the star, nevertheless, had a good first night: "She endowed the Empress Teresa with royal capriciousness and unfailing dignity and personal charm."

"Mary was exhausted by mid-summer of '37," says Jerome Collamore (her stage-manager at that time), and he suggests that the wonder is not that the plays were a bit ragged but that they ever got on at all:

In the case of *Retreat from Folly*, Liagre was the producer of the stock company and he wanted to direct.   M.A. said O.K. (Of course she really did it; Liagre was really just in the way.)   Mary was all right on direction, but she was having a lot of trouble with her lines.   I remember sitting in the set fireplace, giving her her lines when needed.   Liagre thought the show would be a disaster, so he went before the curtain and said that he was not the director as stated in the program, but that Miss Anglin had directed it. Actually we got through not that badly. I remember Tallulah Bankhead came back after the play to see M.A. and pat her on the back.

Arthur Sircomb directed *Marriage Royal*, and when M.A. (because he had wasted hours on costumes the night before) was too pooped to make rehearsal the next day ("Why couldn't the cast come to my bedroom and sit around my bed and run the lines?" she asked), he gave an ultimatum: "Either she shows for this rehearsal, or she doesn't open." Fortunately, Raymond Moore, the manager, who was a prince, intervened. He said, "Why don't you rest today, come to the theatre tonight and have a dress rehearsal. We'll dismiss the audience and open on Tuesday. We got through Tuesday all right and two shows on Wednesday, but she was at the edge of her resources, and if I hadn't cooked her a supper on Wednesday, she wouldn't have eaten. And then I got word that my father was dying, and Mary said, "Jerry, you must go. I'll be all right." (C, 14.9.85)

On 12 July 1937 Howard wrote thus cheerfully (from Cedarwold) to his mother Elinor Vaughn Hull:

Dear Ma Mère,

You see I fall into French; my grandmother was a French woman and, I have heard, not particularly reputable. I am glad there is some distinction in the family. Mab opens tonight in Dennis, Mass., Cape Playhouse in a new play called *Marriage Royal*—one of course hopes something from it. A young woman by the name of Tamara is in it, Herbert Yost, E.H. Fielding and the author of the play whose name is Wallsten. Quote: "Some idea of the excellence of the cast may be gathered from a perusal of the foregoing Broadway names." I think Eddie Plohm and I wrote that phrase forty years ago. It was a good line—Pres. Harrison thought so at the time. . . .

The play called *Retreat from Folly* is, I am sure, going to be a big success. It is a play that Marie Tempest did in London, and Will Hull in the *Courier Journal* says it is rich and warm and will unquestionably appeal to those theatregoers who like the humor and decencies of human folk.

As you know me quite well, you know I will spend the evening praying for the success of the show in Dennis.

Always love,

Howard

On the envelope is written in Elinor's hand "Howard's last letter." Twenty-five days later Howard was dead, and on 16 August 1937, M.A. replied thus to Randolph Somerville's invitation to discuss a theatrical collaboration:

Dear Randolph,

A thousand thanks for your letter and its kind content. I hope I can answer it in the course of the week. Meantime, as you may have guessed from this bordered paper, I have lost my dear Howard.

He passed away at dawn on the 7th of August—just tired out and weakened from his long fight. His heart failed.

I can't do more than send you a few words now, but it will explain another postponement in correspondence.

Affectionately,

Mary

Chapter XIV

The Rivals and Watch on the Rhine: 1937-1958

O, let not virtue seek
Remuneration for the thing it was . . .
(Shakespeare, *Troilus and Cressida*, 3.3.168)

Howard was scarcely cold in the grave when M.A. accepted an offer to do *Retreat* at Ogunquit. She explains herself in the process of turning down an invitation from Randolph Somerville to join him and his students "cavorting with Shakespeare in a sylvan setting":

> Dear Randolph [she responds]: Thank you for your kind letter and its invitation. I can think of nothing that would be nicer than to accept it, but I fear rest, and I can only meet strangers for some time to come.
>
> What a lovely way to go off and study. How fortunate your young people are.
>
> I am going to pick up work again in a post-season at Ogunquit. This will probably make it possible for me to retain an option on the play—hence the effort. (S, 22.8.37)

And "the effort" was surely commendable. It conformed somewhat to the letter she received (30.10.37) from Father John O'Hara, President of Notre Dame University, who wrote to assure her of the "many prayers, Masses and Holy Communions for the repose of [her] husband's soul" which the Congregation of the Holy Cross would "feel privileged to offer up," and finished with an "in perpetuity" offer of "50-yard-line tickets" for her and her brother (Basil) for the Notre Dame-Army game which, he knew, was, for her, the one significant sporting event of the year.

Another of the *many* messages of condolence that she must have especially cherished was this telegram:

> Just heard of your sad loss.
>
> My sincerest loving sympathy.
>
> Virginia Harned Courtenay.

There is a heart-warming assurance in those two lines that the ever-gracious Virginia was glad that her illness forty years earlier (in *Lady Ursula*) had provided M.A. with a stepping-stone to stardom.

In the early 'forties, M.A. did a number of hour and half-hour shows for radio, including some Catholic charity work; she is shown here with Francis Joseph, Cardinal Spellman, c. 1942.

M.A. was indeed ready to make the effort to live up to the troupers' watchword of indomitability, "the show must go on," but, as Emmy says, "The loss of Mr. H. was too much for M.A.: after that she started regaining weight" (W, 16.10.85), and, one may add, steadily losing physical verve and mental acuity—so that, henceforth, only flashes of the former brilliance were possible.

She did play *Fresh Fields* through late June and July at Clinton, Conn. (two weeks) and Gloucester, Mass. (three weeks) in the summer of '38, but, as she observed, a little wearily, to Somerville: "These summer theatre jaunts yield little financial return, . . . small personal satisfaction, and no artistic achievement" (S, 1.8.38).

In the fall of '38, according to Emmy Wittich:

> They were going to do on Broadway a revival of *Outward Bound*. M.A. was asked to play it with Burgess Meredith, but simply couldn't adapt herself to the [rather brash young] company. I remember somebody calling her by her first name. She was shocked. Most of all she didn't like the director, new from Germany [the outrageously rude, thirty-two-year old] Otto Preminger. After a few [fractious] rehearsals she gave it up. (W, 16.10.85)

Outward Bound is the atmospheric, semi-symbolist fantasy by Sutton Vane about the Ship of Death carrying a motley assemblage of the newly dead out into the ocean of eternity. The death-pondering M.A. would have liked to have played it, but not at the expense of having her Christian name bandied about by junior members of the company, and hearing the guttural growls of a director scarcely old enough to be her son. Preminger ultimately chose Laurette Taylor as his female lead. Even though "she had been an alcoholic for ten years" (P, 49), she was apparently easier to direct than Margaret Anglin. Actually, not to spoil a good story, M.A. was reading for the second female part (the raddled ex-beauty, Mrs. Cliveden-Banks) and was replaced, as she was exactly ten years before in *Macbeth*, by her friend Florence Reed.

At this time she was also dickering for production rights to George Kaufmann's "delightful" *Kingdom Come* (S, 8.9.38). But her big project in '38 was trying to sell *The Persians* of Aeschylus to the Greek Theater with herself in the "not overlong or complex role of Atossa." However, it was again an obvious financial no-go, for the University of California wouldn't pick up the tab, and it was no longer possible for her to get a financially offsetting "commercial engagement" in her beloved Golden Gate city (J, 277).   As a sop, President Sproul offered M.A. a summer teaching post at the university, which she wisely declined: "My lectures on Greek tragedy [she admitted] would only be glorified rehearsing, which is all I know how to do" (J, 278).   Incidentally, in the summer of '37 she had tried to interest the Hollywood Bowl in a Margaret Anglin *Electra* to challenge Blanche Yurka's recent *Electra* success and proposed Berkeley performance—fortunately she was turned down flat.   At the end of '37 she had tried to entice Katherine Cornell and Guthrie McClintic into "joining her in a production of *The Trojan Women*," but they had declined "most politely but most succinctly" (J, 274).

Despite the flurry of theatrical activity, 1938 (like most of the remaining active years) was mostly given over to radio and "platform" work, and we hear (S, 17.5.38) of a "Concert series, . . . going to Detroit" in which she was presumably a feature performer, perhaps in "The Happy Prince."   On 16 October 1938, M.A. was in Toronto to do a Shakespeare broadcast for the CBC.   Before the show, she and Jerome Collamore were treated, as the latter recalls, to an "excellent dinner at Arthur's, me beside Mrs. Frank [Harriet], Mary beside Arthur, then to studio for broadcast" (C, 14.9.85).   M.A. did the Katharine scenes from *Henry VIII*.   The performance, Collamore implies, was not conspicuously good, but she did not miss the opportunity of injecting an affecting tremolo into such lines as,

> Sir,
> I am about to weep; but thinking that
> We are a queen—or long have dream'd so,—certain
> The daughter of a king, my drops of tears
> I'll turn to sparks of fire.

and

> O my Lord,
> The times and titles now are alter'd strangely
> With me since first you knew me.

and

> like the lily
> That once was mistress of the field and flourish'd,
> I'll hang my head and perish.

In 1939 M.A. gave up her apartment (130 W. 57th St.) and took to using hotels (first the San Carlos, then the Sevillia) as her New York base; she also began selling off all the well-preserved costumes and props of the palmy days. The tax man had begun to hound her for arrears—"I never paid taxes when I was rich," she told Basile, "why should I now that I'm poor." It was another year of many theatrical projects and pipe-dreams but, so far as one can ascertain, no engagements. She did, however, have a regular Monday evening radio show, and perhaps her most memorable event of '39 (reminiscent of her rolling-chair stage experience of '22) was her "crash" on the "shining floors" of the NBC studios. She writes thus to Somerville on 3 July 1939:

> While I have been very cautious (pedestrianly speaking) ever since I fell over the steps that didn't exist in Maplewood last October, newly polished floors at NBC headed me for a crash on Monday night. I went through the broadcast, and, after it, was ordered to the hospital where the x-ray revealed a fracture, only a small one, I think (and hope!). I didn't ask for details, I was too forlorn to be interested. Anyhow, here I am in a splint, vying in beauty with Epstein at his most Epsteinish. Except for my ribs, I am in no serious pain and will go to work in a "rolling chair" next Monday, but, alas, not, I fear to Cooperstown.

On Monday 4 September 1939 (the day after the declaration of another war), Norah Kelly Worthington left her husband Cyril and *Orphans of Divorce* was on. This was the story of how Norah, a stylish Manhattan matron of fifty, is ditched by her wealthy businessman husband for a gold-digging, oversexed twenty-nine-year old actress. The two sons and a daughter (in their mid-twenties) become their mother's bulldogs as divorce litigation goes forward. So, in order to stop the internecine warfare, Norah Kelly decides to become Norah Knight, and disappear. The stage is set for endless tear-jerking possibilities, and, presumably, an eventual smarmy reunion of the noble Norah and the cynical Cyril. In the second episode Norah gets run over (and amnesia); in the third she gets a marriage proposal from her rescuer. And so it went for eight or ten platitudinous programs. As Emmy Wittich recalls:

> The script was badly written. M.A. re-wrote a lot. The writers and producers didn't like that at all. It was on the air for quite a while. I guess when the writers and producers had had enough of interference they took it off the air. (W, 16.10.85)

The Worthingtons were scarcely more dumpish and dissentious than their creators. M.A. liked the idea of preaching against divorce, but she couldn't come to terms with her text or her acolytes.

In 1940 she was still thinking Greek tragedy, with special reference to the Trojan War. She asked her friend and former press agent Thoda Cocroft to sound out Joan Crawford (Andromache) and Marlene Dietrich (Helen of Troy) for a production of *The Trojan Women* in which M.A. would play Hecuba. Apparently Thoda's soundings fell on deaf, or more likely, incredulous ears (J, 279). Also in 1940, to let Johnson continue:

> She tried to talk Eva Le Gallienne into a production of *Iphigenia in Aulis*. The project was to be for the benefit of various war charities in Europe. She suggested that Washington and Ottawa would be ideal locations for a simple production of the tragedy: "a royal tent set among rocks and trees, voilà tout." She met with Miss Le Gallienne about this and about setting up a classical repertory to produce the Greek plays as well as the plays of Shakespeare, Molière, Racine, Goethe, Schiller, Goldoni, and Restoration comedy. Nothing resulted from this ambitious scheme. (J, 280)

One nice theatrical thing did happen for her in 1940, and that was a successful production of *A Party* (with a college cast, and M.A. as Mrs. Pat and co-director) in Florida. As Emmy Wittich recalls:

> Early in March 1940, the president of Rollins College [Richard Burton], a friend of M.A.'s, asked her to put *Party* on for the students. It was done very well. And 2 weeks at that time of year in Florida [Winter Park] was great. (W, 16.10.85)

She also did *Fresh Fields* ("Will it never die?") with a stock company at Ridgefield, Conn. (sixteen miles from Cedarwold) for a fortnight at midsummer. She certainly *wanted* to do *A Party* or *Kingdom Come* or *Fresh Fields* for Somerville at his little theatre at Cooperstown called The Duke's Oak, but apparently never did. Her health was clearly becoming increasingly precarious—she speaks to Somerville on 3 June as "just finishing off a year of mad physical damage with a sturdy attack of bronchitis." On the 10th she speaks of a "visit to Dr. Hood," and ends: "I have just heard Duff Cooper's speech [on the progress of the blitzkrieg] and my hand is shaking so that I cannot write." She contents herself in August (S, 10.8.40), after more well laid plans had "gane agley," with the simple expletive, "Quel summer!" However, four days later (14.8.40) she recorded an abridged *Evangeline* (ARS) with a piano rendition by George Vause of the orchestral background music by Philip Gordon. This record is still extant. It preserves a full-throated but not always well-modulated rendition. She had, incidentally, performed the fully orchestrated *Evangeline* in Detroit in May of '38 with Henry Ford (a fierce aficionado of all nineteenth-century Americana) as guest of honor. In appreciation of her ardent rendition, Ford presented her with a deluxe set of McGuffey's *Eclectic Readers* (6 vols.), which prize fell a little short of the lucrative recording contract she had been banking on.

M.A.'s only (traceable) histrionic endeavor of 1941 took place in New York on 3 January. This was the radio (WOR) version of R.C. Berkeley's *The Lady with a Lamp*, in which M.A. took the role of Florence Nightingale (C, 16.9.85). This minor achievement may have reminded her of an earlier, loftier wish to create a play called *The Trial of Edith Cavell* in collaboration with Paul Kester (K, 6.6.17). Jerome Collamore also gives us the incidental intelligence that "in the winter of '41 M.A. was living at the Sevillia Hotel on W. 58th St." (C, 16.9.85).

Doubtless there was a fairly steady trickle of radio work coming her way. "All through the late thirties and early forties," says Emmy Wittich, "M.A. did lots of radio work, hour and half-hour shows. She did some Catholic charity things: Cardinal Spellman and Governor Alfred Smith were present" (W, 16.10.85). It might be remarked that Smith's last year as Governor was 1928, and that Francis Joseph Spellman was made Archbishop of New York in 1939 and Cardinal in 1946. M.A. had known Smith since the mid-twenties, and probably first met Spellman in the mid-thirties.

The last word on '41 is a note from M.A. ("in the grip of a devilish cold, and not doing any feasting") to Somerville on 31 December conveying "many good wishes for the coming year and a heartfelt cheerio—before I look at the evening paper and fall into despondency." Oddly enough, the old and tired Margaret Anglin constantly fretted about World War II, whereas the youngish and ebullient Margaret Anglin had seemed almost oblivious to "the Great War"—which may have been why she had an "impervious" tank named after her (*Variety*, 6.11.18).

Nineteen forty-two, against all probability, saw M.A. back on the boards in a major production, with a "very strong" Walter Hampden. It all came about because "Detroit's own" Mary Boland (another Sacred Heart Convent and Charles

Frohman girl) who was playing Mrs. Malaprop in Eva Le
Gallienne's production of *The Rivals* was, as Jerome
Collamore politely puts it, "bending the elbow too much"
(C, 16.9.85).   Emmy Wittich is less metaphorical about the
weakness of the "gentle and generous Mary" (GSAS, 76):

> [In March of 1942] the Theater Guild asked M.A. to go to
> Chicago to replace Mary Boland in *The Rivals*.   The
> reason, Miss Boland was a heavy drinker and was most
> of the time intoxicated—so I heard.   M.A. had one week
> to prepare.   She had a gorgeous costume made of bright
> green heavy taffeta.   Took her long-haired Mary
> Magdalen wig which I put into a coiffure every
> performance. She was still having difficulty remembering
> lines, so she had me stay in the wings with the script
> and I gave her the lines whenever she came towards me.
> From Chicago we went to Boston and from there to
> Baltimore. (W, 16.10.85)

Apparently Miss Boland's indisposition was attributed
to "sinus trouble" but nobody believed that, and when
(after getting bad reviews in Chicago) "she just upped and
quit," pretty Mary was sued ($4,000) for breach of contract
by the Theater Guild and suspended by Equity (of which
M.A. was by now a reluctant member).   In any case,
Hector Charlesworth (*Toronto Globe and Mail*, 28.3.42) paraphrases
the Chicago critic Lloyd Lewis to this effect:

> Miss Boland had punched all the life out of Mrs.
> Malaprop's lines, stressing the malapropisms so far that
> they broke down.   At her first entrance she bounded on,
> blond, loud and hoydenish.   Her interpretation was pure
> vaudeville—not unnaturally, since she had beside her the
> nightly spectacle of Bobby Clark making Bob Acres a
> variety turn instead of a dramatic role.   What we were
> getting from these two was much more in the order of
> slapstick than satirical comedy of manners.
>   Miss Anglin's interpretation, on the other hand, is
> genuine Restoration drama.   Apparently she has put on
> flesh and, following the fashions of Bath in the late
> eighteenth century, wore an enormous henna wig.   She
> entered with stately grace and sweetly regal smiles.   She
> toyed with the malapropisms gently, letting them straggle
> forth as merely the blunders of a silly woman, not at all
> sure of the meaning of words, but very, very certain that
> her position in society demanded their use.   Miss Anglin
> made her an essentially charming but illiterate matron,
> trying to live up to the affectations of the life around
> her, and she carried this idea into the action as well as

the quips. Miss Anglin has, in short, lifted this *Rivals* back onto the track again, and it is now, except for Mr. Clark's incredibly antic scenes, just what Sheridan meant it to be.

All this is very high praise (perhaps too high) for an off-the-shelf has-been, and indeed her opening in Boston was described by Rudolph Elie of the *Boston Herald* (17.3.42) as "not too secure," and he remarks that (in spite of Emmy's ministrations) "she tossed away a few of her lines."

Yet [he concedes] she demonstrated by her skillful stage business a sure hand for the comedy, and seems bound to improve as she becomes more comfortable in the part.

(And she was, indeed, more secure in the Baltimore run.)

The rest of '42 was largely taken up with trying to get performing rights to Emmet Lavery's play version of Eric Shepherd's *Murder in a Nunnery*, and meanwhile doing a lot of rewriting of the script. She wanted, particularly, to keep it out of the hands of Alfred de Liagre to whom it had been submitted and who, she thought, would surely botch the production of a potentially excellent play. ("What hope is there, when people expect anything from that brand of intelligence in the way of comprehension?" [S, 18.6.42].) She was told by Julie Hearnes of MGM that, if the piece played well, MGM would pay liberally for the movie rights. M.A. was clearly keen to do the (again "potentially") "very interesting, very human" part of the Reverend Mother, and much of her rewriting was directed towards "giving the play" to that character. At this time, too, she began her long campaign to mount an American revival of Pinero's "county," "turf" comedy *Dandy Dick* (1887). Neither of these elaborate schemes ever came to fruition, though she kept tinkering away at *Dandy Dick* for years.

Just after New Year's Day in 1943 the Theater Guild again called upon Miss Anglin to replace her fellow native Ottawan, Lucille Watson, in the dowager role of Fanny Farrelly in Lillian Hellman's Pulitzer-Prize-winning cloak-and-dagger piece *Watch on the Rhine*. After having been promised "3 weeks time and 2 weeks rehearsal," she was allowed "only 4 rehearsals in New York," and asked, on that basis, to fit into a more or less seasoned *Watch* cast (S, 31.1.43). Then, in icy-foggy Detroit, she fell victim to a viral cold and earache and she asked the producer, Frank McCoy, to send out an S.O.S. for Lucille Watson to return. McCoy said he'd try (which he didn't), but she'd simply have to tough out the Detroit opening (which she did). And she continued, through much bodily misery, to "rowdy [her] way thro'" for a whole month (13 Jan.-13 Feb.) in Detroit, where one critic was sufficiently taken with *Watch* to call it "a perfect play with a perfect cast" (*Toronto Telegram,* 13.2.43).

In the story, Fanny Farrelly is a wealthy Washington widow (full of eccentric vim and vinegar) whose daughter Sara has married Kurt Müller, a leading actor in the underground anti-Nazi resistance movement. Sara returns to her ancestral home with her husband and three children in the spring of 1940, just when Fanny is hosting her best friend's daughter and her husband, the nefarious Rumanian Count Brancovis. Brancovis recognizes Müller and attempts to blackmail him. Müller kills Brancovis (as the only secure course) and disappears into the night. And the self-centred and insular Fanny is at last moved to compassionate admiration of Kurt's heroic altruistic idealism. She and her smugly complacent family have been, as she says, "shaken out of the magnolias."

Needless to say, the Toronto critics (who are moderately laudatory of the play), save the choicest of their sugar-plums for the dowager, "the Speaker's daughter." Hector Charlesworth of the *Globe and Mail* (16.2.43) observes that:

> The role of the matriarch is so subtly and elaborately drawn that it provides a magnificent opportunity for the flawless finesse and brilliant individuality of Miss Anglin. Her beautiful speaking voice, with its infinite variety of expression, and her sense of poise and pace make the character human and memorable.

Augustus Bridle of the *Star* (16.2.43) recalls Margaret Anglin's having been seen fleetingly in Toronto fifteen years earlier in a glittering cameo part in *Diplomacy*, and delights in having "this splendid veteran actress" back in her home town for a fortnight in a challenging full-length role. The part of the cultivated but shrewish "old-school" American tory "seems to have been made for her; she does it with such wit, poise and alert dignity, and such distinctive musical diction."

Rose MacDonald of the *Telegram* (16.2.43) is even more fulsome:

> It is a captivating performance that she gives, with the light comedy touches which the role of Madame Fanny, so kind, so wilful and, for all her foibles, so much the great lady, contributes to the play. . . . It is an altogether enchanting, amusing and touching portrayal. . . .

Of course, the fact that Miss Anglin had vouchsafed young Rose an altogether gracious pre-performance interview may have added a little rose-color to her spectacles. That interview, published after the opening (17.2.43), had been a little nostalgic, a little rambling. Miss Anglin remembered skating across the bay to Toronto Island, and hitching rides on horse-drawn trams, and Goldwin Smith chatting with her father, and her mother's accounts of Lord Dufferin's soirées, and Sir Wilfrid Laurier showing her her birthplace in the House of Commons, and writing fan letters to young poets (one of whom spoke of the "perfume of melody" in her voice [EWW2]). Rose, incidentally, with the concurrence of the other critics, also tosses a bouquet to Walter Gilbert for a "deeply moving interpretation" of the role of Kurt Müller.

In the last week of the Toronto stand, M.A. accepted the invitation of her brother Arthur to move into his elegant house on Clarendon Avenue; and there, in the conservatory, one afternoon of pale wintry sun, a "plumpish, thirty-fiveish, Swedish maid" accosted her, drew her aside conspiratorially and conveyed to her a budget of horrifying intelligence:

> Mr. Anglin is a Nazi agent [she declared]. I know this out of all doubt. He has many secret meetings in his study after dark with many spies. They are all spies here. I know that you know persons in high places. You must use your influence to have Mr. Anglin arrested. Otherwise. . . .

She then opened her dress to show a hectic rash on her chest, saying "Look what they have done to me!" As these dreadful confidences continued, M.A. felt that she had suddenly been thrust (without a script) into an unwritten fourth act of *Watch*. Ultimately she managed to pacify the "poor demented creature" and to advise the amazed Arthur to put her into the care of an alienist. It was after this unnerving interview that M.A. told her niece Madeleine that this was the latest (and she devoutly hoped the last) of a continuing series of mad persons who seemed irresistibly attracted to her, "like iron filings to a magnet." Whether she had any other such lunatic encounters in her late "spaced-out" days we do not have any way of knowing—nor did she.

The Toronto engagement closed out M.A.'s six-week stint with *Watch on the Rhine*, but she did play it again that

Globe and Mail, *courtesy of Herbert Whittaker*

With Walter Gilbert in *Watch on the Rhine* at the Royal Alexandra; the Toronto critics saved the choicest of their accolades for the dowager, M.A., "The Speaker's daughter" (1943).

June for a fortnight at the Shubert Theatre in New Haven, Conn. Right after that she returned to Mrs. Malaprop. As Emmy recalls:

> In the summer of '43, a man in California [George A. Leal] wanted to produce *The Rivals* on the West Coast. [Leal] was born in Hawaii, had made a lot of money in trucking and was interested in the theatre. M.A. liked the idea. (W, 16.10.85)

After some initial failures of communication and niggling misunderstandings ("such that all courage, patience and certainly joy have oozed out of me" [S, 24.6.43]), a contract was worked out, and the production was launched on 25 July with a Sunday afternoon performance at M.A.'s old stamping-ground, the Greek Theater at Berkeley.

The performance was damned with faint praise by the *S.F. Chronicle* (27.7.43). The callow reviewer was clearly predisposed to see "Margaret Anglin, once a brilliant star," as a museum piece. "The performance," he says, "was possibly of more nostalgic than theatrical value." But the Sheridan material is sufficiently good and was sufficiently crisply presented that the afternoon was at least mildly diverting, "and in spite of a brutal sun which sent many scampering for cover, this somewhat truncated *Rivals* must be counted as a success within the limits Director Reginald Travers has staked out for it." Miss Anglin, opines the bright young critic, was "adequate" but a mite "creaky."

> I gather [he says] that she has no illusions about being "as great as she ever was." Those who saw her in her hey-day tell me she was magnificent and she is wise to want to be remembered that way.

His final prediction, that the production would do much better "when played intimately in something less vast and impersonal that the Greek Theater," was borne out by the polite reception accorded to the rest of the run. Through the rest of July and the first half of August the Leal *Rivals* travelled to "Sacramento, Oakland, Stockton, Santa Barbara, Long Beach, down to San Diego, and so on" (W, 16.10.85), and indeed did better in more intimate, and best in neo-classical, theatres.

"After the tour ended," says Emmy Wittich,

> she and I went to stay for a few weeks with Carrie Jacobs Bond [*aet.* 81], the author of such songs as "I Love You Truly," "Just a-Wearyin' For You," and "A Perfect Day." Mrs. Bond lived in a lovely house in the hills of Hollywood.

> M.A. also wanted to see some people in Hollywood, nothing to do with pictures, she was very camera-shy. (W, 16.10.85)

Nevertheless, we find M.A. writing to Somerville on 25 August:

> I am being deluged with movie offers. My only impression of it all being—they'll take a chance on anything, for fear they might miss or lose something, and for no other sane or intelligent reason.

M.A. apparently knew Carrie Jacobs Bond as far back as the fall of 1909 when she was playing *Helena Richie* at the Savoy. Jerome Collamore tells us that

> M.A. offered her the theatre on a Sunday afternoon when she wasn't playing, for Carrie to give a recital. Carrie sat at the piano and sang (really talked the songs, M.A. said) and that is what brought her to public attention. Later she had her own publishing Co. which brought forth her songs. I remember when Mary was at the apartment on E. 49th St. Carrie came there one evening and we had a very pleasant visit. (C, 3.10.85)

Incidentally, Margaret made use of Carrie's idea of talking songs over background music in her radio renditions of such old chestnuts as "Danny Boy," "In the Gloaming," and "Love's Old Sweet Song."
While she was with Mrs. Bond, M.A. was apparently attempting to recruit Victor McLaglen and Billie Burke (S, 8.18.43) to join her in a west-coast production of *Fresh Fields*, and negotiating with Leal about taking part in his production of the Victorian melodrama *The Drunkard*:

> I am [she concedes] something more than comfortably accommodated here, and it is beautifully situated, but, just to be perverse, a horrid nostalgia floods my senses at times—and I can hardly say for what or where—perhaps merely for things that are gone. (S, 21.8.43)

All the west-coast pipe dreams (including "radio work out here") went up in wistful smoke, and on 15 September she returned to New York where she leased a suite at the Sevillia Hotel ("but spent a lot of time at Cedarwold"). Later that fall she got the best of all the dramatic coaching jobs that occasionally came her way in her declining years. The celebrated (Canadian) conductor Wilfrid Pelletier asked M.A. to coach his wife, the equally celebrated (American) soprano Rose Bampton (*aet.* 35), in the acting of the title role of Gluck's *Alceste* (the opera version of Euripides' *Alcestis*):

> The fee [says Emmy] was generous. M.A. spent some time teaching Rose Bampton on the Met. stage. M.A. had two tickets from Miss Bampton for opening night. She took me. Miss Bampton gave a beautiful performance. (W, 16.10.85)

Nineteen forty-three was the last year of theatrical consequence for M.A., though she continued for some years to get *some* radio and *some* coaching work:

> In 1944 [says Emmy] she did have a couple of students. She rented a large studio apt. on W. 57th St. She had a hard time. She was not well. In '44 I married my husband who was in the army and who soon went overseas. I took a job but still worked mornings and evenings for M.A. until '46 when my husband returned. All the time I was with her in the city, she practically had a guest (one or more) for dinner every night. (W, 16.10.85)

She continued to spend freely both in town and in the country, keeping a housekeeper and caretaker at Cedarwold, and, of course, Neil (the chauffeur), and Emmy. By the mid-forties her brother Basil, at that time director of labor relations for Texaco, was beginning to pick up a number of the outstanding tabs; and his worries were augmented in 1946 when sister Eileen (after the death of her husband) returned from Peking with mem-sahib ways, precious little money, and a conspicuous drinking problem. She, too, ultimately became a charge to the genial and generous Basil.

Jerome Collamore recalls taking in Judith Anderson's highly touted performance of Robinson Jeffers' *Medea* with Margaret and Eileen in 1947. "Anderson," he says, "acted with loudness and deliberation." She was brash and spectacular, but where was the "awful stillness" that Anglin knew so well how to project? She also continuously upstaged Florence Reed, "a far better actress than Anderson ever dreamed of being." "Eileen said to me afterwards, 'Wasn't it awful; let's go back to the apartment and talk about it'" (C, 14.6.85). And so they did that, until the small hours, and doubtless had occasion to remind each other that forty years before, "on her sail to Australia [in 1908], Mary had been given a play by Robinson Jeffers (*aet.* 21) about a woman in love with a horse who was jealous of her husband and stamped him to death when he came into the stall.   Mary considered it filthy and threw it into the Pacific Ocean where it may still be floating" (C, 16.8.85).

The mid-to-late forties were also the time of the "nasal hemorrhages."   "When Eileen went to her [M.A.'s] apartment one morning, she said the bathroom looked as though a pig had been stuck" (C, 18.11.85).   At that point Basil took to phoning M.A. morning and evening to make sure she was all right (C, 30.9.85).   In the late forties, also, she contracted breast cancer and underwent radical mastectomy.   Through all this, her niece Basile says, "She was very stoical and never complained, though she must have been in considerable pain much of the time."   She was well aware of the fact that, with her failing memory and delayed reactions, she was something of a drug on the theatrical market, but she continued to think of herself as a potential play producer, capable of taking secondary parts in her own productions.   Indeed, she had come to believe that this was the only way in which she could "get to tread the boards again."

In 1945 she was much exercised over getting production rights to Zola's *Thérèse Raquin*, and securing a prominent part in it (the mother) for herself.   She sent a script, heavily reworked and annotated, to Eva Le Gallienne, whom she had elected to play the "smouldering" Thérèse.   According to Jerome Collamore:

> Eva replied, "I don't think I'm the smouldering type," and sent it back.   Then she and Margaret Webster took the idea and did it with Dame May Whitty. (C, 3.10.85)

In 1946 M.A. was all wrapped up with Jean Giraudoux's *La Folle de Chaillot* (1945).   She had acquired a French script from Alfred Lunt, via Thornton Wilder, who had decided not to translate it because he didn't like it.   M.A. tried her hand at translating it herself, but she found her French rusty and she couldn't cope with the Paris slang.   She kept translating "maquereau" as "mackerel" and not as "pimp," and wondering why the lines didn't make sense:

> Finally [says Jerome Collamore], she got Blythe Parsons to translate it for her.   Then Mary met a French actress who was a great friend of Madame Giraudoux, and she said, "I'm returning to Paris and will tell M. Giraudoux to give the play to no one but Margaret Anglin."   After waiting several

weeks Mary checked up and found that this French actress
had met an old flame in Montreal and had holed up there
for a while. Meanwhile Laurette Taylor had sent her stage
manager over and tied it up. (She died before getting to
rehearsal.) (C, 16.9.85)

M.A.'s last letter to Randolph Somerville is dated
"Cooperstown, 2 July 1946," and presumably antedates the
Parsons translation. "Miss McManus's sun-dappled velvet
lawn, and this lovely air—only bird twitters and the occasional
long hum of passing motors," has a sweet tranquilizing effect
upon the old campaigner, but the hand is shaky and the drift
is maundering:

> Yesterday [she writes] I worked part of the day on *La Folle*,
> but found myself wandering about from time to time, up the
> hill in search of our little "office," but abandoning the quest,
> as my gait was wobbly and uncertain and there was no
> strong shoulder to hold. . . .
> Last night, quite a thunderstorm about 7, then heavy rain
> till dawn. I closed all the windows in the sunroom and
> made my bed there—leaving the doors open to all I could of
> the rain perfumes. Slept most peacefully, except for one
> short Nazi-ridden dream. I seem to want to voice a *Te
> Deum* every other minute.

> Grateful love,

> Mary.

Perhaps the single most regrettable failure in M.A.'s
declining years was her inability to persuade any angel to
sponsor her in one last histrionic fling as the captivating
madwoman, Aurélie, in Giraudoux's tart but effervescent satire
on profiteering French-style. It really did seem a part tailor-
made for the slightly batty septuagenarian M.A., and
apparently she thought so herself. Ultimately, of course,
Martita Hunt stole Aurelia from her in the Broadway premiere
of *The Madwoman of Chaillot* in 1948.
It is gratifying to note that M.A.'s fear of impairing her
own reputation by undertaking leading roles in the forties was
less important to her than her fear of letting down the play.
Thus, in the spring of '46, when Jerome Collamore asked her
to play the important dowager role in his romantic comedy
Adelaide, in a summer run "on the Cape," she was "very
interested" and "gave it a lot of thought," but in the end "she
turned it down—'I was afraid I'd mess it up for you, Jerry'"
(C, 16.9.85). And in 1947 she "most regretfully decline[d] . . . an
offer from the Near East Relief Society to sponsor her in a

performance of *Electra*," because she was sadly convinced that she was simply not "equal to the demands of the role" (J, 281). Also in '47 (in a letter to the agent Lyman Brown) she turned down the offer of "the role of Queen Charlotte" (*The Queen in Britain*), which she thought so weakly written that only a monumental effort on her part could make anything of it ("enough to satisfy myself")—and there were no monumental efforts left in her. She was now, quite frankly, looking for an untaxing "fool-proof" part—one that might well have to be largely of her own devising.

In December of '48, however, she was happy to reply in the affirmative to this telegram (2.12.48) from the amateur actor-manager Stanley Daley of Saint John, N.B.:

> Newly organized group in Saint John entering play in Dominion Drama Festival. Would like to play under patronage of your distinguished name, with your kind consent to be known as "The Anglin Players." Play selected *Rebecca*. Hoping request finds favor with you. Letter following.

Miss Anglin's gracious response (5.12.48) was:

> Letter received. Certainly. Many thanks for the honor you do me. Margaret Anglin.

"The Anglin players" went on to honor her by meriting an honorable mention in the '49 DDF.

Work in the late forties was reduced to a trickle of small radio-drama parts, the occasional poetry reading, and a few drama classes, which she gave (and hated) "for Clare Tree Major at her school in Chautauqua" (C, 18.11.85). But as late as August 1950 she was still thinking seriously of treading her beloved boards just one last time in her long-pondered revival of Pinero's *Dandy Dick*. To that end (when she was seventy-four and he twenty-eight) she hired Harding Lemay, an out-of-work actor and would-be playwright, to help her rewrite *Dandy Dick* in such a way as to set her up in a fool-proof version of the very British, humorous role of Georgiana Tidman ("George Tid")—"a jovial noisy woman [as Pinero puts it], very horsey in manner and appearance, and dressed in a pronounced masculine style with billy-cock-hat and coaching coat." (Even though "George" is a widow in her mid-fifties, the never-say-die M.A. would still have had to contrive to lose twenty years in order to play her to the life.) The part was to be "reduced in lineage," sharpened in pithiness, and strategically hedged in on all sides with mnemonic jogs imbedded in the speeches of others.

During the two weeks (at $50 per) of drowsy afternoons at summer's end, which Lemay spent with her, the super-annuated diva often skipped the script-doctoring. Instead, she went maundering off into cloudy nostalgia and/or vanity trips for the dubious edification of the young self-avowed "failure," who knew that *he* would never be numbered among the cloud-dwellers:

> She had known Mrs. Pat [she told Lemay], and Duse, and Bernhardt, Coquelin, Henry Irving, and Ellen Terry. . . . Fingering the amber beads that swung against the crepe of her lavender tea gown, she repeated gossip and recalled ovations of fifty years earlier: Ellen Terry was charming, but she could never remember her lines; Duse was extraordinary, but only if she was audible, which wasn't often; and Bernhardt was a perfectly dreadful Roxane in Coquelin's French production of *Cyrano*. (*ILO*, 188)

Then the heavy lids would close upon the far-away look and she would cat-nap off while Lemay fidgeted through the yellowing leaves of her scrapbooks, until he was recalled by her "Forgive me, my dear, an old woman," and yet another half-century old "recollection of Mr. Frohman."

> At the close of each afternoon [Lemay recalls], her maid brought us Manhattans. Settling back against her pillows, Miss Anglin reminisced about old restaurants in New York, London, and Paris, riding in the Park with her husband [sic] before the turn of the century, Calvé and Emma Eames at the Metropolitan, Owen Wister [*The Virginian*], Richard Harding Davis, and William Vaughn Moody, playwrights, politicians, and poets. (*ILO*, 189)

On most evenings after their desultory "work," M.A. would take the lean and hungry Lemay to a good French restaurant just around the corner from the hotel. "During one of those placid meals [recalls Lemay], when she drank three Manhattans and ordered, but did not eat, a bowl of soup, she asked me, without preliminary comment, why I was unhappy." Lemay then confessed that his marriage was unhappy because he was a failure as an actor and his wife ("Priscilla") looked like becoming a success:

> "Give her up," said Miss Anglin, with a curiously dry inflection. I started to rise but her featherweight hand restrained me. "Give her up," she repeated. "She's an actress. Good or bad, she's an actress. She has no need for you, except as a porter, or a bookkeeper, or a nurse. Actresses don't have husbands, they have attendants."

> Taking my hand in hers, she gazed at my fingers as if she'd forgotten what she wanted to say, and then smiled with a tremulous self-mockery, not unlike Priscilla's, and released my hand. "No one knows that better than I," she said, collecting her furs and purse, "for I married a man very much like you."
>
> She didn't mention my marriage again. When the new script of *Dandy Dick* was neatly typed and inserted into its folder, she took me out to a celebration dinner and slipped a bonus check into my pocket. (*ILO*, 190)

On a later meeting she recalled (perhaps a little inaccurately) Howard "walking her home from the old Empire, holding her hand in his, like the country boy he really was. He, too, had been an actor, though not a very good one. 'He was too good a man to be a good actor'" (*ILO*, 191). Perhaps M.A. felt she could allow herself to speak bluntly of Howard's menial status to a relative stranger, since she always spoke of him affectionately (if not reverently) to mutual friends, and since, too, she had for over a dozen years made an annual pilgrimage (with flowers) to Albany's Rural Cemetery on the anniversary (7 August) of Howard's death, and never visited that city without visiting Howard's grave as well.

That last bonus check and those expensive "placid" dinners of "many courses" to which she treated the rather seedy Lemay were little grande-dame flourishes which she could now ill afford, but she could not break the free-spending habits of half a century—and besides, there was always Basil to bail her out. (On 23 July 1950, for instance, she sent a lavish floral tribute to Laurier House in Ottawa on the occasion of the death of her long-time friend Mackenzie King.) Shortly after the Lemay episode, however, Basil was constrained to liquidate *all* of M.A.'s remaining property in order to amortize her debts. He then took her and Eileen into his big house in Greenwich, Conn. (on Long Island Sound) and set the two sisters up, each in her own spacious apartment.

In the spring of '53, Basil, himself in failing health, could no longer cope with his menage or (as he was sometimes constrained to call it) "menagerie" of three high-voltage eccentric women—Eileen, verging on dipsomania, and both Marie, his wife, and Margaret, our heroine, a little batty and more than a little erratic. Margaret, in a moment of sweet reasonableness, volunteered to relieve the pressure by going for an extended visit to her old home-town of Toronto where she could be Arthur's guest. But in 1953 Arthur was an eighty-six-year-old invalid, and the seventy-seven-year-old insolvent and occasionally non-compos Margaret necessarily became a charge to his children. As far as her loyal colleague, friend and admirer Jerome Collamore is concerned,

> M.A.'s physical and mental powers were O.K. right up to the end. Her illness would mix up the expression of her thoughts, but I'm sure she was mentally clear. The last time I saw her was when she left for Canada. Her nephew [Dr. Adrian Anglin] came down and took her back. She thought it was only a trip. But she paced up and down as we waited for a car to take her to the airport. She kept looking over at me anxiously. I was afraid she'd come over and say she wouldn't go. But she finally left—never to return to New York, her real "home." (C, 22.11.85)

The actual date of her ultimate one-way excursion into the grey and oblivious north was 16 May, the feast, as the church-calendar-conscious M.A. would have noted with wry irony, of St. Brendan the Voyager, the first European to reach Canada. She actually rather enjoyed her first-ever plane ride in the company of the urbane Adrian. In a letter to Jerome Collamore, dated 1 June 1953, she remarks that she was almost clear of her maddening speech impediment at 25,000 ft.—"the higher we got, the better my language. Oh, for a cup-full of that air! *It would mend me.*" Unfortunately, she was not able to procure a beaker-full of the pure serene of the ozone layer, and after the descent of TCA 913 it was all down-hill for "la nonpareille," as Don Louis de Bourbon used to call her.

Towards the end of her time in New York she was given to a species of somnambulism which occasionally had her walking the streets at midnight in her nightgown, and on one occasion had her wandering about in the groves and thickets of Central Park searching for her "son" who was "lost." Eileen, commenting on that incident, told Basile that the only lucky thing about Margaret's marriage to Howard was that it was barren. Howard, she insisted, was both a knave *and* a fool—though her basis of judgement would seem to have been a couple of meetings in 1910, when Howard actually looked like a comer.

Basile also remembers having been the nonplussed audience for more than one reverberating, self-questioning soliloquy just before the fluttering M.A. was wafted from her. One of them went, according to Basile's notes, something like this:

> Where are my pretty son and daughter? What did I ever give poor Howard, poor Fido, but table scraps? Whatever became of my command of . . . my command? Electra's occupation's gone.

I remember Eléna, Electra, Orestra, Emnestra—but who am I?
I can't seem to remember myself.   Still, I *was some*body, I
suppose.   I did make *some*thing my own.   I spoke to many
audiences in a mighty civil manner—and said what?   No
matter; I spoke them fair.   We shall not look upon their like
again.   Art thou there, truepenny?   Dost hear this fellow in
the cellarage?

A little spooky, Basile says, this going off into blank verse and
Shakespearean tags, not knowing whom she was talking to.
On a more business-like note, M.A. once told Basile "I made
two million dollars and more out of fifty years of theatre, and
now I am a common almswoman."

Phrases of apologetic exasperation—"I can't remember," "I
can't think," "I cannot speak or spell aright," "I am a dumb
ox," "a shambles"—echo through the last few muddled and
disjointed letters of this splendidly articulate woman; and
there were indeed occasional fits of angry, crockery-crashing
frustration as the physical and mental depredations of her
disease became ever more engulfing and insulting.   Her lapse
into almost total non-responsiveness was essentially the result
of the aphasic component of her affliction—though it is
interesting to note, in this connection, that the French facility
of her youth seemed to return to her near the end.   Bertrand
Le Vay recalls her accessibility in her last days to questions
spoken in French, and recalls especially her sad recollection of
"les temps heureux jadis—les temps d'espérance."

But no one would wish to follow her too closely down
that last sad slope towards "mere oblivion" and the final
baffled and baffling silence.

Rather, at the end, one would surely wish only to hear
again the words of her old friend and admirer, Hector
Charlesworth, recalling Margaret Anglin in her early prime as
"a brilliant young actress" who "excelled in comedy as well as
emotion," as "a girl with beautiful red-gold hair, magnificent
grey eyes, striking animated features, and the bearing of a
princess."   And one would wish to hear again his heartfelt
conclusion: "Stage annals contain no record of an artist more
versatile, and few so richly endowed with personality and
beauty of utterance" (*Toronto Globe and Mail*, 13.2.43).

On 7 January 1958, Mary Margaret Anglin Hull died in
Toronto in a psychiatric nursing home on May Street (#8).
She was eighty-one years and nine months old.   According to
her nephew, Dr. Adrian Anglin, "She died of gradual
disintegration—the death certificate says 'pulmonary pneumonia.'"   Her death-bed was attended by her nephew, the

Reverend Gerald Falconbridge Anglin, C.S.B., who administered the last rites. She was laid to rest just south of her brothers, Frank and Arthur, and just west of her parents, Timothy and Ellen, under a handsome Celtic cross in Mount Hope Cemetery, while a dozen chilly nephews and nieces tried to remember something of her past glory.

The journalistic obituaries were more successful in this respect. They were replete with tributes to her dramatic "wit," "intelligence," "poise," "instinct," and "intransigence." One spoke of her "serene tragic features," another (the *N.Y. Times*) of the "cold, square-jawed intelligence" with which she played classic Greek tragedy. Many spoke of the excellence of her voice and of her rendition of dramatic poetry.

But the word which is, almost accidentally, exactly right is the "statuesque" of the *N.Y. Times* obituary. What she was, at her best, was *iconic*. She was a specific state of soul monumentally embodied, made statuesque—like the "statue-like . . . Psyche" in her favorite Poe poem ("To Helen"). The voice, too, was cunningly modulated, sculptural in its cadences. Like a mana-invested icon, her fully achieved "creations" were, and were intended to be, unforgettable. "Who will ever forget her poignant Mimi?" asks Morgan-Powell (*Montreal Star*, 18.2.43). The question, he would assure us, couldn't even arise in respect of Joan and Helen, Rosalind and Viola, Electra and Medea.

EPILOGUE

Lines Composed by the Grave of Margaret Anglin
May 1986

I lingered in the graveyard of Mount Hope
By Margaret Anglin's tomb,
Desiring something of this woman's scope,
That woman's art, in shifting gloom
And sunshafts, and I wondered,
In a little wisp of rain,
As a distant scene-shift thundered,
And the sun bowed out again,
Tears, is it tears, in the grey wind—?
I thought of Ruth, Helen and Magdalen,
Of wild Antigone, her father blind,
Her brother beastly dead on the bleak fen,
Of Phaedra and Medea, passion-torn,
Of Joan of Arc, how beyond reason brave,
Iphigenia, innocent, forlorn,
And deep clouds gloomed your grave.
And now the light laughed in the linden tree,
And now the sun danced in the green-gold wind,
And now I am in Arden or in Arcady,
Losing my way with wayward Rosalind,
Or was it Viola in Padua, or was it Kate—?
And Mrs. Malaprop arrived and Mistress Ford
As the light mellowed and the day grew late,
And I had done my alms, had my reward.

Envoy

Thanks, Princess, for your hospitality.
In the bright lights, and in the failing light,
Always your bright or sad smile welcomed me.
And even now it almost seems you might
Give me a ghostly hand familiarly,
A curtain call from the hushed house of night.

Index

318